BEHAVIOR ADJUSTMENT TRAINING

BAT for Fear, Frustration, and Aggression in Dogs

Grisha Stewart, M.A., CPDT-KA

Wenatchee, Washington U.S.A.

Behavior Adjustment Training
BAT for Fear, Frustration, and Aggression in Dogs
Grisha Stewart, M.A., CPDT-KA

Dogwise Publishing
A Division of Direct Book Service, Inc.
403 South Mission Street, Wenatchee, Washington 98801
509-663-9115, 1-800-776-2665
www.dogwisepublishing.com / info@dogwisepublishing.com

Graphic design: Lindsay Peternell
Cover and interior illustrations: Lili Chin, www.doggiedrawings.net
Interior photographs: Animals Plus, Company of Animals, Dan Catchpole, Simon Conner, Aaron Lieberman, Dana Litt, Stevie Mathre, Midwest Metal, Premier Pet Products, J. Nichole Smith, Thundershirt, Melissa McDaniel

Some text has appeared previously in the *Ahimsa Dog Training: Training Handbook.*

Limits of Liability and Disclaimer of Warranty:
The author and publisher shall not be liable in the event of incidental or consequential damages in connection with, or arising out of, the furnishing, performance, or use of the instructions and suggestions contained in this book.

ISBN 978-1-61781-050-3

Library of Congress Cataloging-in-Publication Data
Stewart, Grisha, 1954-
  Behavior adjustment training : BAT for fear, frustration, and aggression in dogs / Grisha Stewart.
     p. cm.
  Includes bibliographical references and index.
  ISBN 978-1-61781-050-3 (alk. paper)
  1. Dogs--Training. 2. Dogs--Behavior. I. Title.
  SF431.S745 2012
  636.7'0835--dc23
                              2011029180

Printed in the U.S.A.

More praise for *Behavior Ajustment Training*

Behavior Adjustment Training is an excellent resource for people who have reactive dogs, and the professional trainers who help them. Grisha Stewart's instruction is easy to understand, enhanced by wonderful illustrations, and she includes the "technical jargon" for pros who crave the science! I especially loved the section on management, which is often overlooked but so critical to a dog's success. Grisha shares details on HOW to effectively manage dogs to reduce incidents. She also offers a variety of BAT options that are easily adjustable based on a dog's environment and specific triggers. There are books that decorate your shelf and books you use on a regular basis—this book is one I'll definitely be using with my clients!

Teoti E. Anderson, CPDT-KA, KPA-CTP, Owner, Pawsitive Results, LLC, Lexington, SC, APDT Past President Delta Society® Team Evaluator, Instructor and Pet Partner®, author *Your Outta Control Puppy, Super Simple Guide to Housetraining, Quick & Easy Crate Training and Puppy Care and Training*

Every trainer who works with dogs that aren't completely bombproof should have both the technical skills of BAT and the learning theory behind it in their toolbox. Stewart presents a thoughtful, reader-friendly protocol that is appropriate for both professionals and laypeople. Both scientific and entertaining, this book will skillfully guide you through a sticky subject, that of negative reinforcement, and explain clearly how this quadrant, when humanely applied as part of a broader intervention, can empower dogs to learn to make choices about their behavior in socially pressured environments. This book will deservedly become a popular resource in the reactive dog literature.

Leslie McDevitt, MLA, CPDT-KA, CDBC, author *Control Unleashed: Creating a Focused and Confident Dog*

I'm glad more people are taking an interest in this important topic.

Terry Ryan, author *The Toolbox for Building a Great Family Dog, Coaching People to Train Their Dogs, Outwitting Dogs* and *The Puppy Primer*

This book will be very useful for trainers and pet owners alike as they work with fearful and/or reactive dogs. Grisha combines desensitization, counter-conditioning, and positive and negative reinforcement, describing the steps for her BAT protocol in a user-friendly way.

I especially like her use of functional rewards, i.e. choosing what the dog would most value in a given training context. She also emphasizes the importance of safe management, and provides many great suggestions for equipment and tools to help set the people and dogs up for success. The illustrations are very helpful, and charming, too! I would definitely recommend this book!

Virginia Broitman, Trainer and Behavior Counselor (30 years), North Star Canines, Take a Bow Wow, Head Trainer for Pixie's Pen Pals, a shelter dog/prison program (www.fetchacure.com), Producer of the *Bow Wow* series of training DVDs (www.take-abowwow.com) (*Take a Bow Wow & Bow Wow Take 2, The How of Bow Wow, The Shape of Bow Wow, Fido Refined, Teaching Impulse-Control to Your Excitable Dog*)

For Peanut: my soulmate dog,
teacher, and muse.

Thanks for being patient with me until I finally
learned to pay attention to your choices.

TABLE OF CONTENTS

ACKNOWLEDGMENTS

I am grateful to many people in the creation of BAT in general and this book in particular. First, I have so much gratitude to Peanut and Boo Boo, for showing me that there is a wise dog underneath the bluster, and for being patient as I looked for what was under my nose.

Thank you to:

My wife, Jill Olkoski, for her patience during this process and for trusting me to train her dog (whose caricature is on the cover).

All of the people who developed the many methods from which I drew inspiration for BAT (see Appendix 2—Other Methods That Use Functional Rewards) plus Leslie McDevitt (for *Control Unleashed*) and Karen Pryor and all the great clicker trainers.

Guild Certified TTouch Practitioner Lori Stevens for engaging conversation and idea-bouncing during my initial brainstorm on BAT.

Alta Tawzer of Tawzer Dog Videos for her unbelievable support; I wouldn't be this far so fast without you!

Trainers Kathy Sdao and Joey Iversen for their training wisdom and insight with Peanut and general training.

Virginia Broitman for being a liaison with the handlers in the Fluvanna Correctional Center for Women.

The trainers and dog lovers in the FunctionalRewards Yahoo! group around the world (including Sarah Owings, Jude Azaren, Donna Savoie, Irith Bloom, Dani Weinberg, David Smelzer, Barrie Lynn, Susan Mitchell, Danielle Theule, Rachel Bowman, Dennis Fehling, and many others), for their great ideas and for bringing BAT to the dogs in their lives.

The many decoys that have helped BAT dogs learn and change.

The many proofreaders for this book, including Nan Arthur, Jude Azaren, Judith Bell, Ann Blake, Mary Blanton, Monica Hadfield, Susan Kennedy, Dana Litt, Monica McFadden, Laura Monaco-Torelli, Shelly Volsche, and others. (Drat, I know I missed some of you!)

The lovely folks who submitted write-ups on their experiences with BAT: Teoti Anderson, Jude Azaren, Sally Bushwaller, Deborah Campbell, Leonard "Buzz" Cecil, Bev Courtney, Elizabeth Haysom, Susan Kennedy, Jennifer Kszepka, Casey Lomonaco, Lisa Mullinax, Lauren O'Dell, Chirag Patel, Ryan Neile, Alice Tong, Jonas Valanius, Shelly Volsche, Dani Weinberg, Kiki Yablon, and Nancy Yamin.

Artist extraordinaire, Lili Chin for her lovely illustrations throughout this book and her efficient, friendly attitude during the process.

Dogwise for publishing this book, especially Charlene Woodward for contacting me and getting things going and Lindsay Peternell and Larry Woodward for pushing this forward in a timely way, even as I pushed for "just one more change."

INTRODUCTION

This book will teach you how to use Behavior Adjustment Training, or BAT, to rehabilitate dogs with reactivity issues, including fear, aggression, and frustration, and how to keep reactivity problems from developing in puppies. While BAT is not the only tool in my training toolbox, it has become the central way that I help clients with reactive dogs. I'm simply amazed at how much faster the dogs are progressing than they did before. Trainers around the world are seeing this with their clients, too.

Experienced trainers and shelter staff should be able to readily understand this book and use it to help dogs with reactivity issues. I highly recommend that trainers try BAT first with friends' or neighbors' dogs so you can experiment with the techniques more freely than you can with paying clients. For extra help along the way, join the BAT Yahoo! group (visit http://FunctionalRewards.com).

If you are not well versed in training, but still want to work with a puppy or a dog with fear or aggression issues, this book, including the appendices and Glossary of Key Terms, should be very helpful to you. However, if you have any safety concerns or any difficulty understanding your dog or predicting what your dog will do, I recommend hiring a professional dog trainer or behaviorist who is familiar with BAT to help you learn how to apply these techniques to your dog. If you can't find such a trainer in your area, look for a positive dog trainer who already works with dog reactivity and encourage her or him to learn about BAT by reading this book or watching one of the BAT DVDs and then practicing with you and your dog. It's a good sign if you find a trainer who is willing to learn new techniques.

I almost called this book "BATting 1000" because it's the perfect batting average in baseball, i.e., the player has hit the ball safely every time he or she is up at bat. With BAT, your job is to set your dog up for success, with the goal of having your dog practice making good choices over and over again, and to avoid the rehearsal effect of doing the behaviors you don't want. Avoid the strikeouts and try to keep your dog's BATting average high!

Throughout this book, I swap dog genders back and forth, to avoid the awkward "s/he," "he or she," or referring to a dog impersonally as "that" or "it." Also, terms that may be unfamiliar to some readers are printed in **bold type** the first time they appear in the text and are fully defined in the Glossary at the end of the book.

In this book, I focus on applying particular concepts to either dog-dog reactivity or dog-human reactivity, but almost all of what I teach can be generalized to other objects of reactivity, meaning that the concept or technique also applies to dogs who are **reactive** to other species or objects in their environment and can even be used with reactive animals of different species. If my example is about dogs who are reactive to humans and your dog is only reactive to dogs or umbrellas, please understand that the concepts are the same. Be creative and don't skip over a section thinking that it doesn't apply to your issue!

This book is meant for anyone who needs help with a reactive dog, but it also has several features meant just for professional dog trainers and behaviorists. These are included in "Notes for Pros" sidebars throughout the book with extra information for people using BAT to help other people's dogs. Chapter 11 is specifically designed to help professionals use BAT with clients. Appendix 2 is a history of other methods that use functional rewards in some way and Appendix 3 is a discussion of all things geeky, like which learning theory quadrant applies to BAT. Both of those appendices are meant for dog reactivity specialists. My goal with that section is to help you put BAT into context so that you can differentiate BAT from other techniques and integrate BAT with the training methods that you currently use.

I see BAT as a constantly evolving process and my formal research isn't finished yet. Based on what I have seen with clients, I have been hesitant to date to write out the details of BAT in book form. That said, I know that many of us (myself included) learn well from reading and love the clarity that a book can provide. So please enjoy this book for what it is: the most current version of BAT at the time it was written. Please learn from this book, use the techniques in it, discuss what you've learned with other people, attend seminars, and combine BAT with other training methods to fit the needs of the dogs in your life. **Above all, let dogs learn to make good choices, without fear, pain, or force.**

CHAPTER 1

Understanding BAT:
Key Concepts

Since you're reading this book, your dog probably exhibits some behaviors that you'd like to change or you are a dog trainer helping other people change dog behavior. Or both. I've only ever had two clients say to me, "My dog is perfect. We just need some training ideas for entertainment," so I'm guessing you're probably in the first category. That's me, too. I developed Behavior Adjustment Training (BAT) not only to help my clients, but also to rehabilitate my own reactive dog, Peanut.

There are a number of key concepts to grasp in BAT. This chapter will serve as a brief introduction to these concepts while the rest of the book will provide more details and examples, including the next chapter about how I began to utilize them when working with Peanut. These key concepts include:

- Functional Rewards
- Relacement Behaviors
- Default Behaviors
- Thresholds and sub-thresholds
- Triggers
- Set-ups
- Reinforcements
- Bonus Rewards

Ask yourself "why?"

If your dog is exhibiting some behavior you don't want, you may have wondered, "Why is he doing it?" Does he not love you? Is he trying to dominate you? If he knows you don't like whatever it is he is doing, then why does he keep doing it? Is he not your best friend, after all? I think the answer is that he behaves the way he does simply because he has some need that the behavior helps him meet. He may not even find the behavior particularly fun to do, as is the case with most reactivity. *But your dog has learned that behavior is a way to get what he wants or needs.*

Think creatively about what your dog gets as a result of doing a **problem behavior** (whatever he's doing that you want to change). In other words, what is the **functional reward** for his behavior? Think of the functional reward as a "real life" consequence that reinforces the problem behavior. Has your dog learned that barking at strangers makes them move away? The fact that the person moves away creates safety in the dog's mind by putting more distance between him and a stranger. That is the functional reward for his barking.

Once you know the functional reward(s) for your dog's problem behavior, the next step is to find other behaviors you can encourage your dog to do that can reasonably lead to that same reward. For example, you can reward your dog's choice to turn his head away from approaching strangers instead of barking at them. That would make looking away a **replacement behavior** for the problem behavior of barking. Sniffing the ground, yawning, sitting, or looking at you are also appropriate possible replacement behaviors for reactivity. Reinforce the replacement behavior(s) by using the same functional reward that your dog earned from doing the problem behavior. For example, when he looks away (a replacement behavior), happily walk your dog away from the stranger, thereby increasing the distance between dog and stranger (the functional reward). That's the core concept of Functional Analysis—using the functional reward of the problem behavior to pay for more appropriate behaviors. The functional reward concept can be applied to just about any problem behavior. Behavioral Adjustment Training is a way to apply the scientific concept of Functional Analysis to reactivity problems: use the functional reward of reactivity to pay for more appropriate social behaviors.

Staying below threshold

Left to their own devices, dogs will resort to behaviors that have been working for them, like barking. To use Behavior Adjustment Training you will temporarily need to micro-manage your dog's life. This means arranging his routine so that he is not faced with situations that trigger him to react with barking, growling, lunging, etc. Trainers call that "staying below **threshold**" or "working **sub-threshold**." The term "threshold" has various meanings and interpretations, depending on who you're talking to, so let me define how I use it. Unless otherwise specified, when I use the word threshold, I mean the line between being relaxed and freaking out. When working sub-threshold, your dog's level of stress is low enough that she's still able to self-soothe. The **trigger** (an approaching stranger, for example) is just barely in the foreground for a dog who is sub-threshold, meaning that the trigger has just begun to stand out from the rest of the perceived environment. If you mess up and put her over threshold, she'll react with aggression, panic, or some other display of reactivity.

REACTIVITY CHART

WHEN DOG ENCOUNTERS A TRIGGER

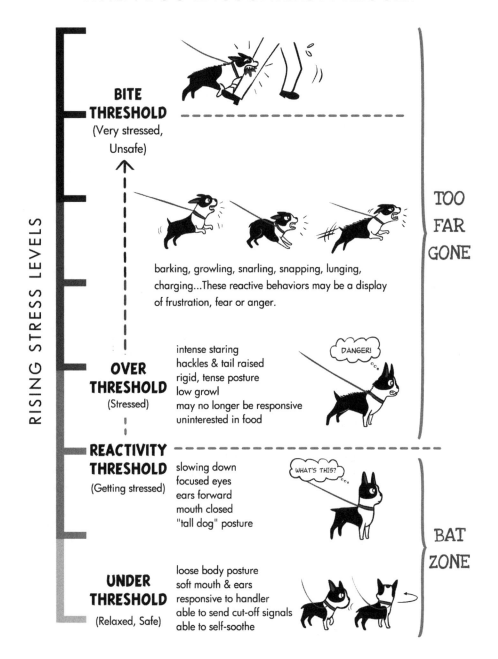

RISING STRESS LEVELS

BITE THRESHOLD
(Very stressed, Unsafe)

TOO FAR GONE

barking, growling, snarling, snapping, lunging, charging...These reactive behaviors may be a display of frustration, fear or anger.

OVER THRESHOLD
(Stressed)

intense staring
hackles & tail raised
rigid, tense posture
low growl
may no longer be responsive
uninterested in food

DANGER!

REACTIVITY THRESHOLD
(Getting stressed)

slowing down
focused eyes
ears forward
mouth closed
"tall dog" posture

WHAT'S THIS?

BAT ZONE

UNDER THRESHOLD
(Relaxed, Safe)

loose body posture
soft mouth & ears
responsive to handler
able to send cut-off signals
able to self-soothe

Reactivity: fear, aggression, or frustration responses that are over the level that dog-savvy humans consider "normal."

Here's a visual. Your dog is just inside the threshold of a doorway feeling safe and secure. If he ventures beyond that doorway he encounters a scary world, which causes him to bark, pace, stress drool, growl, or display another 'bad' behavior—generally, all of the things we want to avoid. If your dog stays within the bounds of the threshold, he can shut that door himself, metaphorically speaking, and self-soothe. As soon as he goes over threshold, he gets sucked through the reactivity doorway. Without a heart monitor or other ways of determining stress, we can only rely on behaviors visible to the naked (human) eye. Depending on your dog and his ability to recover, you might consider pupil dilation, staring, and a slightly increased rate of breathing to be under or over threshold. What you will do with BAT is create situations in which your dog is always able to self-soothe.

Set-ups

In Behavior Adjustment Training, you will use **set-ups** that are sub-threshold 'dress rehearsals' for a dog in which he can practice making good choices and repeat appropriate replacement behaviors over and over again. One successful run-through is helpful, but *repetition is what creates a new neural pathway in your dog's brain.* In the final picture, your dog's **default behaviors** will change, but the environment and the consequences that keep the new behaviors strong will stay the same. That's why it's called Behavior Adjustment Training. You will learn to adjust your dog's behavioral response to his environment, so that she can rehearse the new behavior, over and over.

In theatre, rehearsals should be accurate, even if it means that actors need to use the script along the way or have someone prompt them with their lines. To give your dog the chance to repeatedly practice doing the behaviors you like—and keep her below threshold—start by putting her in a very watered-down version of whatever situation normally triggers the problem behaviors, and then provide a reward that she finds most meaningful in that situation.

Let's say, for example, that your dog bites men (a problem behavior) who lean over to pet her (the men being the trigger). If you have observed that when your dog sees a man far enough away, say fifty feet, she stares for a second and then just turns away from him (a replacement behavior), you actually have a great opportunity to build a new default behavior (turning away rather than biting). In order to make turning away in the presence of men your dog's default behavior, you will need to rehearse this behavior over and over again. This is where BAT set-ups come into play.

I will discuss set-ups in much more detail later, but here's a quick overview. Normally you will need helpers to play the role of the trigger (unless the trigger is an inanimate object). In this example, since your hypothetical dog has shown she does not react badly at fifty feet, start your BAT set-up with the dog seeing a male helper at a distance of fifty feet. The sight of the man is a tiny, tiny bit stressful, so if your dog turns her head away from him, you can mark and then reward that behavior by walking the dog happily away from the man and praising her intelligent and brave choice, say 3-5 feet closer. Once she's doing well at fifty feet, gradually work closer to the man. This predictable approach teaches her that she can control the safety of her situation without resorting to biting. Because she has learned that she can safely get away from the trigger, the end result is usually confident curiosity and trust.

Clicker/marker training

BAT uses clicker training, which is a type of training that uses an event marker, like an audible click sound, to tell your dog exactly which behaviors you are rewarding. This event marker lets you teach your dog more quickly, because she doesn't need to guess at which behaviors she's doing to earn the reward. All of the stages of BAT use some kind of event marker, either a verbal/visual marker or an actual clicker, to tell your dog that she has earned the functional reward (see Appendix 1 for more details on clicker training). The functional reward is the main **reinforcement** in BAT, but you can also use food and toy rewards in situations where you find they help your dog stay below threshold, and avoid them when they are more distracting than helpful. This is an important point and I'll talk more about these **bonus rewards** later.

> Reinforcement is any consequence to a behavior that makes a behavior more likely to occur in the future. That consequence can include treats, toys, or relief from something unpleasant, like social pressure.

If you are familiar with clicker training, good for you! You'll see a lot of clicker training concepts in BAT. If you are new to clicker training, read through Appendix 1 for ways to use the clicker to train some behaviors that come in handy with barky, growly, fearful, or frustrated dogs. The clicker comes in very handy when doing BAT on walks.

There's a lot more to BAT, as you'll see in the chapters that follow, but that's the gist of it. You'll get a lot of different examples of how BAT works in this book, especially for reactivity, like barking, lunging, and other negative reactions. In all of the examples, there is a common thread of using the natural consequences of the problem behavior to reinforce behaviors that you can live with.

CHAPTER 2

BAT Boy:
Peanut's Transformation

Peanut was the dog who led me to BAT. When I walked with Peanut and my students tried to say "hi," I couldn't hear them over the sound of my dog's barking. You can imagine that it was pretty embarrassing for me, a professional dog trainer! Peanut would not have the social skills he has today without Behavior Adjustment Training. Peanut was my muse and guinea pig for BAT. It might not even have been developed without him. Here is Peanut's story.

Peanut: 8-year-old, neutered herding dog mix
Presenting issue: Fear barking at humans

Peanut had a rough start. When he was eight weeks old, Peanut, his five littermates, and their fear-aggressive mother were taken to the shelter just after Christmas. The shelter staff separated Peanut's mother from the six puppies and assessed her to be too reactive to place. She was put to sleep. They spayed and neutered the puppies, vaccinated them, and pronounced them ready to adopt when they were ten weeks old.

Unfortunately for Peanut, a puppy's fear response develops between eight and ten weeks old, so he and his littermates were right in the middle of a sensitive developmental period during all of the stress involved with being moved to the

Grisha and Peanut.

shelter. Peanut's amygdala, the almond-shaped part of mammalian brains that responds to danger (among other things) was just coming online when Peanut was in the shelter. The amygdala is what turns on the fear switch in a dog at the first sign of danger. When you spot a curved stick on the ground and jump away before thinking, that's your amygdala making a snap-judgment to save you from the 'snake.' The amygdala helps dogs react quickly to get out of harm's way. It's useful for quick escapes, but sometimes the amygdala can be like a thermostat stuck on high. That was certainly the case for Peanut, because he reacted like he was in extreme danger even when there was only a mild threat or no threat at all.

Peanut probably got the impression that the world was not safe during those two critical weeks—he was taken from his mother, moved to a new location, neutered, and surrounded by the smell of fearful dogs just as his brain was beginning to discover things in his environment were dangerous. Peanut's whole litter probably wound up with a triple dose of sensitivity to danger: genetic (inherited from the mother); chemical (in utero stress from the mother); and environmental (stress of moving and being in the shelter during a sensitive period and lack of early socialization).

Trauma aside, Peanut was an adorable two-pound ball of fluff at ten weeks old. I was volunteering at his shelter and was on the lookout for another dog. I looked at his litter and quickly fell in love. I chose Peanut because he was neither the most outgoing nor the shyest puppy in his litter, but I hadn't really thought through the fact that the whole litter was probably a bit shell-shocked.

Peanut went to two six-week puppy kindergarten classes and two six-week adolescent dog classes because I was intent on socializing the fear out of him. I primarily used **systematic desensitization** and **classical counter-conditioning** to help him overcome his fears: I kept his stress level low and every time he saw a person, dog, or something else that was potentially scary, I immediately fed him tasty treats. I also taught him a solid auto-watch through that process. That is, he learned to turn to automatically look at me to get a treat if he encountered one of his many triggers. If you're not familiar with those helpful techniques, you can learn about them in Patricia McConnell's *Feisty Fido*, Nicole Wilde's *Help for Your Fearful Dog*, and Ali Brown's *Focus Not Fear* (see Resources).

There were a few bad incidents in his puppy class with a classmate. The other puppy was a bully, inappropriate for a socialization class for young puppies. He would consistently charge right at the other dogs, pin them to the ground, and growl in a serious way until the instructor pulled him off. That only took a few repetitions, with Peanut on the bottom with his throat in the other puppy's mouth, before he was sure that other dogs were a danger.

Peanut never played in puppy class and he barked at the children in the classroom. I have a very clear memory of three-month-old Peanut's muffled bark at a child who had tossed him a tennis ball. I wish I had realized that his puppy class was not a good fit for him. Even though Peanut was a rock star in the training exercises in class, he entirely missed the socialization aspect of puppy kindergarten because it was too stressful for him, and he could not interact with other dogs and people successfully. To make things worse, at four months old, he also was on the losing end of a two-on-one scuffle at the dog park. If I could turn back time, I would've been more careful in puppy class and I would have avoided the dog park, especially a park where people simply stand around drinking coffee as the dogs 'play.'

Because of the early socialization and genetics issues mentioned above, along with his bad experiences with dogs in puppy class, Peanut developed several phobias: including humans (any age and size), wheeled objects, dogs, basketballs, etc. He was very sensitive to loud noises and fast motions. Using classical counter-conditioning on walks, I was eventually able to get Peanut completely past many of his fears, including bicycles, Frisbees, and basketballs. He and I could walk on a busy hiking trail or a city street, but I still needed to constantly use treats, toys, or continual praise when we encountered people, his main remaining fear. Even after five years of classical counter-conditioning on walks, Peanut's threshold distance without my micro-managing was still about eighty feet for adults and one hundred plus feet for children. Unless he was actively being fed, played with, or talked to, he would tip back his head, stand tall, and bark in alarm if people got any closer than that.

Except for his family, Peanut didn't seem to remember people he had met and no one else but us could pet him. We would shower him with treats for being around strangers, but Peanut's list of Trusted Humans never went beyond the seven people with whom he had had extended contact as a puppy. I think that was because he didn't actually pay that much attention to people, except inasmuch as that they caused us to feed him.

Using BAT with Peanut

The problems I had in reducing Peanut's threshold level with both adults and kids led me to work on trying to get better results than I had with classical counter-conditioning techniques. I started with adult humans as the decoys for my BAT sessions with Peanut. The goal was to work at enough of a distance that Peanut did not have a bad reaction, and having human helpers and decoy dogs that I could control was helpful for him.

> Human helpers and decoy dogs are critical to using BAT. They play the role of triggers that can cause reactivity on the part of a student dog, but because you are coordinating their actions, the dog can stay calm.

Like most fear barkers, Peanut felt safer when people were further away from him. He had learned that his barking was effective, because it resulted in people leaving him alone or I walked him away from them. With BAT, I used an increase in distance as a reward to teach him replacement behaviors, like looking away from the approaching people, shaking off (as if wet), sniffing the ground, and other actions. Here's how that looked. In my BAT set-ups, the helpers posed as 'scary people' loitering down the block and Peanut and I would approach them, just to the edge of his comfort zone so there was a very good chance he would not bark. If instead of barking, he looked away or sniffed the ground or did something I asked him to (like Sit), I said, "Yes" (my event marker) and walked him away from the people (the functional reward). We practiced this over and over in different locations.

Whenever I accidentally walked Peanut too close and he started barking, I helped him calm down by calling him away or using some smaller signal, like a kissy noise or even shifting my weight. From that new position, further away from the trigger, I would give him another chance to offer a replacement behavior and get the reward of walking away again. I didn't use food during Peanut's BAT set-ups, so he paid more attention to the helpers than he had when we used classical counter-conditioning. I recommend doing BAT without food or toys whenever you can, especially for set-ups. Working without these distractions allowed Peanut to focus more on the social situation and gather more information about the helpers or decoy dogs.

It quickly became obvious that Peanut didn't have a memory problem when he met people this way. My helpers acted in set-ups only a few times before they joined Peanut's quickly expanding 'Trusted Humans' list. After twenty BAT set-ups with ten different people, Peanut got to the point where he actually seemed to want adult strangers to pet him on walks! When he was ignored, he would go up to them and lean into their legs. He'd stay for petting and then walk away when he was done. Peanut progressed so much that he and I began volunteering as a therapy dog team at an assisted living facility. Children were still an issue for him at that point, but fortunately there weren't many around the nursing home that we visited. I grinned from ear to ear when residents commented that Peanut was the perfect dog! He made an excellent therapy dog—interested in them, welcoming their attention, but polite and not pushy.

After the success with adults, I took about a year and half off of officially working with Peanut's issues before returning to training to help him get over his fear of children. Doing a single BAT approach/retreat with the occasional children that we'd see on walks, I found that Peanut's comfort buffer near children had shrunk, so that he could now be within twenty feet from them in a busy area. However, he still needed one hundred feet when it was just Peanut, me, and an approaching child, unless I actively distracted him. If you have my DVDs, you have seen how far away I started Peanut's first BAT session with kids.

I wasn't sure how much Peanut would **generalize** his prior training with adults to the trigger of children. Dogs are very good at **discrimination**—i.e, noticing that trigger X and trigger Y are different. In this situation, generalization is the process of learning that X and Y are similar enough and should both trigger the same behaviors. He clearly did not put children in the same category as adults at that point, because children triggered a barking reaction and adults triggered him to solicit attention. Would he need another twenty set-ups to see that what he learned before applied to children, too? It turned out that the answer was a resounding no. He learned to trust children in less than half of the number of set-ups that we had needed for adults.

The scientist in me has to note that I can't draw a lot of conclusions from this good result, for many reasons. For one thing, Peanut had experienced some Behavior Adjustment Training between the work with adults and the formal work with children, from chance encounters with children on walks. On the other hand, he didn't have the repetitions that he would get from staged BAT set-ups. Furthermore, I had refined the techniques of BAT in between Peanut's work with adults and his work with children. But anecdotally, his progress was a great sign!

The eight BAT set-ups with children were spread out over five months and included a total of nine different children (some sessions had two kids). The first BAT set-up with a child started at one hundred feet and ended up with Peanut sniffing the girl as she sat in the lap of her mother, who was petting Peanut. During our first session, I got greedy and accidentally put him over threshold a lot, but I interrupted his outbursts and he recovered well each time. I think we would have made faster progress if I had been as careful with him as I am with my clients. I've seen several trainers work their own dogs and I think it's hard to be careful with your own dog's threshold! Fortunately, I video-taped the session so that I was able to see my mistakes and fix them in the next session.

At the beginning of the second set-up, a month later with a different child, Peanut was able to begin just twenty feet from a seated child and fifty feet from her when the child was walking around. That session finished with the child petting Peanut with the child sitting beside her mother. The third set-up was with two children eating at an outdoor restaurant, so they were sitting the whole time. Peanut made pretty quick progress and finished by hanging out with them and getting some of their food. The food wasn't part of his BAT training, but it's always helpful to end on a pleasant note, one way or another. The fourth set-up began at twenty feet from a standing child and ended with the child and Peanut walking around together. In the fifth set-up, we added in some motion and also worked closer to home.

The last three BAT set-ups (six through eight) were informal, more like a social gathering rather than the more formal approach/retreat training pattern we had done in earlier sessions. Peanut and the children were allowed to interact naturally while I continued to watch for behaviors to reward. In the sixth and seventh set-up with kids, Peanut was off-leash in a safely contained outdoor setting, walking around with two boys (one was new, one he had met before). He saw more realistic behavior from the boys, including some running, a few fits of frustrated crying, and lots of happy laughter. During the eighth set-up, Peanut was able to be off-leash and calmly interact with two girls at their home, with no need for treats or micromanagement, and not a single bark. He had done BAT with only one of the two girls before.

Note for Pros: Unlike most of the dogs that I use BAT with, Peanut has no history of biting or snapping and he has a great warning system, so I chose not to use a muzzle. If the dog you work with has any history of biting, or you are not sure of what might happen, train her to be comfortable wearing a muzzle, and use it during the session. See Chapter 2 on safety for more tips.

In that last encounter with kids, Peanut went up to the girls and leaned in for petting, but he still occasionally seemed to feel uncomfortable when the girls approached him. The good news is that instead of barking at them, as he would have done in the past, he just moved himself to a safer position. The children could have kept pestering him, but they didn't, because I was watching and told them not to follow Peanut around. Until he learns to be very persistent with his new skills, I will need to help the children he encounters reinforce Peanut's attempts to create safety. That is, I need to notice when Peanut is trying to get away from children and honor his need for distance by having the children leave him alone. Considering that Peanut went from barking at children from one hundred feet away to actual interaction, I was thrilled with his rapid progress.

For the visual learners: my BAT DVDs have a lot of footage of Peanut's training and progress over time. The *Organic Socialization DVD* has footage of several set-ups and *Full Day Seminar DVD* has the most video of him.

Peanut seems to be learning more on his own every day. My clients and the people who have tried BAT around the globe are seeing the same type of success with fear, aggression, and other kinds of reactivity. One of the great aspects of is BAT that it allows dogs to manipulate their regular environment to meet their needs, instead of manipulating their owners for food or other rewards. *BAT creates dogs that seem to have a better understanding of how the world really works, which in turn makes them feel safer.* I can't get inside of dogs' little heads to know that for sure, but they behave as if they trust the world more. That newfound trust causes dogs to be curious and learn more about the stimuli around them, realizing that life is safer than they previously believed. And whenever they feel threatened, they have a safe way to self-soothe, so they are ready to take on the world again. How cool is that?

When I work with clients, they are excited to get on with the business of fixing their dogs' problems. I imagine you may be, too. I want to make sure to get you the information you need on BAT, but skilled trainers are kind of like trauma surgeons—first you need to save the patient, then you can work on the finer points of treatment. That is why the next chapter goes through tips on how to make the dog's situation as safe as possible before getting into all of the details of BAT. If you're a professional trainer who is familiar with reactivity, you are probably already advising your clients on many of the management solutions in the next chapter and may want to skip to Chapter 4.

Peanut doing agility with human jumps and weave poles post-BAT.

CHAPTER 3

Quick Fixes:
Safety and Management Essentials

Management is the trainer buzzword for changing your dog's environment to make it impossible or unlikely that he'll be triggered to engage in the problem behaviors. Behavior Adjustment Training and management go hand in hand; when using BAT to rehabilitate a reactive dog, you will also need to implement management to keep your dog out of trouble. Management is essential to keep your dog sub-threshold in relation to environmental triggers—that is, your dog's life should be set up to help him stay calm, relaxed, and safe. Behaviorist B.F. Skinner called it "environmental engineering" (see Appendix 2). In this chapter, I'll talk about the management strategies that are especially helpful for reactive dogs.

Management solutions can create a safe situation right away, because they don't require training your dog, but rather making some environmental changes that can set the dog up for success. Generally, that means installing some piece of equipment or changing the way you expose your dog to the environment. Building a fence is an example of management. A fence is a simple device that keeps dogs from escaping the yard and requires no training. Putting up a baby gate and giving the dog a Kong before visitors come over are management techniques, as is walking your dog on a leash. Most cities have leash laws, so there will most likely always be some level of management in your dog's life.

If you find that your dog frequently barks, lunges, growls, or cowers at some sort of trigger, please read this chapter carefully. Creating a safe environment is critical for successfully rehabilitating a reactive dog. Management solutions can make you feel like you're living in a prison, but they are immediate, effective, and not necessarily permanent. My goal with most management strategies is to put them into place right away to prevent trouble, and then change the dog's response to triggers using BAT and other techniques so that management can be minimized or becomes no longer necessary over the long run.

If BAT is going to help your dog, why do you even need to know about management solutions in the first place? Because the dog needs to feel safe as often as possible in order to thrive. Here's an anology. In the HBO hit television series "The Sopranos," Mafioso Tony Soprano repeatedly visits a therapist to help stop his panic attacks. Meanwhile, opposing gangs try to kill him, he strangles his rivals, his marriage is in shambles, his children are in trouble, and he even has issues with his girlfriend. Even if his therapist were a genius, Tony's recovery would come slowly, if at all, because he is fully aware that there's more danger in his world than he can handle and he shows no real willingness to change his environment. Unfortunately, this is the sort of situation people put their dogs in all the time. We humans want our dogs to change their behavior without changing our behavior or their environment. We want them to feel safe while loose dogs run down the street, kids pop into elevators, and loud motorcycles whiz by. But, in the dog's mind, the mafia is out to get them, they are in way over their heads, and they know it.

For any training plan based on reinforcement to work, you have to tone down the environmental stimulation that sets up dogs to fail, like exposure to loud noises or windows with views. Just as you might use fencing to keep a toddler out of the pool, physical barriers can help keep dogs away from situations that they aren't yet trained to handle. If BAT and management are used properly, your dog will be given multiple chances to succeed and little or no chance to panic or rehearse unwanted behaviors. Why is it so important to set dogs up for success? Whether you use them intentionally or not, consequences change behaviors. If your dog's reactivity is significant enough that you're reading this book, chances are that your dog has been routinely rewarded for unwanted behaviors. It's important to prevent your dog from being rewarded for unwanted behaviors with basic problems like jumping up or pulling on-leash, but *setting your dog up for success and preventing failure is even more critical for reactivity, because reactivity is emotionally driven and can have dangerous consequences.*

Let's discuss some management steps that increase safety and reduce your dog's overall stress level. These include:

- Reducing visual stimulation
- Reducing face-to-face encounters
- Avoiding problems while on walks
- Muzzles and other safety related equipment

Out of sight (and sound), out of mind—reducing visual stimulation

Starting at home, one simple solution to reducing visual triggers for your dog is to eliminate any perches from which your dog can spy on passing dogs or people. Reactive dogs with lookout posts successfully practice barking all day long, and the training time you put in is nothing compared to your dog's nine-hour shift of guarding the house! Dogs need entertainment, but working for Homeland Security all day is not fun, it's stressful. Just imagine this from the dog's perspective. She barks, the boy or dog walking by goes out of sight, and she thinks her behavior has worked to protect the house—but then it happens again and again! Her barking becomes a stronger habit with each passing day. A home with a perch is like a giant Skinner box (operant conditioning chamber); it automatically trains the dog to bark.

> Note for Pros: If your clients aren't willing to make environmental changes to prevent the reinforcement of problem behaviors, they might as well just hand over your fee and send you on your way without even bothering to hear the rest of what you have to say. Don't just ditch them, of course, but to make any improvement, you must convince them to change their home and habits to prevent auto-training of unwanted behaviors.

To get rid of perches, you can move furniture, use baby gates or exercise pens to block off an area, and/or install Roman shades that allow a human to see out of the top while the bottom is closed off. During our gloomy Seattle winters, I find that Roman shades that let light in at the top are much better for my mood than fully closed top-down shades! Hardware stores carry a plastic film that will cover existing windows and make them look like stained or smoky glass, fluffy clouds, or other patterns. The fake snow that comes in a spray instantly removes distractions and is easy for renters to clean off of windows. This spray can also be gradually removed by wiping away little bits to make the outside world more visible. For a cheap solution, you can tape waxed paper onto the window. Waxed paper is the squirrel-barking solution I used on the bottom half of my sliding glass doors. I only have so much time to train and turning off the 'backyard TV' was a quick fix for my dogs' barking.

My quick fix to prevent barking at squirrels.

If you are an apartment or condo dweller, you may need to find ways to keep your alert-barking dogs from being able to hear (and bark at) people in the hallway or neighboring units. To keep dogs from noticing and barking at noises outside, play sound recordings that are mostly monotonous, with occasional changes—like ocean waves with high-pitched birdcalls. Because sudden changes are specifically what tend to snag a dog's attention and make him bark, variations in the sound recording are important, because then the dog gets used to the environment changing. Turn down the volume as weeks or months go on, so that the dog begins to hear more and more of the 'real' environment.

There is also a lot you may need to change outside as well. For example, I love dog doors, but they should not be open without a human at home to supervise. Dog doors can lead to the same sort of reactivity rehearsal problem as perches. Fences should be sturdy and, ideally, not allow the dog to look through. Privacy fencing that completely encloses the dog's area is my favorite way to fence a yard. *The main criterion for a fence is that it actually prevents escapes and intrusions.* That may sound too basic to mention, but it is not. A student in my Growly Dog class complained that his dog kept getting out and chasing other dogs down the block. How did she get out, you might ask? There was a lovely fence around the house, but no gate! Another client complained of the same problem, except that his dog was jumping his three-foot fence. This was an athletic thirty-five pound dog, and I'm pretty sure even a five-foot fence would have not been a challenge.

Make sure your fence is really secure.

I have seen a surprising number of clients for aggression and fear issues whose fences were inadequate. They had holes under the fence, broken slats, areas only secured by bushes that the dog could get through, you name it—somehow people just expect their dogs to understand the concept of a fence and respect it, even if it's not secure. I always recommend clients install a real, physical fence. Aside from the ethics of electronic fences, an 'invisible' fence that you cannot even see does not keep people or other dogs from coming in and teasing, attacking, or getting bitten by your dog.

Even if you have a solid fence, don't leave your dog alert barking in the yard when you are not home. Although the dog may not be able to see through the fence, he can certainly hear what is going on beyond the fence. Extensive yard time is a privilege, not a right, and barking dogs should lose that privilege until they have cooled off. Any benefit your dog may get from the chance to exercise is outweighed by the chance to practice unwanted behavior. Spending time in the yard alone, with no human at home to hear barking and do something about it, trains the dog to bark. As with the indoor perch where they can bark at passersby, the yard is like a giant auto-shaping machine for barking, with the functional reward of getting the dog or person walking by to keep going. If your dog has this problem, be sure to read the section on Fence Fighting in Chapter 9.

> Note for Pros: If you have an intake questionnaire, ask about the existence, state of repair, and visibility of their fence, as well as whether the dog is supervised while in the yard.

If you need proof that being left alone in a yard can lead to barking, just take a walk in the suburbs during a weekday. For example, on our first walk in a new neighborhood, Peanut and I passed by seven yards with unsupervised dogs. Every single one of the dogs barked at us, and they were reinforced for that barking as we walked away. That's just what's happening to your dog if you are leaving her in the yard (even if fenced) while you go to work. In one of the yards we passed by, a fight actually broke out. First, the Doberman and Corgi in the yard began barking at us. Then the Doberman quieted down, followed by the Corgi. When the Corgi started barking again, the Doberman redirected her aggression to the Corgi, pinning him to the ground with her mouth around his neck! The Corgi squealed. I yelled and threw a small rock at the Doberman. Fortunately, they broke apart before I needed to use my SprayShield (citronella spray for breaking up dog fights) to stop the attack, but how many other times has this happened? Replacing their reactivity with better behaviors will take some practice and their training will go nowhere if the dogs continue to be left out in the yard during the day.

Reducing the amount of stimulation your dog encounters will help her relax and keep the home quieter, which should drastically improve your family's quality of life. However, giving your dog down-time from her job as Chief of Security is more than just simply covering up the problem. Setting up your dog's environment to prevent barking is essential for successful treatment.

Preventing accidental close encounters

In addition to practicing the rehearsal of stress and barking from a distance caused by poor fencing and perches, you need to protect your dog by making accidental run-ins with their triggers impossible. Well, anything's possible, *but opportunities to bite another dog or a person should be made extremely unlikely.* Even a one percent chance of escape when you go out your front door means that your dog can get out over ten times on an average year, since your door probably opens over a thousand times a year.

One of the most effective solutions is to install some kind of **airlock** on all exits to unfenced areas, to help prevent escapes and reduce the opportunity for aggression. An airlock is a physical buffer that keeps your dog from escaping even if the door is left ajar. Even if one door is open, there is another that blocks the exit. Most daycares, dog parks, and training centers have airlocks for each exit, so dogs don't get loose. An airlock for the exterior doors of the home gives your family a place to welcome guests without dogs escaping from the property or coming face-to-face with guests. You can just open the door to your house, close the dogs in the house behind you, and then let the guest into your airlock. If you are getting a pizza, the delivery driver never comes into contact with your dogs. Because freedom is no longer just on the other side of the front door, dogs also make fewer mad dashes outside. Why bother, when it's just another room of the house?

An airlock prevents escapes.

If you really want to be safe and keep your dogs calmer, put a lock on the gate to prevent people from coming up to the door. Installing a wireless doorbell and mailbox on the gate are a must if the mailman and visitors are locked out, but even if the gate is unlocked, putting the mailbox out at the fence will prevent or reduce the once-daily rehearsal of aggression toward the mail carrier.

Installing a doorbell along with instructions on the gate will further reduce unwanted encounters.

> Note for Pros: A nice side effect of a new doorbell is that it has no negative association, so you can easily teach the dog that the doorbell is a new cue for "Go to Bed."

Even children can understand safety concepts, like airlocks, with some training. I worked with a family whose dog, Roxy, had bitten a neighbor's son. The reason they first contacted me was that their daughter had opened the door and their barking dog charged out and bit the visiting child on the upper thigh, leaving a nasty bruise through layers of clothing. They have installed an airlock and a system of gates in their home, so that Roxy has to go through an internal gate, a door, and the gate on the porch to get to a visitor.

A warning sign is not enough if the gate is left open.

I recommend putting in extra safety steps with children, because they can't always be relied upon to make good choices. A system needs to be made childproof, or as much as any system can be. Now, Roxy hangs out in her internal pen (the kitchen and living room). It's really helpful to have an area of the house that Roxy can be in that is away from the doorway. This was created with tall baby gates, but you can also do this with exercise pens, which are available at pet stores. We found that Roxy was happiest when she could interact with the family, so the baby gates keep her with them but away from the front door. An exercise pen is another good alternative which has the advantage of being mobile.

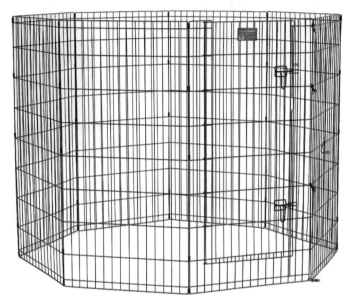

Exercise pens are flexible management tools.

When the doorbell rings, the children are supposed to ask mom or dad to open the door for them. The guest is still outside of the gate, not at the door, because their doorbell is outside of the airlock. Mom can then double-check that Roxy is in her pen, and then open the door, go out, open the gate, and let the guest in. If the child forgets the rules and opens the door herself, the visitor is still protected, because of the airlock. If the child opens the gate to Roxy's pen while mom is in the airlock with the guest, mom will hear barking and knows not to open the door. If the guest ignores the note on the airlock and walks in without an invitation, the guest is still safe, because Roxy is still penned up within the house. In order for Roxy to be set up to bite another guest, all three safety systems would have to fail at once, which is unlikely.

These steps are a lot to go through, but the emergency room for a child and euthanasia for a dog are also a big deal. A bite is very unlikely, but the consequence is so bad that prevention is of the utmost importance. These extreme measures are not something I would expect a family with children to do forever. Many families with young children simply cannot be expected to make enough changes to keep everyone safe, and the family dog must find a new home or be put to sleep. Contrary to popular belief, there are not a lot of homes out there that are willing to take a dog with a bite history, and these steps can help keep your dog's record clean while you improve the dog's behavior with BAT and look for a new home. These steps can also give your dog a chance to relax until the training kicks in enough for him to be trustworthy.

Putting your dog in a crate, behind a strong, tall baby gate, in a bedroom, or on a tether (short leash attached to a wall or heavy object) with a tasty bone or food-stuffed puzzle toy can allow you to have visitors over without causing your dog stress. Having visitors is stressful and potentially unsafe when your reactive dog is loose in the house. A spot that allows your dog to get used to the guests in the home is the best location for the crate or tether, unless there is just too much stimulation. You might have tried putting the dog away, but simply being put away is not enough. Without the proper (edible) distraction, your dog is likely to become more and more stressed by the visit, and your training may backslide. I have food-stuffed toys in the freezer at all times so that my dogs can enjoy the special times that they get them. In my house, we reserve those high-value items for non-social visitors, like a cable technician or the electrician. If your dog continues to bark regardless of the distraction of food puzzles, she should be in the car or some other location out of the home when people come over. Otherwise, she will get an even more negative association with visitors. Continue keeping her off-site until your BAT sessions make her able to handle visitors in her home.

Keep in mind that items that are valuable enough to distract a dog from a scary visitor are extraordinarily 'valuable' and might cause fights in multiple dog households. If you have more than one dog, you may need to give your dogs their bones in crates, separate rooms, or otherwise safely separate them to keep the peace. To prevent crate guarding, close the crates when the bones are picked up. Do not allow visitors to greet or taunt the dogs while they are eating. Even when dogs are being quiet, they are still aroused by the visitor's presence, so it's a good idea to ask visitors to ignore them.

Braving the great outdoors—avoiding problems on walks

As you know, your home is not the only place where training can be sabotaged by overexposure to triggers. Walks are a big challenge for reactive dogs. The one important aspect of keeping your walks peaceful is making sure you can physically hold your dog back. To walk a reactive dog, or any dog, really, I recommend using a leash that you can grab without hurting your hands. That means no cord-type retractable leashes, chain leashes, or other leashes that might tear your skin. The leash should be long enough for your dog to feel free, but not so long that she can go around a corner without you. If you take proper care, you can walk your dog with a longer leash, taking up the slack before you go around corners, or a tape-type retractable leash, used in the same way. If you do use a long leash, attach it to the back of a harness, to avoid choking or body-slamming your dog (if dogs hit the end of the leash with a lot of momentum, front-clip harnesses flip them over). It's really hard to use a retractable leash without letting the dog get into trouble (think of the momentum a dog can build up in twenty feet!), so I usually recommend a six- or eight-foot leash made of leather, Pleather (fake leather), or a comfortable fabric. Longer leashes are better for dogs who are fearful, but not reactive in a threatening way, because it gives them room to maneuver.

Long lines combine safety and freedom.

Attach your long lead to the back attachment of a harness for safety. You might also use a bungee attachment in between the long lead and the harness.

The Freedom harness allows full range of motion but allows you control.

There are lots of good harnesses currently on the market. My current favorite is the Freedom harness by "Wiggles, Wags, and Whiskers" because it has an attachment in the front and back (used separately or using both ends of the leash), velvet in the armpit areas, and a correct fit, so that dogs are allowed their full range of leg motion. Front-attachment harnesses give your dog the freedom to choose how to move his head, but you can still safely pull him away if you accidentally put him into a stressful situation that makes him flee in panic or bark/lunge. I recommend head collars and harnesses for dogs that are much stronger than their humans, but I prefer no-pull harnesses whenever they are sufficient. If you do need to use a head collar, attach one end of a European-style leash to the head collar and one to the harness, so you are primarily using the harness, but have the hand collar for back-up. Take time to get your dog used to wearing a head collar, using the same steps as for a muzzle (see page 34).

Whatever your dog wears, you should feel like you have enough control over your dog, while allowing him to avoid triggers on walks.

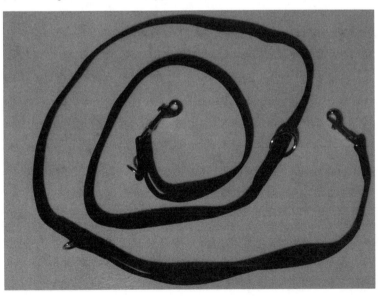

A double-ended leash allows for two points of contact.

Two points of contact increases safety and reduces the pressure on a head collar. This is a double-ended leash attached to the K9 Bridle head collar and the back attachment of the Freedom Harness.

On urban dog walks, the first step out the door can be dangerous, especially if you live in a building with indoor corridors or elevators. The higher the building, the more likely it is that your dog will be trapped in a tight space with his trigger, unable to escape. You can help your dog avoid triggers in tight quarters in several different ways, balancing inconvenience and safety. For freedom of movement and fewer surprise encounters than the elevator, you can opt for the stairs with your dog. If you have a small dog, you can pick up your dog and face him toward the wall. The Calming Cap is a semi-transparent hood that covers your dog's eyes and reduces the visual aspect of people or dogs in the elevator with them. Feeding your dog a constant stream of treats can also help elevator rides become more pleasant. Wearing the Calming Cap can allow some dogs to take the elevator without showing aggression.

A sod patch or some other way for your dog to eliminate indoors reduces the number of required walks, so that walks can be exclusively for training. Moving to a house with a securely fenced yard, or at least a first-floor apartment, is the ultimate environmental engineering for a reactive dog. When moving is impossible and other changes are insufficient, medication or other stress reducers may be necessary to allow apartment dogs to go through their days without freaking out every time they head out on a walk.

Suburban dogs can have more peaceful walks than their urban cousins because they are not trapped in elevators, hallways and noisy sidewalks with other dogs and people, but as I mentioned in the section above, they do tend to have a constant barrage of

dogs barking at them from their yards. Imagine that your neighbors shouted obsceni-
ties at you whenever you went for a walk by their houses. How long would it be before
you developed some reactivity?

If you experience barking from the canine residents on your walks, note which homes
have barking dogs and cross the street, if possible, so that your dog doesn't have to
walk right past them. You can reduce the chances of being barked at by silencing your
dog's jingling tags, which keeps the dogs that are inside of houses blissfully unaware of
your dog's presence. You can attach the tags directly to the collar by drilling a second
hole in the tag and sewing both ends to the fabric of the collar. Another option is to
get some kind of tag silencer. A rubber band works fine for that, or there are com-
mercial tag silencers available.

I have successfully trained most of the single yard dogs in my new neighborhood to
stop barking at Peanut and me as we go by, and we avoid the rest. I trained them using pure classical counter-conditioning. I just happily shout, "Treats," in an inviting
voice, as if I were calling the dog over to join us, and toss in a few pieces of stinky
treats. The treats I toss often actually hit the dogs in the yards so that they'll notice
the flying food. I then give a few pieces to my dog, say "Treats" again, and toss some
more in, followed by more treats for Peanut for putting up with all of this. If your dog
can't get close enough to a yard with a barking dog to be able to feed the dog, you can
either set aside time to train this without your dog or just work on your own dog and
let the dogs in the yard keep barking. Talking about the barking dogs in a normal tone
seems to help Peanut think that everything's ok. "That's just Ginger," I say to Peanut,
making up the name on the fly, "She has a fence." I use the same sort of tone that I
would use if I were pointing out something mildly interesting to a friend on a walk, as
in, "Looks like Bob got a new car" or "I think Mina trimmed her roses a little short."

Sometimes when I toss treats to yard dogs, they immediately stop barking and start
scarfing up the treats, or even offer Sits. Other dogs will not eat the treats and bark like
mad anyway, but eat the treats after we walk away. But each time I show up and say
"Treats," most of the dogs are less and less likely to bark. Eventually, once they hear
the word "treats" they just quietly await their rewards. I gradually start weaning off of
the treats once the dogs are quiet, over the course of a few weeks to a month.

I have to throw in some words of warning about training other people's dogs on your
walk. First, it's a good idea to get permission first, as doing so without permission
may be illegal. If you don't get permission, that's your choice, but for your dog's sake,
be ready to just walk away or have a short explanation ready if someone comes up
to yell at you. Everybody I've encountered has been fine with it, but Seattle, where
I live, is a pretty friendly place. Second, their dog may be allergic to your treats, so
use simple treats without grains or nuts. Third, their dog may be on a diet, so try to
use low-fat treats, but not at the expense of taste or smell. Fourth, if there is more
than one dog, the treats may cause a fight, so I only use this for dogs who are alone
in their yards. (My Corgi-Doberman story earlier did not involve any treats.) Finally,

be careful about feeding treats through the crack of a fence. A dog may decide to bite your hand instead of the treats! I tend to toss the treats over (or through) until I'm really sure about the dog. A few dogs on my walk lean into the fence for petting, but that's not where we started!

Even if other dogs are not barking at your dog from behind fences, she may be overwhelmed by the proximity or intensity of her triggers on walks. For example, an off-leash dog running full-tilt toward a reactive dog is like a tarantula falling on an arachnophobic person's head. It doesn't help you a bit to hear a happy reassurance that their loose dog is "friendly." If I had a dollar for every time I have had that shouted at me as a big dog came running up to mine, that money would buy a lot of dog training books!

Off-leash dogs are a big hazard on walks. If you routinely encounter loose dogs, you should consider changing your route, unless you can manage to convince all of the humans there to keep their dogs on-leash. I have clients who live next to a lovely forest park within Seattle. They delighted in walking through the park with their dog, but they encountered off-leash dogs several times a week. Progress in training had been slow, and we tracked the problem down to over-the-top meetings with loose dogs at the park. Imagine going for a daily walk in a place where you get mugged at knifepoint a few times a week. Would those walks help you relax? Fortunately, they realized what their 'peaceful' walks in the forest were doing to their dog and began taking their daily walks through their neighborhood, instead. Eliminating encounters with off-leash dogs helped this client's dog gain confidence and by doing BAT, the dog is now able to meet calm (leashed) dogs on his neighborhood walks. To avoid off-leash dogs, some of my other clients exercise their dogs indoors or drive their dogs to walking paths by busy roads.

Here are a few indoor exercise ideas:

- Hide and seek games where the dog finds you or toys/treats/objects (my personal favorite)

- Clicker training new physically or mentally demanding tricks, including Touch from a distance and Heel or loose leash walking (see Appendix 1)

- Food puzzles

Food puzzles are great for relieving pent-up energy. The Wobbler dispenses food as it wobbles (left). The Scrambler Plus is a big egg shaped toy that moves in crazy ways (right).

- Treadmill: regular human treadmill or a dog treadmill (off-leash only using treats to encourage the dog to enjoy the treadmill)
- Fetch (with calming time between throws—not ideal for all dogs)
- Tug (with calming time between tugs—not ideal for all dogs)
- Puppy pushups: alternating Sit, Down, and/or Stand

When off-leash dogs are a possibility on a walk, I recommend carrying SprayShield citronella spray. As I mentioned earlier, I had a can of that spray when I saw the Doberman go after the Corgi. To break up a fight with SprayShield, spray it directly at the nose of the more intense dog(s), which usually results in sneezing. A trainer friend of mine accidentally sprayed his own face with SprayShield and he said that it does sting, but that it's still a lot better than a dogfight. I have successfully broken up four fights with SprayShield—real fights, in which one dog had latched onto the other and would not let go. Trainers have different rules about citronella spray. I reserve it for fights where other methods of keeping the peace have failed; others use it as their first line of defense. Another option for repelling oncoming dogs is a squirt bottle or Pet Corrector, which makes a hissing noise. I don't recommend using an aversive like that for training, but I pull out all the stops when breaking up fights.

SprayShield is a good product to break up dog fights.

Most loose dogs are not looking to start a fight, they are just coming over to sniff your dog, but because your dog is reactive, that's still dangerous. Here's my hierarchy for repelling loose dogs and dogs on unlocked retractable leashes. If one step doesn't work, move on to the next.

1. When you see a loose dog far ahead of you, do an emergency U-turn (see Appendix 1 for training tips) and cross the street or turn and walk the other way.

2. If the off-leash dog is too close to just walk away without causing a scene, then shout, "Call your dog" with a hand out, like a traffic cop, toward the dog and as you do your U-turn. Repeat that statement in response to whatever the person says. Negotiation wastes time. Adding "my dog is contagious" can be helpful, though!

3. Toss a big handful of treats or rocks at the other dog.

4. If the loose dog follows, **body block** by quickly moving between the loose dog and your dog and stepping toward the loose dog to back him up (note that this can be dangerous to you).

5. While holding the leash to keep your dog's face away from the oncoming dog, use your foot to move the loose dog away (can also be dangerous to you, so only do this at your own risk).

6. Use SprayShield if a fight breaks out, and then grab the upper thighs and pull the dogs apart as soon as possible.

Avoiding loose dogs is safer than repelling them, so I'll say it again here: *if you commonly run into loose dogs on your walk, change your walking route!*

Even encountering a leashed dog up close can be trouble, but it's much easier to get away. The first thing to do is avoid head-on meetings by having reactive dogs wait for you to check for dogs (or people) at corners, blind alleys, at curbs, in and out of cars, and in and out of the house. Practice short stays with a release word at the end, like "Free," and gradually build up time. The reward can be a treat, praise, or simply permission to move again. For times when you do get surprised by a trigger, it's helpful to teach the emergency U-turn that I mentioned before. That helps with off-leash dogs, children popping out of SUVs, and anything else that might suddenly put your dog out of her comfort zone. The emergency U-turn is like a flotation device tossed to get a drowning child out of the deep end of the pool. This book covers the U-turn in detail in Appendix I.

Scan for trouble as you walk, but don't dart your head and eyes around, because it will probably freak out your dog. Dogs will pick up on your nervousness if you are constantly looking about, so make sure that you are relaxed, breathe calmly, and look around without appearing nervous to your dog. The easiest way to do this is to have a friend who can scan for you. Have pre-arranged cues so that you can quickly get the information from him/her that a loose dog, child, or object is coming, and from where. If you are on your own during a walk, then you can feed your dog for polite walking and look around with each treat. Calmly look around instead of darting your head about like a nervous Border Collie.

Take a walk without your dog, on your usual walking route. Notice your stress level and think about whether your dog's issues have influenced that. Take some time to learn about breathing techniques for relaxation via a yoga course, meditation class or books on breathing. I like the audiobook *Breathing—the Master Key to Self-Healing* (see Resources) by Andrew Weil. It has potential suggestions for breathing for health and relaxation.

Another helpful way to avoid danger on a walk is to know where you are walking—where the yards with dogs are, where the lady who usually lets her dog out lives, etc. Take short walks on paths that you know, but gradually push the envelope and take slightly different walks each time, to keep things interesting. If you want to take a new path with a reactive dog, you might want to walk it alone first, keeping track of the triggers that you see along the way. Be aware of the various triggers that might be present on a particular walking path. Many reactive dogs are very sensitive to noises, so walking along a busy street with cars may make them more likely to react to other triggers along that route.

Many dogs seem to handle noisy locations better if they are wearing some kind of body wrap, like the Anxiety Wrap or Thundershirt. The wraps physically calm dogs in the same way that swaddling helps calm a baby. Other dogs may need medication

Thundershirt

to handle the city or even need to move to a quieter neighborhood. I worked with a human-reactive bulldog mix that lived in downtown Seattle. I felt terribly for this poor dog. A loud cacophony hit our ears as soon as we walked out of her apartment building: giant duck-shaped tour buses with loudspeakers, three fire trucks, hundreds of pedestrians talking, cars honking, and a dog barking. I can only imagine the smells that went along with that for a dog. She would walk about half of a block to eliminate and then would pull like mad on her prong collar to get back inside the apartment. She was fine with dogs at daycare or walks on quiet streets, but with so much going on downtown, she also began to react aggressively to other dogs on walks. She was treated with a combination of anti-anxiety medications, the Thundershirt, BAT, and switching from the prong collar to a front-attachment harness. She will also be moving somewhere quieter soon.

Some dogs do better on walks close to home, some need to be further away to avoid territoriality, and some dogs are so reactive to everything that their walks need to be indoors, just around the house. For those walks, you can put out interesting smells or do training along the indoor route. Some dogs do well if they have a constant stream of dogs versus one or two along the way. For dogs who react to sudden changes in their environment, a walk on a busy urban walking path would be better than a walk in the neighborhood, especially if off-leash greeters or front-yard barkers surprise you on your neighborhood walk.

Anxiety Wrap

Speaking of barking, talking to people that you see on a walk may cause your dog to start barking. Why? I don't know, but one good reason is that your dog thinks you are barking at the other person. Think about it from a dog's perspective: you are facing directly at the person, staring, and you've suddenly stopped walking and started making noise on an otherwise quiet walk. Sometimes you even start wrestling (known to humans as a 'hug' or a 'handshake'). What's a dog to do? So I find it helpful to normalize the concept of talking on a walk by saying a quiet hello to everyone we meet, plus several hellos just out of the blue, to nobody at all. If this is a problem for your dog, keep that in mind as a trigger for when you are actually doing BAT set-ups.

Pay close attention to your dog when you walk her. If your dog is ignoring you, it might be because you've been ignoring her. Give her a reason to pay more attention to you. Leave the cell phone in your pocket. If you need to walk or run for exercise and can't focus on your dog, then don't bring her! You can run on a treadmill after your walk if you need a little more exercise. The moment you see her stop paying attention to you, you can call her name or walk the other way, so she learns to always keep some of her focus on you. Or use that treadmill to give her some exercise before the walk. There are even treadmills made just for dogs, but you can use clicker training to teach a dog to run on a regular treadmill.

When I say that your dog should pay attention to you, I don't mean that he should stare at you during the whole walk or walk precisely in Heel position. If that's what you want, fine, but I like to let dogs be dogs. Half the fun of going on a walk with my dog is watching what he sees or smells on walks, watching him prance along in doggie bliss. Being able to sniff on their walks allows dogs to learn what's out there. I think letting them sniff is an important factor in handling the world with confidence. Dogs very often have to sniff after they've encountered something scary; it's self-soothing.

When walking a reactive dog, leave your other dogs at home so that you can pay attention to him and so that your dog is not triggered by another dog's behavior. Reactivity can be contagious, so if you have one dog that does well with dogs and people, keep it that way by walking him alone, away from the influence of your reactive other dog. Walking your dogs separately also prevents any redirection, where your reactive dog goes after your other dog because he can't reach the real target. Having said that, there are benefits from social facilitation. If your reactive dog sees and smells a dog that he is familiar with having a good time meeting other dogs or people, then it may make him more comfortable. If you have two people, one can handle the reactive dog and the other can handle the confident dog, who can serve as a role model. Keep the reactive dog at a distance that alllows him to stay below threshold.

I met with a family who had two Rat Terriers with a host of self-control issues. Sophia, the dog who I was there to see, was very reactive to other dogs. Sophia would scream her little head off when she caught a glimpse of another dog, even from several blocks away. People thought her humans were torturing her! Being humans, the owners were convinced that we needed to walk both dogs together, out of fairness, even though the other dog had some reactivity issues as well. One dog shouldn't get a walk without the other, right? When we walked the dogs separately, Sophia's reactivity dropped to about thirty percent of what it had been, so we first did BAT with her alone, and then together with her littermate after the reactivity improved. Because of this, their other dog's reactivity immediately dropped down to almost nothing and they could all enjoy an easy walk without even training her at all!

Muzzles can be effective safety tools

Muzzles are a relatively easy way to prevent bites. I think a lot of people are afraid to use them, because it's an admission that their dog really does have a problem. It also just 'looks bad' and there's the stigma that a dog in a muzzle is worse than a dog not in a muzzle. It's ironic, really, because the dog in a well-fitted muzzle can't bite you! If you have muzzle phobia, I'd like you to think about how calm you would feel if you knew that your dog could not bite another person or dog. If that's not enough, go ahead and do a quick exercise. I'm not kidding. Get some of your favorite 'human treats,' like a candy bar chopped into little pieces. Visualize your dog wearing a muzzle, and then eat a piece of candy. Relax and repeat.

> Note for Pros: Make it easy for your clients to find the right kind of muzzle by referring them to specific places to purchase it. It's hard enough to get over muzzle phobia, much less have to drive around to ten different stores to find the right one.

In terms of which type of muzzle to use, I like the plastic Italian basket muzzles and the Baskerville Ultra because they allow the dog to pant, breathe, move their whiskers, drink, and eat treats (put the treats between the bars or use squeeze cheese). They don't allow ears from another dog to slip in, as the nylon grooming muzzles do. Here's a grizzly example of why I never use the grooming muzzles. I know a dog who

was wearing a grooming muzzle during an on-leash introduction. A fight broke out and the other dog's ear somehow made it inside of the dog's muzzle. Grooming muzzles fit fairly tightly, so after biting down on the ear, the dog didn't have much choice but to tear it off and swallow. Ick." So basket muzzles are the way to go. The rubber Baskerville Ultra muzzles are softer than the hard plastic and metal ones, so if they run into you or punch into one of their triggers, it won't hurt as much.

An Italian basket muzzle with a K9 Bridle head collar underneath.

The flexible, treat-friendly Baskerville Ultra.

I have three rules for muzzles: 1) train your dog to get used to wearing a muzzle rather than just putting it on your dog; 2) always set up your dog to be below threshold; and 3) always supervise a dog in a muzzle to avoid accidents. I make an exception to the second rule when it's a safety issue and there's no way to avoid the stress. For example, if a dog who is reactive toward people injures herself and must be inspected by a veterinarian, that's an appropriate time to muzzle the dog.

When in doubt, use the muzzle or put a fence between your dog and the trigger for up-close work. Keep in mind that your dog can still 'muzzle punch,' i.e., run into the target at top speed, which can hurt a child or smaller dog. Make sure the muzzle fits well, so that neither the dog nor their opponent can slip it off.

Never just put a muzzle on your dog without proper training. Imagine that you are a dog that has never worn a muzzle before, and you find yourself wearing a muzzle at the veterinarian's office. For one thing, this unfamiliar piece of plastic is suddenly stuck to your face. But it gets worse: once you have this thing on your face, the vet proceeds to be much ruder to you than ever before, poking, prodding, and generally wreaking havoc on your nervous system. Now something that started as just uncomfortable is a big tip-off that bad things will happen to you. If you've already put a muzzle on your dog and had a bad response, it'll take more time to get her comfortable wearing it, but please persist, because it's worth it.

There are many ways to get a dog used to a muzzle, but using clicker training to teach your dog to put her own snout into the muzzle is an elegant solution. You can start by treating your dog for just looking at the muzzle and gradually **raise criteria** (get pickier about which behavior earns a treat). Soon your dog will be actively seeking out the muzzle to target, and then eventually holding her snout inside the muzzle. It becomes a sort of game to your dog. Here are the steps:

1. With the muzzle in one hand and treats in the other, present the muzzle to your dog. As soon as she looks at it, say "Yes" and feed a treat. Just as she finishes the treat, hide the remaining treats and the muzzle behind your back. Repeat until your dog happily looks at the muzzle.

2. Cup your hand around the front of the muzzle so that you can put treats in the muzzle (on your hand) without the treats falling out and tuck the straps out of the way. Repeat the step above (marking for looking at the muzzle), but put each treat reward in the muzzle for your dog to eat, and then step back after your dog gets the treat, so you relieve any pressure of being around the muzzle, and so your dog has to follow you to get to the muzzle. Repeat ten times.

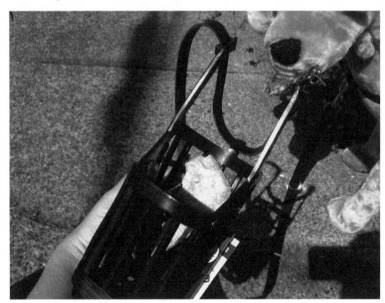

Turn the muzzle into a food dish in your hand.

3. Raise criteria by waiting for your dog to move toward the muzzle before you mark and reward in the muzzle (continue stepping away after your dog eats the treat). Repeat until your dog is moving toward the muzzle eight times out of ten.

4. Raise criteria by waiting for your dog to put her nose into the muzzle before you mark and reward in the muzzle. Repeat until your dog is touching the muzzle eight times out of ten.

5. Working in blocks of ten touches, start marking only if your dog holds her nose in the muzzle for at least one second. Repeat until she is able to stay there for one second at least eight times out of then, then change criteria to 2, 4, 8, 10, 15, 20, 25, and 30 seconds. If this is a challenge for your dog, I recommend targeting a Post-It note or other target and teaching her to hold her nose to it for longer and longer periods of time. The paper target can then be put into the basket of the muzzle to help her learn to put her nose in there for a long time.

6. Now start to work from farther away, so she has to come further to the muzzle to target. She's already had to move a little because you have been retreating away from her after she eats each treat. Start stepping three feet away after she eats each treat, then raise criteria to six feet once she's doing well. When you change the distance, lower criteria to touching the muzzle at all for ten times, then raise your criteria to a nose hold ten times, then do ten trials each of 2, 8, 15, and 30 seconds.

7. Now that your dog is diving into the muzzle when you bring it out, you can pretend to put the straps on (just holding them in your hand), for half a second. Mark and reward in the muzzle. Repeat about ten times.

8. Gradually increase the duration of how long you have the straps over the back of her neck, and then start attaching the clips. Continue marking and rewarding duration. If she starts to paw at it, it means you have probably asked for too much, too soon. Just ask her to do something, like a Sit, and then reward by treating through the muzzle and use the time that she's chewing to take it off.

9. Practice in different locations and with different amount of distractions. You can also attach the collar part of the muzzle, with the basket just hanging down, and play fetch with a ball or do a Find it session with treats.

10. Continue rewarding your dog every time you put the muzzle on—either with food, toys, attention, or something else that she loves.

Always remember that dogs are fabulous at learning what predicts danger or safety, so never do something 'mean' to your dog in the thirty seconds after you first put the muzzle on. That might mean toenail trimming, a vet examination, greeting another dog if they're afraid of that, or walking outside for those who are scared to go outside. Even though the muzzle is for bite prevention, put it on at some other times when you are just hanging out and loving on your dog, so that it becomes a very normal piece of equipment. For visual learners, I recommend watching a video by UK dog trainer Chirag Patel on how to condition a muzzle, which is similar to the steps I've written above. You can see it on my website at http://doggiezen.com/muzzle or search for "domesticated manners" and "muzzle" on YouTube.

One way I've thought of to help make the muzzle a great thing is to make a "Muzzle-cicle." Tightly wrap the nose-end of the muzzle with plastic wrap. Put about a half an inch of wet dog food in and mush it into the end, so the muzzle is basically like a bowl with some dog food at the bottom. Put that in the freezer. Once it is frozen, remove the plastic wrap and put it on your muzzle-trained dog. This is a great way to have visitors over, too. Again, your dog should be 99.99% fine with visitors, but the muzzle is there as a just-in-case. The Muzzle-cicle helps distract your dog when visitors first come in and makes that 99.99% into 99.999999%. Either put the Muzzle-cicle on at least thirty seconds before your dog notices the visitors, or put it on just after she (safely) notices that you have company. I would only do the latter if your dog truly loved her Muzzle-cicle!

In case you can't tell by now, I think that bites must be strictly prevented. As Yoda sagely said in *Star Wars*, "Do, or do not. There is no try." Engineering your dog's environment for safety is essential when you choose to keep a dog with a bite history in your home, and it's still important even if your dog hasn't bitten yet. Any dog will bite, with enough provocation. Many jurisdictions allow "one free bite," but even a single bite can be enough to have the dog euthanized, depending on local laws and the severity of the bite. For example, a dog in Seattle that inflicts an injury requiring two or more stitches to a person would be immediately considered "dangerous" and must be euthanized or removed from the city (see Resources). Given the severity of the consequences of a bite, preventing bites is critical. Training takes time, and good management gives dogs an opportunity to change their behavior patterns.

Checklist of useful products for reactive dogs

- **Calming Cap:** Worn over the eyes to calm the dog, especially useful for reducing visual stimuli, as when the dog is riding in the car or elevator. Developed by Trish King.

- **Clicker:** Little hand-held box that makes a sound, which the trainer always follows with a reinforcer. I use the clicker only with tangible reinforcers, like food and toys.

Box clicker.

- **Exercise Pen:** An "ex-pen" is a portable fence, like a baby gate with multiple panels. Used to block off areas that you want to keep the dog in or out of, as well as a barrier for greetings between dogs and decoys. Comes in metal and plastic.

- **Front-attachment harness:** Harnesses where the leash clips to a ring at the dog's chest to give you leverage if your dog lunges or pulls (visualize the physics). My favorite harness is the Freedom harness by Wiggles, Wags, and Whiskers. It has velvet armpit straps and two leash attachment points, for more control, and you can attach to just the back attachment to give the dog freedom during BAT set-ups.

- **Head Halter:** These are collars with a loop around the nose and around the neck, like a horse bridle. They come in various brands and designs like K9 Bridle, Comfort Trainer, Halti, and Gentle Leader. Head halters help you control the movement of your dog's head, which is like having power steering for your dog. Acclimate to head collar before using, as you would with a muzzle. Use only if other leash walking devices are insufficient, with a double-ended leash attached to a harness or other point of contact.

- **Leash:** Reactive dogs should be on-leash when out in public, especially if your dog may scare, bite, or overwhelm someone with over-friendliness. In areas that are tempting to let your dog off-leash, a twenty foot leash provides plenty of exercise without completely compromising safety.

- **Mobile Phone:** Bringing your phone lets you call for help, if necessary. Focus on your dog, instead of chatting while you're walking, but do bring a phone for safety.

- **Muzzle:** Having your dog wear a basket muzzle drastically increases the safety of working up close. Use with supervision.

- **SprayShield:** Citronella spray that can repel oncoming dogs and break up most fights.

- **Thundershirt and Anxiety Wrap:** Body wraps that reduce anxiety by swaddling the dog. Especially useful for sound-sensitive dogs.

- **Treat Pouch:** Convenient access for treats, especially helpful for walks

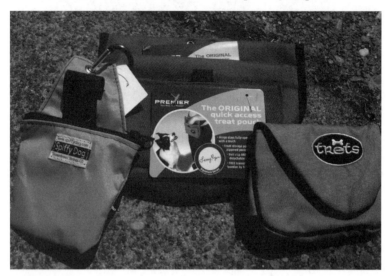

Treat pouches are a convenient way to access treats on walks. WoofHoof TRETS magnetic Reward Pouch, Spiffy Dog zipper Pocket Treat Bag, and the Premier Gentle Leader Treat Pouch are three good options.

The Premier treat pouch developed by Terry Ryan.

I imagine that you're ready to get working on BAT! Let's start with an in-depth discussion of functional rewards and replacement behaviors.

CHAPTER 4

Functional Rewards and Replacement Behaviors: An Introduction

---

We've all heard the saying, "You get what you pay for," and that applies to dog behavior even more than the department store. As much as we would like dogs to listen because they love us so much, chances are your dog does what you ask if and when it works for him in some way. Dogs also have a reason for jumping up, pulling on the leash, and racing to the door when you grab your keys. For example, a puppy pulls on the leash because she has twice as many legs as you and wants to go faster! Forward motion—if you allow it—is her functional reward. Thinking in terms of functional rewards can be really helpful no matter which behavior issue you're working on.

This chapter covers in detail two of the key concepts for BAT—functional rewards and replacement behaviors—so please read it carefully. Understanding the terminology and concepts from this chapter will make it easier for you to follow the rest of the book so that you can more quickly learn how to use BAT to deal with the problems associated with reactive dogs.

Definition and examples of functional rewards
A functional reward is a naturally occurring consequence of a behavior that makes a behavior more likely to occur in the future.

By "naturally occurring," I mean that the consequence regularly occurs outside of a formal training scenario. In short, functional rewards are real-life rewards that are logically paired with the behavior (using the dog's logic and history). Functional rewards are consequences that provide such things as safety, attention, and fun. Functional rewards often accidentally create, maintain, or enhance problem behaviors as well, especially if you are not aware of what the dog finds rewarding.

> I think of BAT as a kind of dog training *tai chi,* where you don't fight the reactivity directly, you just use the force behind the behavior (the functional reward) and the dog's underlying curiosity to overpower the reactivity for you.

You are probably already using functional rewards with your dog to make your life easier or more fun, even if you are not aware of the term. One of the classics is the dog who runs to the door and sits politely as soon as you grab your keys or his leash, even if you don't say anything. Your dog has learned that a ride in the car or a walk is about to happen after you grab the leash, and by sitting in front of the door he will get the functional reward of a fun outing with you even quicker. On the other hand, if your dog races to the door and acts crazy, guess what? You've trained *that* crazy behavior chain inadvertently if you continue to let the dog have the functional reward of going for a walk.

Now let's look at jumping up to greet through the lens of functional rewards. Your attention (even negative attention like telling her to stop jumping or sit) is likely the functional reward for jumping up. If so, you need to stop paying attention to your dog when she jumps to stop her habit of jumping. For example, if you always slowly turn away when she jumps up on you (and ask others to do so as well), the result is that jumping up is no longer worth the effort. The dog still craves attention, so use attention as a functional reward for some better behavior, like sitting to greet.

Here's another example. Puppies have a natural instinct to get back with their families for protection when they are alone. Because of that instinct, puppies whine and bark when left alone too long in a crate and try to escape to bring their family members closer. We can't get inside their heads or ask them directly, but behaviorally, we know that puppies become quiet when a person comes back and lets them out. Your return to the puppy provides companionship and safety, which is the functional reward for the puppy's whining. Interestingly enough, *your dog may have trained you* to let her out when she cries, because you also get a functional reward for the 'letting out' behavior—the puppy's silence. So you can see that functional rewards reinforce behavior in *both* the puppy and the human in this example. If you were to go stand near the crate but wait for ten seconds of silence before opening the crate, then waiting in silence would be the replacement behavior for the puppy, earning the same reward of companionship and safety. Waiting to let the puppy out of the crate to reward quiet behavior (rather than whining) is now an example of a common training trick for ordinary behavior problems. But more important to our subject here is this type of approach can also be applied to more serious issues like aggression, reactivity, and fear, because those behaviors are also maintained by functional rewards. Note: returning to the crate is also a functional reward. However, I think reassuring the puppy with your presence, while still telling her (with your behavior) that she can only get out when quiet is better than letting the puppy panic. If the puppy is just frustrated, not panicking, then wait for silence to return to the crate. I'm wiling to put a puppy through a tantrum, but not a panic attack.

Knowing what is rewarding your dog is the key to understanding his behavior. It's not always obvious, but if you take the time to observe your dog you can usually figure it out. Your ability to understand and recognize functional rewards is the first step to making BAT work.

Replacement behaviors

A replacement behavior is what you teach your dog to do instead of the problem behavior. The key to making this work is when replacement behavior becomes a more efficient or more effective way for the dog to earn the functional reward than the original problem behavior(s). Let's go back to the example given above of the dog who rushes across the room, barks, and scratches the door when you reach for your keys or his leash. If you clip on the leash and open the door to let the dog out after he does all of that, you are providing him a functional reward (the fun outing) for his behavior and you will have to repaint your door much more often. If that has happened with your dog, your best strategy is to start requiring him to sit before you clip the leash on. If the dog is bouncing around, simply set down the leash and patiently, silently refuse to clip the leash to the collar until he sits. Sitting becomes the replacement behavior for jumping and acting crazy because you have made going for a walk contingent upon polite behavior: your dog gets to go on a walk if, and only if, he is calm. Making the functional reward of walks and car rides contingent upon sitting will quickly calm down the situation at your door.

Ideal replacement behaviors should be naturally or easily linked to the functional reward of the problem behavior. Replacement behaviors should 'work' for your dog in that he gets the same result as from doing the problem behavior.

Old habit: Problem Behavior → Functional Reward

New habit: Replacement Behavior → Functional Reward

Think again about a dog who jumps up on people with the hope of getting attention or getting petted. If this behavior works, attention or affection is the functional reward. As I mentioned above, part of correcting this behavior is to slowly pivot away from your dog whenever he jumps at you. But, if you simply ignore or punish a dog who has been successful in getting attention for a long time by jumping up on people, the dog will get creative in his attempts to get attention. This may include more enthusiastic jumping, barking, or nipping. This is why it's important to find a replacement behavior that is naturally linked with the functional reward of getting attention. I recommend teaching the dog a play bow since dogs often use play bows instinctively to engage other dogs in play (a training tip I picked up from my friend Joey Iversen). Then, by either prompting or waiting for the dog to do a play bow, reward this new replacement behavior with the attention and petting he was trying to get by jumping up. You can add in treats as a reward, too, but over time, use petting and paying attention to reinforce bowing. See Appendix 1 for more details on teaching your dog to bow.

Here's one more example. Even though polite walking is not naturally linked with the functional reward of getting to walk forward, it is *easily* linked if the person holding the leash is consistent in rewarding polite walking and not pulling. The connection between polite walking and forward motion can be enforced every time your dog is on-leash. That means polite walking is a great replacement behavior for pulling.

Requirements for a functional approach to problem behaviors

There are three simple requirements for using the concept of functional rewards to fix problems in your dog (or other animals, including your human family). Functional rewards aren't a cure-all, but they do work in a lot of different situations, because dogs tend to do whatever works.

First, you need to be able to pinpoint the functional reward that is maintaining the problem behavior. There may be more than one functional reward that is 'paying' the dog to do the behavior you are trying to eliminate. It may help to film the dog doing the behavior in her daily life so that you can see what the regular consequences are for the problem behavior. A professional trainer or behaviorist can also help you figure out what's motivating your dog to do the behavior (hint, it's some kind of functional reward, probably not 'dominance').

Second, you also need to be able to find a replacement behavior that reasonably earns the same functional reward. The dog had some reason for doing the problem behavior, and she still needs to have her needs met. I've given several examples of that above and we will get into more detail on replacement behaviors for reactivity in the next chapter.

Finally, using a functional approach also requires that you are able to control access to the functional reward, at least temporarily, so the dog is consistently getting it only (or primarily) for doing the replacement behaviors. For example, you can consistently control attention given to the dog, access to a fun walk, or the forward motion that he loves. If you can't control access to the functional rewards, then you will need to use some other kind of reward to build behavior. But any time that you can use functional rewards, you can create powerful, long-lasting change.

To summarize

When you have a problem behavior that you're trying to fix, look at the consequences of that behavior from your dog's perspective. One or many different consequences are maintaining the problem. To adjust your dog's behavior, teach her that a replacement behavior will earn the same functional reward.

Knowing the functional reward for the problem behaviors is one of the three requirements for using a functional approach with an individual dog's issue. The other two requirements are: being able to control access to the functional rewards; and having an appropriate replacement behavior.

Requirements for a functional approach to behavior problems:
- Functional reward is known
- Functional reward is controllable
- Replacement behavior exists.

CHAPTER 5

Functional Rewards and Replacement Behaviors for Reactivity

Most dogs who bark, lunge, or bite aren't chemically imbalanced killers, out to injure other dogs or people for sport. If we could translate what their barking or lunging at some trigger means, it would generally be either "Go away!" (anger), "Get over here and play with me!" (frustration), or "Let me get out of here safely!" (fear). When the behaviors become over-the-top or obnoxious, we call that "reactivity." The point of reactive behavior usually seems to boil down to increasing or decreasing distance between the dog and the trigger. That means that, in most reactivity cases, *the functional reward is an increase in distance from the trigger. In other words, walking away from the trigger is usually a reward.* That's even true for dogs who run toward the trigger like a bullet to fight and often true for the ones who just want to play.

I split reactivity into three main emotional buckets because of their influence on the variety of functional rewards a dog may perceive:

- **Fear.** "I want to get away." Walking away from trigger is the best functional reward and the trigger leaving is also reinforcing. Visual clues: the dog's center of gravity is low and away from the trigger (rear end tucked under, legs bent) or the dog alternates between lunging forward and bouncing away.

- **Anger.** "I want you to go away." The trigger leaving is most reinforcing. However, I usually have the student dog walk away anyway as the functional reward, because it's a good pattern for the dog and owner and it's still reinforcing because it reduces stress by increasing distance to the trigger. Visual clues: the dog is standing up high and stiff on his toes, squarely facing the trigger.

- **Frustration.** "I want to get closer to you." Ironically, both walking toward the trigger and away from the trigger can be used as the functional reward. I'll go into this in detail in Chapter 8. Visual clues: the dog is fairly bouncy, vocal, and greets without fighting when allowed to get up close, although the dog's rude greeting may cause the other dog to start a fight.

Dogs may have a combination of the above emotions. For example, a dog who is normally fearful of people may also show territorial aggression near her home, so she is both fearful and angry. Anger is a reaction to a violation of what the dog might perceive as 'rules,' so territoriality and resource guarding are both examples of anger. While science has traditionally avoided using anthropomorphic terms like fear and anger, recent research seems to indicate that dogs definitely do have these primal emotions. Read Patricia McConnell's excellent book, *For the Love of a Dog* and Alexandra Horowitz's *Inside of a Dog* for more information about recent research on dog emotions and cognition (see Resources).

In a social situation, the trigger itself has some 'magnetic power' for reactive dogs who show aggressive displays, no matter what emotion is driving the behavior. I call this the **magnet effect.** What I mean by that is that once the dog gets too close, it's like she's sucked in and can't seem to help herself. She might prefer to put a lot of distance between herself and the scary monster, but first she just has to bark, growl, or even bite. That probably serves the purpose of making sure the scary monster will let her get away, or will stay away from her next time. Whenever barking, growling, or biting work to make a dog feel safe, she's just gotten a functional reward and she is even more likely to repeat those behaviors next time. That's why I spent so much time discussing management in the Chapter 3—you need to help your dog avoid rehearsing reactivity, because it's a lose-lose proposition.

During a recent initial consultation, I explained the concept of functional rewards to a couple with a dog I will call Gigi, a Cattle Dog mix with fear and territorial issues. My clients said that they didn't think Gigi would want to put distance between her and other dogs, because she always ran toward other dogs. She had escaped from the yard once and chased a dog way down the alley before attacking him, inflicting wounds that required veterinary attention. I asked whether they thought she wanted the other dog to be close to her, as though the purpose of chasing the other dog down was to keep him around. They laughed and said, of course not, she wanted to get rid of this dog! I think Gigi was explaining, in no uncertain terms, that she didn't want the other dog anywhere near her house. A good offense is the best defense, right?

They still weren't entirely convinced that Gigi would find walking away reinforcing until we took her outside for a set-up. There is always some distance, outside of the threshold boundary where the dogs are not 'magnetically' drawn in and are happy to create space by moving their own bodies away from the trigger. We quickly found that spot for Gigi. She would briefly stare at the decoy dog and then look away. Her owners then walked her away from the other dog. Her body language was relaxed and happy as she left. The couple commented that Gigi looked so proud of herself and that she seemed to be paying more attention to them than usual. If we had walked Gigi too close to the decoy dog, we definitely would have gotten barking and lunging, and they probably would have had to pull her away instead of her happily trotting away with them. The magnet is too strong up close when training begins, but there's always some distance at which reactive dogs are happy to walk away from the trigger. Using BAT, that distance can eventually shrink to nothing.

Controlling access to functional rewards

Aggression, reactivity, and fear are particularly well-suited to a functional approach because distance to the trigger is usually controllable, especially in set-ups. To control your dog's access to functional rewards outside of BAT set-ups, you need to use management. That means you may need to walk in a different location or use distractions like treats until your dog can handle his neighborhood walks. You may need to put up better fencing or close window blinds so your dog is not tempted to bark at passersby. If you have more than one dog and they fight with each other, you may need to separate the dogs when you aren't home until training is completed. But all of those things are possible!

If the functional reward of your dog's reactivity is chasing prey, then you may not be able to use that exact functional reward. For a dog with a strong prey drive, you can't usually control access to the functional reward as prey tend to appear in random fashion and letting the dog get to the prey is usually hard on the prey. Well, you could, but it may not be humane or ethical. You can prevent your dog from having access to squirrels or small dogs, but you shouldn't let him go kill the other animal as a reward. You can use squirrel chasing as a reward once the squirrels are safely in their trees, but I can't justify using the chance to chase a cat or a small dog as a reward. To use BAT in this situation, I use a substitute reward that serves a similar function as the predation, like the bite/hold/shake sequence that he gets while playing tug of war. So instead of letting your dog chase the squirrel as the functional reward for good behavior, you could play tug.

If your dog panics at the sound of loud noises, achieving safety is the functional reward for her behavior. You can control the volume of recorded noises easily, but during thunderstorm season, you can't control external noises. Jude Azaren reported to the FunctionalRewards Yahoo! group (see Resources) that she used running back inside the house as a reward for her thunder-phobic dog's brave choice to go out into a storm with her. That effectively controlled the functional reward by reducing the noise from the thunder outside and helping her dog feel safe.

Polite cut-off signals as replacement behavior for reactivity

Let's say that your dog barks, lunges, or growls as a way of saying "go away, or I will fight you!" What your dog is doing has been labeled **cut-off signals,** or distance increasing behaviors, by behaviorists. However, growling and lunging are the kinds of behaviors you are trying to avoid. Fortunately, not all cut-off signals so directly signal aggression. Looking away (head turns) and turning ones backs on the trigger also serve as cut-off signals. Barbara Handelman defines cut-off signals as being used to "interrupt behavior coming at them from another animal. Cut-off displays unequivocally signal that further interaction is not desired" (see Resources). Learning to recognize and eventually reward *polite or acceptable* cut-off signals can allow you to train dogs in a way that honors their need for safety and distance. My training goal is to help reactive dogs rely on the more polite cut-off signals instead of behaviors that look like aggression. I use the term 'polite' cut-off signals (or 'good choices') to mean the non-confrontational cut-off signals which, while more subtle, are also understood by most dogs. I should probably use something that sounds less judgmental than 'good' choices, because the opposite would be a 'bad' choice and it's not a far stretch to a 'bad dog,' a phrase I can't stand. But clients seem to understand the phrase 'good choices' a lot faster than 'replacement behaviors' or even 'polite cut-off signals,' so I use it, with a small inner twinge each time.

Polite cut-off signals are pretty much the same set of behaviors that you might do if a creepy stranger tries to make eye contact with you in an elevator. These are ways of saying, "please stay away and leave me alone." Take a second to picture what you do in that situation. I know that I break eye contact, turn my head or body away, avoid sudden movements, maybe do some grooming behavior like looking at my fingernails, or even exit the elevator.

Dogs do many of the same cut-off signals that we do, and meeting another dog on-leash must feel a little bit like being stuck on an elevator with a creepy stranger. There are a lot of individual behaviors you could reward when using BAT with your dog, but generally speaking, watch your dog until you see a polite cut-off signal, which tells you that your dog is done gathering information. (Note, however, these behaviors vary by dog.) Here are some examples of what typical polite cut-off signals might look like:

- Look away from the trigger (not necessarily 'done'—depends on the dog)
- Head turns laterally away from the trigger
- Lip lick
- Turn body away from the trigger
- Ground sniff
- Sigh
- Shake off (as if wet).

Lip lick can be a polite cut-off signal indicating stress or anticipation.

Polite cut-off signals, like look-aways and body turns, make excellent replacement behaviors for aggression and panic, because they have the exact same functional reward: putting distance between your dog and the trigger. To anthropomorphize a bit, that increase in distance and safety is what your dog is trying to achieve with a cut-off signal, be it a polite or an aggressive display. BAT can teach him that he can get what he wants efficiently by doing an easier, more polite behavior.

Head turns and other polite cut-off signals are probably already in your dog's repertoire when he encounters something slightly stressful, but he just doesn't use them persistently or you don't recognize them for what they are when he's up close with his trigger. BAT rewards replacement behaviors frequently enough that dogs begin to use them automatically, instead of resorting to aggression or panic. *BAT works well because you pick replacement behaviors that your dog is naturally disposed to, meaning that your dog's brain already links the replacement behaviors to the same functional reward when the trigger is mild enough.* If your dog saw another dog from a long way away, he would probably look for a bit and then spontaneously do polite cut-off signals without any prompting from you. That's the foundation that BAT builds upon.

For dogs who don't show any kind of aggression and only try to flee, you reward polite cut-off signals but also try to set up the situation so that the dog does **pro-social behaviors.** Pro-social behaviors are your dog's version of flirting with someone across a crowded a bar, something you want to encourage in a timid dog. Such behaviors can lead to a rebuff (cut-off signals) from the decoy dog, but the goal is to elicit social behaviors and information from the other dog. The following are examples of pro-social replacement behavior:

- Look at, lean toward, or walk toward the trigger
- Sniff, gather information about the trigger
- Offer distance-decreasing or 'friendly' behaviors toward the trigger—play bow with rear in air, bend joints, look goofy, etc.
- Lift tail from a tucked position
- Mouth softening.

Note for Pros: Replacement behaviors are species-specific, but can also vary within the species. When you do BAT with other species, like birds, horses, or humans, reinforce replacement behaviors that 'normal' animals of that species naturally do.

Choosing a replacement behavior that is naturally linked with the functional reward has a great side effect: automatic training. Once your dog understands the linkage, the environment will begin to train your dog for you. For example, if you've taught your dog to walk away from a person if she wants some distance, that should work in real life, too. Most people will leave your dog alone if your dog walks away from them. I've seen that happen time and again with clients and with Peanut.

GOOD CHOICES

These REPLACEMENT BEHAVIORS for reactivity
reduce the tension of a greeting.

HEAD TURN

or look away from trigger

SNIFF GROUND

BODY TURN

loose spine

SCRATCH

YAWN

somewhat stressed

SHAKE-OFF

stress release

SOFTEN EYES

"I'm friendly"

EARS TO NEUTRAL

relaxed

LIP-LICK

or nose-lick

PLAY BOW

"I'm friendly"

When a replacement behavior isn't naturally linked to the functional reward you use in training, the dog's behaviors may fall apart in real life instead of being maintained by the environment. For example, you could theoretically teach a reactive dog to do a play bow to make other dogs go away, but play bows are not going to be rewarded that way in your dog's natural environment, because play bows are distance-decreasing behaviors. That's like teaching a child to say, "More, please," instead of "No, thanks," to stop dad from piling more vegetables on her plate. It may work in your house, but when she tries saying that at someone else's table, she'll be disappointed and confused.

It helps to pick replacement behaviors that are less expensive for your dog to do than the problem behavior, meaning that they take less energy or are easier for your dog to do. Let's go back to the replacement behaviors we looked at before, the polite distance-increasing signals. Turning the head, sighing, or walking away are less expensive behaviors than barking and lunging and potentially starting a fight. Given a choice of two behaviors that earn the same functional reward, a dog is likely to choose the one that's easier. Dogs are masters of efficiency.

Bark, Lunge, Bite (problem behavior) → Safety (reward)

Polite distance-increasing signals (replacement behavior) → Safety (same reward)

Problem behavior: Reactivity → Safety

Replacement behavior: Polite cut-off signals → Safety

Sniffing the ground is a great replacement behavior, in that it is natural, very visible to the handler, and easy to reinforce.

To summarize, if you know the functional reward for your dog's reactivity and you can control access to that reward, and if you have a replacement behavior that can be paired well with the functional reward, then BAT should be a great tool for your dog. BAT has worked well with my private clients and trainers around the world report similar success. We also use BAT in our Growly Dog class at Ahimsa Dog Training in Seattle and the technique has been very effective for dogs with a variety of barking, lunging, growling, and/or biting issues.

And now…the moment you've all been waiting for. Let's look at how to do BAT set-ups!

CHAPTER 6

BAT Set-ups for Reactivity

This chapter walks you through the details of using Behavior Adjustment Training to help reduce dog reactivity. As I mentioned before, all training with BAT is done sub-threshold, meaning that your dog is exposed only at a level of stimulation that allows them to react well, without rehearsing the behavior that you are trying to change. Keeping your dog below threshold is easiest to do when you have a carefully arranged situation with helper humans and/or dogs to practice with, but it can usually be done on walks, too. Keep thresholds in mind at all times as you work with your dog.

In order for BAT to work, you must be able to recognize when your dog is at or below threshold level versus when he is over threshold. The following two photos show examples of each.

Wait for a good choice here, but be ready to prompt. Dog is at or below threshold: mouth open, tail slower, center of gravity neutral. However, facial muscles are tense and leash is tight.

Time for graduated prompting! Dog is starting to go over threshold: mouth closed, forehand wrinkled, tail moving fast, body coiled and ready for action.

Choice points

A **choice point** is a situation in which a dog approaching his threshold level must make a decision to do something, like choosing between two paths in a maze. To do BAT, set up situations in which your dog must make a choice between doing the reactivity or a replacement behavior where your dog has a really high chance of getting it right doing the replacement behavior. That's not any old point—the deck is stacked so that your dog is very likely to do a polite cut-off signal instead of panicking or being aggressive. I suppose I could coin a new term for that, like a "favorable choice point" because the odds of your dog offering the desired behavior are in your favor. But I'm the sort of trainer who never wants to give dogs a strong chance to do behavior I want to eliminate, so any choice point I set up would be a favorable one. Let's stick with the simpler term: whenever I use the term "choice point," please take that to mean "favorable choice point." Your dog's arrival at a choice point is the beginning of a BAT trial. Receiving the functional reward ends the BAT trial.

At a choice point, there must actually be a choice to be made, so that your dog practices the act of choosing the new behavior. As training goes on, keep the probabilities about the same, so your dog is choosing what you want, over and over. What changes is the choice point itself: the training environment becomes more and more realistic as you move closer to the trigger and the dog's threshold level and work in different settings. Let's use the analogy of rehearsing a theatrical play again. The first set of choice points is like reading the script in a quiet coffee shop; the middle stages are rehearsing with other actors; dress rehearsals get the actors used to the distraction of costumes and sets; and the final choice points are like performing on Broadway. For example, in Peanut's first BAT session with a child, he was on-leash, with a single child sitting on an adult's lap behind a barrier, far, far away. In the final sessions, Peanut was off-leash and two children were running around a room with him. You wouldn't perform on Broadway without a lot of rehearsal. The same is true for training—performing well takes lots of rehearsal, at the right difficulty level. In all of your dog's encounters with their triggers, especially the ones in which your dog is off-leash, the chance of a successful 'performance' should be very high.

Here's another example of a choice point, from Kathy Sdao's *I-Cue* seminar, which is where I first heard the term applied to dog training (see Resources). Kathy played a video of her teaching puppy raisers at Guide Dogs for the Blind in which she demonstrated how to set up choice points to train polite walking around distractions. The puppy was to walk in a straight path that was marked on the ground, with a distraction off to the side. The distraction was close enough to get the puppy's attention, but far enough that the puppy was likely to turn away from it and keep walking. The choice point began the instant the puppy noticed the distraction. Just as the puppy chose to look away from the distraction, the handler clicked and rewarded with a treat, praise, and continuation of the walk. Genius!

Good trainers can understand the concept of choice points. Great trainers can apply the concept of choice points to replace any acquired behavior, from leash pulling to jumping to reactivity. BAT prevents and rehabilitates reactivity by using the choice point concept to reinforce non-aggressive or even friendly behaviors with fundamental rewards.

BAT session preview

A Behavioral Adjustment Training "session" consists of a series of **trials** in which your dog encounters a choice point, offers a replacement behavior, and gets her functional reward. A BAT session can be an unrehearsed encounter out in the world (see Chapter 7 for full details) or it can be carefully orchestrated as a set-up which I'll cover in detail in this chapter. As I said before, a set-up is like a dress rehearsal, where your dog practices making good choices, over and over, which creates a most powerful change.

The basic steps of one BAT trial are:

1. **Choice Point:** engage with the trigger at a safe distance.

2. **Wait** for an appropriate replacement behavior from the dog or prompt a replacement behavior if your dog begins to go over threshold instead.

3. **Mark** to pinpoint the correct behavior using a verbal marker for set-ups.

4. **Functional Reward:** usually walking/jogging about ten to twenty feet away from the trigger.

5. **Bonus Reward:** praise, petting—something that your dog likes. On walks, you can use other kinds of bonus rewards. I'll give more info on that later.

BASIC BAT SET-UP

STEP 1: CHOICE POINT. Dog notices the trigger from a safe distance.

*Pick a distance where the dog is below threshold and not likely to overreact.

STUDENT
* loose leash
* under threshold

DECOY
(another dog
or human)

SAFE DISTANCE

STEP 2: WAIT FOR A GOOD CHOICE. Prompt if you have to.

*Look for an ENGAGE- DISENGAGE pattern or a CUT-OFF SIGNAL

1.

HEAD TURN
YES!

2.

SNIFF SNIFF
YES!

3.

YAWN
YES!

STEP 3: MARK the good choice at the precise moment.

* For example, use a verbal marker like "YES!"
You may use a clicker only if you are using
FOOD or TOYS as a Bonus Reward (STEP 5)

CLICK!

STEP 4: FUNCTIONAL REWARD = distance from the trigger.

*Walk or jog the dog away from the trigger on loose leash

SAFER DISTANCE

STEP 5: (OPTIONAL) BONUS REWARD = Food or Toys

*The optional treat/toy comes AFTER the Functional Reward.

GOOD BOY!

RINSE, REPEAT...

If Your Dog Goes Over Threshold

If the trigger is too close, suddenly moves, and if your dog gets STUCK at a choice point or goes OVER THRESHOLD...

* accelerated breathing
* up on toes
* intense stiffness
* pulling tight on leash
* unresponsive to handler, magnetized by trigger
* or any change for the worse...

GGRRRRRR

PERHAPS **NOT** SO SAFE A DISTANCE?

ABORT this trial by calling his name, making a sound, or shaking the leash to get his attention. Don't yell at him.

Move dog a few feet away with the trigger still in view or turn and walk away in the opposite or diagonal direction.

EXAMPLES:

BOOGIE!

VIBRATE LEASH

LET'S GO!

BUTT TAP

"KISS KISS" SOUND

TURN AND GO.
Avoid JERKING OR dragging, if possible.

RETURN TO STEP 1
Look at the trigger from a safer distance

* loose leash
* under threshold

INCREASE THE DISTANCE

How to make your set-up a success

Successful set-ups don't usually happen by luck or accident. Sessions that maximize learning and minimize stress take careful planning and preparation for the various issues that may crop up.

Plan the session in advance and communicate throughout. Before your dog and the trigger come into contact, discuss your plan with the helpers. Who is going where and in what order? Choreograph the introduction very carefully. It seems to help to have the decoy in place and then walk the student dog into the scene. If you're specifically working on dealing with sudden appearances of the trigger, then you could have the student dog arrive first, and then bring in the decoy, at enough distance so that there is no bad reaction.

Check in frequently with the helpers to discuss how things are going. You can do this as a running commentary during the session or by stopping to take breaks and putting the dog away so you can talk. The former has the benefit of getting your dog used to conversation with strangers if your dog has issues with people. The latter has the benefit of being able to concentrate on the dog(s) instead of chatting. Walkie talkies or a cell phone with a hands-free set can be used to communicate to helpers who have to be far away.

Any talking, or lack thereof, will be part of the stimulus conditions, i.e., part of what your dog is noticing and taking in as part of the training. I have had some client dogs who are only reactive if their handler is talking to the stranger, and the reverse has also happened—the dog is only reactive if the handler does not talk to the stranger in a friendly way.

Keep sessions upbeat. Make the sessions pleasant for the sake of all involved: dogs and people. Take multiple breaks, especially if any of the dogs ask for one by sniffing a particularly interesting spot on the ground. A lot of the time, dogs sniff to displace their stress. Even if it's not displacement (there really is a good smell there), sniffing is a lovely way to relax. If something has stressed your dog, or his behavior seems to be getting worse instead of better, take a break to discuss it. For breaks, move your dog and the decoy further away from each other, or completely out of sight.

Breathe, but keep your breathing calm and steady most of the time. When working up close, do your best to actually breathe, to help the dog relax. Kathy Sdao has suggested singing happy birthday to bring one's breathing back to normal for the sake of the dog. I made up a little song for Peanut, too, to the tune of "I'm a Little Teapot." You might want to try it! I have also had some success relaxing Peanut just by thinking of things that make my own mouth water, like a bowl of ice cream or Thai food from a certain restaurant in Seattle that I adore. He is a mama's boy and even though I'm pretty sure he can't read my mind, you can bet that he's paying attention to my stress level by smell or some other sense. Conversely, I have accidentally caused him to pace around the house in a stressed-out state by practicing a certain kind of energetic yoga breathing.

Plan escape routes in advance. Unless you're training in a locked room where nobody else has the key, it's possible that a person or dog may come and surprise your dog. Most of my set-ups are outdoors, in public spaces, so we expect passersby as a matter of course. Choose a spot for your set-up that has easy escape routes if there is someone walking down the street toward you. I like to use places that have good visibility, so that I can see triggers coming from very far away—enough time to calmly move your dog to a better location. For urban dogs, that can mean driving to a better spot for the set-ups, or practicing in the hallway by the door of one's apartment, so it's easy to duck back inside.

Watch for intruders. If you have a dog-reactive dog, be ready for off-leash dogs who can intrude on your set-ups; it can be disastrous if they run up to your dog. It's critical for training and safety that the dog stays sub-threshold as much as possible, so when I do set-ups with clients, I often park my car nearby, unlocked, so that my client and the dog can pop inside in case there's a loose dog. Another option is to have the set-up on the sidewalk or road just outside of your home, so it's easy to quickly run back inside.

Designate one of the people in your set-up as the loose dog wrangler, so if there's a loose dog in the neighborhood, you and your dog can disappear into a car, behind a fence, down the street, or elsewhere, while the wrangler intercepts the off-leash dog and returns him to his owner. If you have one reactive dog, her human, and a decoy dog with his person, then the latter are the designated dog wranglers. Friendly dogs make excellent dog wranglers, since they are drawn to their own species like a magnet. This is less necessary when you are working with a human-reactive dog, but it's still a good idea to designate someone to intercept curious bystanders or running children chanting "Doggy!!!"

If you're working indoors, you don't have to be as careful about random triggers just showing up, but it's often more stressful for the dog because of the smaller space. I've had a few dogs who were lovely and friendly up close inside of a building (any building) and ferocious at a distance outside, but those are the exception, not the rule. I tend to do outdoor work on fairly neutral territory first, like down the street or even in a different neighborhood, unless the dog is able to stay below threshold at her house. A good general rule is that you should work at the most challenging location at which the dog will not be too stressed. BAT sessions should be pleasant.

Film your sessions if possible. Filming your training set-up seems to discourage random intruders—somehow people are more hesitant to interrupt a video shoot than a training session. You and the other owner are going to be looking very intensely at your own dogs and may have trouble scanning the neighborhood. I'm speaking from experience here. I like to think of myself as being pretty aware of my surroundings as I work, but that's not one hundred percent true. I know this because I have a video of myself being completely unaware of danger.

I often film my sessions close up and go over them later because I am so focused when working close to the trigger. I see things I completely missed during the session. In the video I mentioned above, a client and I were doing a BAT session with her dog and mine. Two dogs were being walked along the sidewalk across the street from our session. The client and I were doing an up-close introduction, but stopped doing so as we focused on our dogs' reactions to the dogs across the street. Then a third dog and handler came walking down the sidewalk toward us. Fortunately, they saw the setup with the camera and crossed the street when they were about fifteen feet away. Disaster averted, no thanks to us! Neither of us even saw them during the session. Eek! That's why I recommend having a third person there, if you can manage it. I know it's hard enough just to get the decoys, but it's helpful.

Keep your dog sub-threshold. If a dog, person, or noise interrupts your session, watch for **trigger stacking,** i.e., the stress levels pile up enough to put the dog over threshold. The various stimuli that concern a dog have an additive property, so that if they are stressed 5% by hats and 10% by strangers, the total stress is not 10% (the larger of the two) but 15%, because now the dog is concerned about both scary things. Let's say that a dog named Charlie bites someone when he reaches a 30% stress level. If it happens to be a hat-wearing stranger, he is well on his way to getting bitten by Charlie. If he is also stressed 10% by someone at the door and 10% by the sound of the doorbell, then a hat-wearing stranger who rings the doorbell and comes inside will push Charlie past his **bite threshold** and get bitten.

The illustration on the next page should give you more of an idea of how trigger stacking works. The top graph shows how much stress a dog experiences when he encounters his triggers one at a time. The bottom graph shows how that stress is additive when two or more triggers happen at the same time (or close together in time). This phenomenon of trigger stacking is one reason why your dog's behavior may seem unpredictable.

Back to your set-up, once you know that your dog has been stressed by something in the environment, decrease the stress of his exposure to the trigger by working farther away, having the trigger behave more calmly, or even take a break. I once worked with a Chihuahua who had gotten to the point where she'd come up and I could pet her under the chin. The upstairs neighbor made a noise and she barked once, and we got back to work. At the next trial, I attempted to pet her, just like before, and she air snapped a warning at me. Trigger stacking can sneak up on you if you aren't paying attention!

Have SprayShield or some other way to safely break up fights. There's always the possibility that the loose dog wrangler cannot keep other dogs away from your dog, that someone accidentally slips and drops a leash, or that a greeting goes completely awry. While I've never had to use SprayShield during a set-up (knock on wood), I plan for the worst-case scenario. Have it accessible during the session, and if you have a helper, both of you should have a can of it. You might even want to have a blanket

TRIGGER-STACKING

Example: Some triggers and their intensities

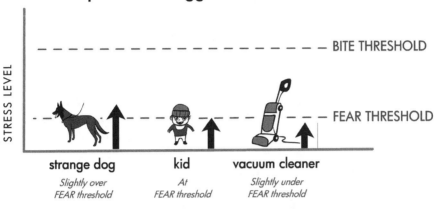

Each time a dog is exposed to a trigger, stress hormones are dumped into the brain and they build up over time.

Regardless of where each dog's "Fear Threshold" or "Bite Threshold" is, THE STRESS OF TRIGGERS IS ADDITIVE.

Dogs don't bite out of the blue.

handy, in case the SprayShield fails. If a dog is latched on and won't let go, you can use a blanket to cover up the attacker's head and eventually get her to open her mouth, while minimizing the possibility of a bite to you. Wrap the blanket over the eyes and mouth and either just wait and pull the dog back when he lets go, or if the other dog is in danger of further injury or death, twist the biting dog's collar to cut off the air supply. Having safe gear, working below threshold, and wearing muzzles during set-ups in which the dogs may come into contact will make this highly unlikely, but it is good to know what to do, just in case everything goes wrong.

Rehearse breaking up a dog fight in advance. You can do an actual reenactment or at least mentally rehearse having a fight break out. I say this because I have forgotten to use the SpraySheild before. I have such a history of reaching into rough puppy play and grabbing the upper part of the back legs (a safe-ish place to grab if you need to separate scuffling dogs) that I automatically did that, even in real fights where the dogs were latched onto each other, rather than grabbing for the SprayShield. So now I rehearse using the spray by grabbing it every time I see an off-leash dog. Even though I don't use it on them, my brain is getting ready, and I was able to remember to use it when I saw a bite-and-hold fight break out at the park.

Check leash connections and gear. Do this *before* each session begins. Check your dog and the decoy dog, and look for chewed or frayed leashes, loose collars, harnesses, or muzzles, and leashes that are painful to grip. For example, the chest strap of the EasyWalk harness tends to loosen while the dog is wearing it; in our regular training classes, I have seen several dogs come right out of the front of that harness. The chest straps had gotten so loose that the neck holes were bigger than the dogs, and the harnesses just slipped over their bodies! To prevent that, you can clip the leash to both the collar and the front clip of the harness at the same time. Or better yet, get a harness like the Freedom harness, which doesn't loosen without your help. If you use a head collar, make sure it has a safety strap if there's a possibility that it'll come off, or better attach the other end of the leash to a harness.

If you are using a decoy dog and they show up with an extendible leash or a bungee leash, replace that leash with a regular four- or six-foot leash that is comfortable to hold. The same goes for the thin puppy leashes that can easily tear through someone's hand. Look for anything that is unsafe and fix issues right away.

Condition your dog to be comfortable wearing a muzzle, if needed, so your dog can wear it for close-up work with the decoy, or choose a location where a fence can stand between your dog and the decoy for greetings. I use muzzles for close-up greetings whenever the dog either has a damaging bite history, I don't know the bite history, or I just want to be extra safe with the decoy (especially children). Muzzles must be properly fitted, so check the fit of the muzzle before allowing any greetings.

Have a back-up plan. In case of emergency, it's most efficient to tell people what to do, by name. In order to do that, *you must learn your human helpers' names!* Use them from time to time during the session, to keep yourself fresh. Besides, people prefer being known by their own names instead of just, "Hey you" or "Fifi's mom." Your back-up plan should have a back-up plan. Know the closest open vet's office and program their contact information into your phone, or write it out on a piece of paper. Most decoys seem to be available on evenings and weekends, so that limits the possible vets to go to.

Keep records on how the session went. This allows you to see what needs to be changed, what your dog did well, and gives you a very clear picture of your dog's progress. That progress is what will motivate you to do another session, and another, so it's helpful to collect at least a little data. One data point that I find helpful is the number of trials before we get to a certain distance with a new decoy. For example, in the the first BAT set-up with a student dog named Sully it took fifty-five trials to get within "muzzle distance"—about six feet (with the handlers standing on the outside). In the second session, it was forty trials to muzzle distance, then twenty, and then seven. Seeing that clear improvement was extremely motivating to Sully's family.

As a final bit of advice on keeping sessions successful, make sure to give everyone *"veto power,"* as trainer and speaker Kathy Sdao says. If anybody feels the slightest bit uncomfortable about the safety or wisdom of a particular set-up, they should feel comfortable speaking up.

> Note for Pros: Veto power is especially important to point out in set-ups with your clients, because people are socialized to respect authority figures and tend not to question a trainers' judgment, especially in the moment. They need your explicit permission to speak up for safety, at anytime, even if it's just a hunch.

Set-up Step 1: Dog sees the trigger.

Set-up Step 2: Wait for a good choice—be sure to breathe. You can stand up straight, too (we did exaggerated postures for photos).

Set-up Step 3: Dog chooses a body turn—mark with "yes."

Set-up Step 4: Happily walk or jog away with dog as the functional reward.

BAT Set-Ups

The following steps will help you prepare and execute a successful BAT set-up like the one shown in the series of photos above.

Step 1: Create a choice point (engagement with trigger)

Before actually starting a BAT session, choose the trigger you'll be working with for your dog (people, dogs, a slippery floor, etc.). Think about the variables for the trigger that you want to focus on. The lists below give some important dimensions to consider for each variable. For example, one dog may not distinguish between an intact male and a neutered female dog, but another dog will think that's a huge difference.

Location:

- Distance to trigger
- Distance to support (mom / dad / sibling)
- Direction to trigger—ahead / behind.

Motion:

- Trigger speed
- Student dog's speed
- Trigger moving / student moving / both moving
- Erratic motion / gait of decoy
- Direction of motion (parallel / opposite / angle/ arc)

- Significant motions (reaching to pet / kneeling / leaning over / play bows / other).

Sounds:
- Trigger making noise (talking / jingling tags / barking / whining)
- Handler talking to trigger
- Other sounds in the environment
- Meaning of sound
- Volume and quality of sound.

Timing:
- How long dog performs before reward
- How long a session lasts (or in real life, how long is your dog expected to be around the trigger?)
- Amount of time since last break
- How long between trials.

Other trigger dimensions to vary:
- Temperament of decoy
- Objects (hats, umbrellas, boxes)
- Smells (smoke, alcohol, etc.)
- Eye contact (none, soft/blinking, staring)
- On-leash / Off-leash (student and helper/decoy)
- Decoy dog: size / age / breed / color / coat type
- Decoy human: size / age / voice pitch / ethnicity / hair color (yes, dogs can be racist, unfortunately)
- Neuter status / sex / heat status of decoy.

Obviously there are many variables that one could choose to work on, and you can't work on all of them in a given session. I recommend that you introduce just a few variables, one at a time, into a session. You might start with the helper wearing a hat, then trade the hat for a walker or a cane, then crutches, then no props as you work on eye contact with you as a replacement behavior.

Your main set-up for exposing your dog to the trigger can be arranged in different ways, but however you do it, your dog should be sub-threshold. Since this is the chapter on the basic set-up, I'll describe how my basic set-ups are usually arranged. Varying the set-up is an essential part of the game, too, so be sure to read the next section on variations.

I like to start with the helper fairly stationary, but allowed to interact with the dog, as in real life. Have your dog approach the helper from far enough away so that she does not go over threshold. Let's say that I'm the helper for a client's human-reactive dog. I might be sitting or standing and talking with the client in a regular tone, giving directions and occasionally looking at the dog. The client has her dog on a leash, usually with a harness, at a distance away from me that is very comfortable to the dog. Next, the client walks her dog ten to fifteen feet closer, either directly toward me or in a curved arc. The dog is not cued to do a formal heel, but rather allowed to walk freely on a loose leash until she notices me or we decide to stop for some other reason.

Here are the ways that you can tell that it's time to stop walking your dog toward the helper during the first trial:

- Dog focuses gaze on helper
- Dog's ears flick toward helper
- Dog breathes faster
- Dog stops moving forward
- Or you just know that it's close enough.

When any of these happen, you know that your dog is at a choice point—he must choose how to deal with the exposure to what normally results in reactivity. If you have set it up correctly, so that the dog is at a choice point where he clearly notices the decoy but is under threshold, he is very likely to choose one of the replacement behaviors.

Finding the right distance or amount of stimulation for your dog at the choice point will take some experimentation at the beginning of each session. Your first trial may be too easy or too hard, so be ready to adjust accordingly. For example, I recently met with a Jack Russell Terrier named Lulu. We started Lulu at one hundred feet from the trigger, which was too easy—she barely noticed the decoy dog. For the next trial, we had her walk up to an approach point that was eighty feet from the decoy. That was slightly too much stimulation, and we had to call her away to avoid an outburst. Eighty-five feet away was a perfect start point for our next trial, and we stayed at that distance for three trials, and then moved our approach point to eighty-two feet for the next trial. If you get an outburst, as we did, you might even find that going back to one hundred feet away from the trigger subsequently becomes a perfect place to begin again if your dog is still aroused. Finding the right starting distance can be tricky, but you'll get the hang of it. As animal trainer Bob Bailey is fond of saying "simple, but not easy." As you work, the distance of the choice point will generally decrease. However, you must always pay attention to the dog's behavior, and stop at the point when the dog engages with the trigger by showing any of the behaviors listed above and illustrated on pages 68 and 69.

SIGNS OF STRESS

There's always an emotional lesson. If your dog is stressed, take a break and do easier trials with more time in between.

YAWNING

TONGUE FLICKS

DRY PANTING

STOPPING TO SNIFF

REFUSING TO
GO FORWARD

DELIBERATELY IGNORING
THE TRIGGER

CROUCHED, SHIVERING,
WORRIED FACE

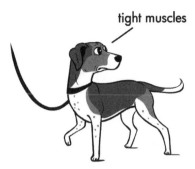

tight muscles

STARING AT TRIGGER
AT REWARD POINT

SWEATY FEET,
DANDRUFF & SHEDDING

FLEEING FROM TRIGGER

SCANNING AROUND
FOR DANGER

REACTING OR
NEEDING PROMPTING

Step 2: Wait for replacement behavior

As you wait at the choice point, look for a number of replacement behaviors to mark and reward. The best replacement behaviors to focus on are polite cut-off signals that follow engagement, so *look for an engage/disengage pattern.*

When you do BAT, help your dog stay on the more relaxed end of the spectrum so that he is able to do the replacement behaviors on his own. However, if your dog starts to go over threshold, use **graduated prompting** i.e., help him choose to do a replacement behavior in the smallest, least intrusive way that works. Start with something as mild as a shift in your weight, sighing, or tapping your fingers on the leash to send a tiny vibration down to your dog. We discussed these "Good Choices" in detail in Chapter 5.

Here is a graduated list of prompts to help tip the scale toward calmness if your dog is about to do the problem behavior, starting with the least intrusive, and building up to the most assertive. Use the ones at the top of the list first, because they give your dog more of a chance to learn without relying on your signals. The goal is to arrange the situation so that your dog can make the decision without your help and doesn't need any prompting at all. Dogs will have varying responses to these prompts, so the order is different for different dogs:

- Relax your shoulders
- Shift your weight
- Calmly praise dog for looking
- Shuffle your feet
- Sigh or yawn
- Tap or move leash
- Cough
- Move your hand or body in the dog's peripheral vision (it's 270°, unlike our 180° vision)
- Kissy noise
- Name
- "Leave it" cue
- "Come" or "Let's go" cue
- Pull dog away (can trigger an outburst).

Behaviors at Choice Point
that indicate YOU SHOULD PROMPT*

Your dog may have a full-blown reaction unless you quickly prompt or reduce the trigger intensity.

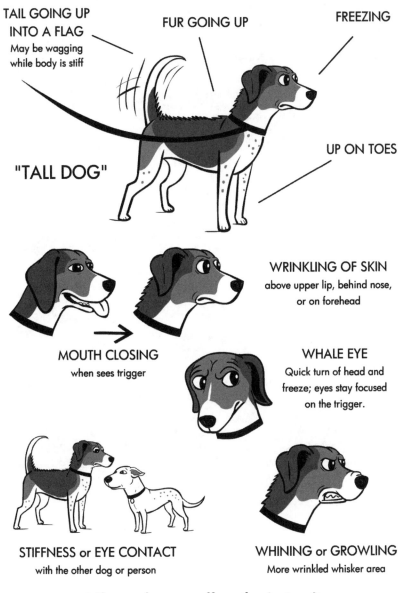

TAIL GOING UP INTO A FLAG
May be wagging while body is stiff

FUR GOING UP

FREEZING

UP ON TOES

"TALL DOG"

MOUTH CLOSING
when sees trigger

WRINKLING OF SKIN
above upper lip, behind nose, or on forehead

WHALE EYE
Quick turn of head and freeze; eyes stay focused on the trigger.

STIFFNESS or EYE CONTACT
with the other dog or person

WHINING or GROWLING
More wrinkled whisker area

* If your dog can self-soothe, just wait.

The following five photos show an example of how to use graduated prompts to encourage a dog at a choice point to walk away.

Tail begins to rise, so handler made a kissy noise to prompt dog to turn.

Kissy noise plus finger lightly touching dog.

The touch worked!

Mark the turn with "Yes!"

Reward by walking away, as dog did head turn without barking.

Step 3: Mark the replacement behavior (pinpoint the good choice)

The moment that the dog offers a replacement behavior, pinpoint the behavior with some kind of marker signal. I use a verbal "Yes" as the marker when I am giving just the functional reward and a clicker when I give food or a toy as a bonus reward after the functional reward. Only use distracting bonus rewards when you need that distraction, like during walks where you can't control the triggers. Use just the functional reward whenever you can. I'll get into more details on using tangible bonus rewards in the chapter on using BAT on walks.

Step 4: Functional reward (move your dog and the trigger apart)

After you mark a replacement behavior, your dog gets her functional reward. For dogs who panic, bark, growl, and bite, an increase in distance to the trigger is usually the functional reward. It's no surprise that distance-increasing behaviors are rewarded by increasing distance! Happily walking your dog away on a loose leash is a great way to do that, because it's something that they can do on their own after training is complete. You can also have the trigger walk away, which is especially appropriate in real-life situations where that happens anyway, like people passing by the dog's yard.

The functional reward won't reinforce behavior if your dog is disappointed to leave, so your job is to set the scene for the dog to easily walk away. It's important to avoid the magnet effect that I mentioned before. This effect can draw your dog in over her head, just the opposite of what you are trying to achieve. When she gets too close, it's like she just *has* to deal with the situation by reacting, as if she doesn't feel safe just walking away at that point. Within that magnetic field, the dog is over threshold and her behaviors change for the worse; it is not likely that walking away will be a reward for your dog once she starts to feel the magnetic pull of the other dog, scary mailman, or other trigger. However, if you are working outside of the trigger's magnetic field, your dog can move around freely and walking away becomes much more attractive. Your job with BAT is to decrease the power of the trigger's magnetic field, so that your dog can move freely.

Because of the magnet effect, many dogs will charge in like a bullet toward a fight, but if you are far enough away, they are happy just to leave—when they are actually done gathering information. For those dogs, you can't necessarily reward the smaller behaviors, like blinking, sighing, or softening the jaw by walking them away because they don't want to leave until they are done checking the trigger out. You could have the trigger leave instead, but it might be that your dog would prefer the chance to gather information. If I want to reward smaller behaviors in that kind of dog, I tend to give a bonus reward at the end of the trial because the trigger loses its magnetic pull in the presence of a treat. Since I'm giving an actual tangible reward, I can also use the clicker: click to mark the good behavior; walk or jog away (call dog if necessary); and give a treat or toy. Walking away also becomes more rewarding because it leads to a treat. Once a dog gets into the habit of walking away, the dog gets less stuck around the trigger. Make sure to do the full retreat first, so the dog notices that they've earned the functional reward, and then you can give the bonus reward of food, toy, play, or other reward.

Some timid dogs, on the other hand, are not magnetized toward the trigger, but repelled instead. Your dog's flight response may be triggered and he may avoid even looking at the trigger. In this case, you would need to work far enough away from the decoy dog that the dog is able to do a **pro-social replacement behavior,** like approaching the decoy first and then reward him with the chance to walk away.

At first glance, it seems odd that *walking away from the trigger reinforces a fearful dog for walking toward the trigger,* but it works! I think one reason they gain confidence is that dogs learn that they won't get stuck and be forced to engage with the trigger. When they have the ability to control their exposure to danger, their natural curiosity can take over. I usually reward pro-social behavior with the dog himself retreating because otherwise you're teaching the dog something that just isn't true in the real world: play bows do not make other dogs go away, they signal them to come closer. However, dogs can always get away from social triggers eventually, especially with the help of their humans.

Step 5: Non-tangible bonus reward

After you've moved away, praise your dog. Tell your dog that he's fabulous and brave. If he really likes petting, do that. However, don't overdo it because the main reward is the functional reward and you don't want to distract him too much. But praising and petting probably produce serotonin in the same way that play does, and its fun for you, too.

BAT SET-UP Variations

A SET-UP is like a dress-rehearsal, where your dog encounters a CHOICE POINT, and practices making good choices over and over.

1. "MONSTER IN THE MIDDLE"

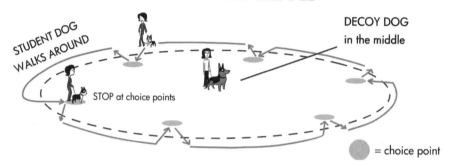

2. "SPIRALING MONSTER"

3. "PARALLEL WALKING"

The paths are not literally 'parallel'. The STUDENT DOG walks side-by-side, behind or towards the DECOY DOG and is encouraged to veer off on an angle or an arc. Reward any GOOD CHOICES by allowing your student dog to move away.

Give your dog about fifteen seconds or more to relax and enjoy the fact that he's gotten away from the trigger before you start another trial. Some dogs may need more than a few seconds to enjoy their functional reward. If your dog sniffs the ground, pees, yawns, shakes off (as if wet), or tries to get away while you are waiting, give him a break, anywhere from another thirty seconds to several minutes. Remember, there's always an emotional learning component, and if you're getting stress signs like yawning, you may be pushing too hard, so tone down the stress.

These five steps constitute one trial of a basic BAT set-up. In the real world, your dog is exposed to triggers in a lot of different ways, so your dog will learn to cope sooner by doing BAT in a variety of situations. Dogs are scenario learners, meaning that while they can learn that something applies in scenario A, they don't automatically generalize that information to scenario B. They seem to be able to transfer fear between situations really well, unfortunately, but they don't tend to generalize safety. Luckily for you, changing the way you expose your dog to the trigger also helps relieve boredom for the humans and dogs during training. Let's discuss some of the ways you can vary the set-ups to fit your dog's needs.

More set-ups: variations on the theme

I usually start my clients off with the basic set-up and then explain how to vary it in a different lesson, so you may want to practice the basic version of BAT and come back to read this later. Many creative clients, especially dog trainers, are able to set up a variety of BAT encounters on their own after learning the basic concepts of BAT. I hope that you will also come up with ways that are different than what I describe here. This is a starter set on the variations of BAT. Most of the variation is in the exposure step, since that allows your dog to get used to a bigger set of triggering stimuli. Another aspect to vary is the functional reward itself and there are also many ways to reduce the intensity of the trigger.

Monster in the Middle is a circular set-up, in which your dog can view the trigger from all angles. Your dog is on the outside of the circle and the 'Scary Monster' is on the inside. The size of the circle is limited only by your space. Empty parking lots of stores that are closed are great for this set-up, because there is a lot of room and there are virtually no other people or dogs. Most of my Monster in the Middle set-ups use a circular space with a radius of about thirty feet. If you don't have that much space, you can do a semi-circle or a quarter-circle. If your dog needs more distance than your circle can provide, just do the more linear version of BAT that I described above until the threshold distance has shrunk enough to use the space you have for Monster in the Middle.

Mark several approach paths from the outside of the circle toward the center. You can use sidewalk chalk or physical markers like leashes or rocks. Do fewer approach paths if you have a smaller radius, more if you have a huge circle. One way to do the Monster in the Middle is to walk along the circle and then directly approach the decoy. So you'd walk around the circle clockwise with your dog on your left side, then turn onto one of the approach paths and stop at the end of that path, which becomes the choice point. Mark good behavior, then pivot to your right and retreat back along the same path. Continue along the circle until the next approach path and repeat. If you walk your dog on the right, as in the previous illustration, then you would walk around counter-clockwise and pivot to your left. Walking this way keeps you from pushing into your dog or restricting his choices.

For a more indirect approach and retreat, you can walk along the circle, then, ten feet before the approach path, walk at an angle toward the tip of the approach path. That's still the choice point. For the retreat, pivot to your right and walk your dog back to the circle—not along the same path that you approached on, but in the same sort of angle, in the opposite direction. So your approach and retreat make a sort of V-shape that's inside the circle, with the choice point at the tip of the V. You skip over the ten feet of the circle before the approach line and the ten feet after the approach path.

Monster in the Middle can be challenging for the decoy dog in the center, so if your dog is reactive to dogs, either keep the session short (a few minutes), have an assistant give treats to the decoy dog, or both. If the decoy dog's handler isn't feeding treats to keep him in one position as your dog circles around, then definitely allow the decoy dog to pivot, so he can continue to face your dog. The last thing you want to do is give the decoy dogs a reactivity problem!

Monster in the Middle is especially useful for human-reactive dogs, because you get all of the benefits and none of the drawbacks; the decoys have volunteered and understand that this is a set-up. Helpers should remain facing one particular direction during the session, unless they are a trainer who needs to watch and give instructions to the student with their dog. It gives your dog a sort of built-in break, because approaching a human from the rear is less stressful for your dog than approaching them head-on.

Spiraling Monster is another circular BAT set-up, which allows your dog to experience the trigger in many different locations, relative to his own body—in front, behind, to the side. The players simply reverse their roles from Monster in the Middle, so this could also be called Student in the Middle. The reactive dog stands at the center of the circle and the decoy walks around the circle, approaching and retreating based on the student dog's behavior. The student dog can also walk away during the reward phase, which means he moves out of the center away from the decoy. He returns to the center for the next trial. Marking your dog's replacement behavior also tells the decoy (or their handler) to retreat. I call it Spiraling Monster because you decrease the distance, at some point, so the circle gets smaller and smaller. The monster is slowly spiraling in.

Circular BAT set-ups are not for every dog. For both Spiraling Monster and Monster in the Middle, the dog walking along the circle needs to have fairly good leash walking skills. The dog in the center, however, does not need any particular talents, since he is just standing there.

Another form of Spiraling Monster is to have the decoy move in a circle around your dog in a continuous motion until you get an acceptable behavior from your reactive dog. Usually the reactive dog watches the decoy circle them for a little while and then looks away. At that point, verbally mark your dog's behavior with "Yes," which tells the decoy dog to stop moving. Walk or jog with your dog directly away from the decoy, about fifteen to twenty additional feet away. After your dog has a chance to enjoy the functional reward (distance), come back to the center of the circle and tell the decoy to resume circling around you. Repeat.

Remember, interrupting panic/aggression before it can build up is part of BAT, no matter how you do the set-ups. If your dog starts to shift into aggression or panic, interrupt and move him a little farther away from the decoy. This is the new choice point, so you wait for the dog to offer a replacement behavior from there.

Parallel Walking is a core component of most dog trainers' toolboxes. With BAT, parallel walking is sort of a misnomer, because you aren't just walking on two parallel paths. I usually have the decoy dog walking on a straight path with the student dog veering off of the path, away from the decoy dog, to reinforce good choices. With parallel walking, your dog and the decoy can walk directly toward each other or walk in the same direction. They can be side by side, or with one following the other. Walking in the same direction with your dog following the trigger is much easier than walking toward the other dog head on.

Parallel walking is great for getting a dog comfortable with the movement of other dogs and people. It also keeps your dog calmer because he is in balance and focused on his own motion. Dogs tend to be less explosive when moving, versus holding still. Dogs also learn to offer appropriate behaviors while still moving, versus only doing them at times when you stop or tighten the leash. If you are doing parallel work close up, then you might consider using a fence in between your dog and the decoy dog, or using a muzzle if your dog has been trained to wear one comfortably.

When walking in the same direction, it's a good idea to merge slowly, as you would on a freeway, rather than walking directly at each other and then heading off together. So if you and your dog are following the trigger, have the trigger walk ahead and then arc in to follow them, slowly catching up. Allow your dog to move away after any cut-off signal.

> Note for Pros: When I do a private session at the home of dogs who are territorial or afraid of strangers I start out by going for a walk, using the merging concept mentioned above. I walk around their block and then the client and their dog come outside and gradually catch up to me, over the course of a

block or so. I ignore the dog at first and they naturally just approach to gather info and then retreat. Some will still bark at me, but most dogs feel brave enough to check out a person who is walking ahead and ignoring them. Note that I only do this if the dog has no history of biting, or if the bite history clearly involves a perceived threat from the human.

For parallel walking in the same direction, *the dog is at a choice point during the whole time that they are walking near the trigger.* Mark any replacement behaviors that you see and then continue walking in the same general direction, but move about ten feet further away from the trigger. After twenty to thirty seconds, move closer again for another trial.

When walking toward each other, set it up so that your dog and the decoy dog are offset by some distance, say ten feet, so that you are walking on two parallel lines that are ten feet apart. Reward any replacement behaviors you get as you walk by reversing course, or calmly stop when you are even with the trigger and wait for a good choice. Reward that good choice by continuing on in the direction you were walking. The closest distance that you get to (in this case, ten feet) should be bigger than distances you've already rehearsed with other versions of BAT, since having the decoy moving is already harder for your dog than approaching a stationary decoy.

Sudden Environmental Contrast or **Sudden Environmental Change** (SEC) is very problematic for most of my clients' reactive dogs, so your dog probably has an issue with it too. SEC is a change in the surroundings that happens quickly, like a child suddenly coming around a corner, a dog suddenly appearing out of a car, or a guest standing up to leave the house. For some dogs, the appearance of a trash bin in a different place than yesterday's walk can stress them out. As I said before, dogs are not great at generalizing learning—especially learning that something is safe, so the concept of SEC needs specific work.

Most of the time with BAT, the helper or decoy dog is in view throughout the session, so that your dog can observe them at a comfortable distance. This is the primary way BAT teaches dogs to be comfortable with the triggers. It takes some extra training to teach them that when the triggers suddenly appear, or suddenly move, they are no more dangerous than before. So first get your dog comfortable in the presence of the trigger, and then begin to work on SEC. This can be at the end of a session with a helper, woven in during the session when your dog is comfortable at a particular distance from the decoy, or in a separate session. Also practice SEC with helpers your dog hasn't worked with before.

Having enough distance between your dog and the helper is the key for SEC. When you change any aspect of the trigger, you may need to work at a greater distance from the helper, and that's especially true for SEC. Let's say that your dog, Lola, is comfortable with the helper at five feet away, but has trouble with the helper suddenly appearing. Start with Lola walking and suddenly encountering the helper, say around a corner, at fifty feet away. Note that the helper is not moving toward your dog at that point, just standing there. Practice this concept at gradually shrinking distances, in various locations, so you don't end up with a dog who thinks that the hedge at the corner of 5th Avenue and Main Street is okay, but surprises everywhere else are scary.

After doing set-ups to get Lola comfortable with encountering a sudden Scary Monster, you could have her stationary or moving and have the trigger pop into view at fifty feet during SEC training (notice that I bumped the distance back up again). For SEC training with your dog, you can remove the trigger between trials or you can also do one SEC trial, followed by a few regular trials, where the trigger stays in view between trials. The latter is a nice way to work SEC training into your regular BAT set-ups. Just make sure it's not stressing your dog; if you learn nothing else from this book, learn this: *there is always an emotional take-home message for your dog.*

With Peanut, the initial BAT training made him become comfortable with walking down the sidewalk and encountering a trigger at a distance, and moving up close, but if he was standing still and the trigger suddenly appeared, it was a different story. So, we worked SEC on scenarios where humans would suddenly appear from behind a hedge, get out of a car, walk around a corner, or otherwise suddenly appear.

We began by having helpers surprise him from one hundred feet away, which was interesting, but not enough to elicit a bark. That was a great starting distance. He turned away, sniffed the ground, looked at me, or offered another replacement behavior and was rewarded with a verbal "Yes" and walking away. The helper then ducked out of sight and we turned around and headed toward them again. We used cell phones with hands-free sets to coordinate the training. That way, we didn't accidentally surprise him at only twenty feet away and end up with a barking episode.

Some SEC variations:

- Your dog suddenly encounters trigger while walking

- Trigger suddenly appears (around a corner, through a doorway, etc.)

- Trigger suddenly moves (turn to go, face away and pivot toward your dog, stand up, lift hand to pet, clap hands, jump, trip over something, etc.)

- Trigger suddenly makes noise or pays attention to your dog

- Moving trigger suddenly stops

- In a group of people or dogs, one does something different from the rest—steps out of the group, stands while they move, etc. This is especially important for herding breeds.

If you do accidentally put your dog over threshold in an SEC trial, keep the trigger in view, because removing it is too reinforcing. Just use graduated prompting to get your dog back to a thinking state (move him a few feet away). Then do a few regular BAT trials with the trigger in view. Since you've already taught your dog to

BAT for GREETINGS

After you've done set-ups further away and your dog is no longer reactive toward a particular decoy at a distance, begin to work on up-close greetings. For safety, use a muzzle or have a **FENCE** between your dog and the decoy.

STAGE 1

1.Click!   **2. Move Away**   **3. Treat**

STAGE 2

cut-off signal: Looking away

1. Wait or Call   **2. Mark Good Choice**   **3. Move Away**   **4. Treat**

STAGE 3

cut-off signal: Nose lick

1. Wait   **2. Mark Good Choice**   **3. Move Away**

There are dogs who love people/other dogs and want to greet but don't have good interaction skills and don't know how to COOL OFF greetings with cut-off signals. BAT is useful to teach dogs that in order to get close to a friend (old or new) they have to be polite.

be comfortable with a stationary trigger, your dog should quickly acclimate to the situation. Remember, it's not just about behavior, it's about teaching the dog that the world is not so scary or angry-making, after all.

Varying the exposure step of BAT allows your dog to encounter the trigger in more natural ways. Depending on the situation, you may also need to vary the way that you provide the functional reward. For example, I worked with a Great Dane in a small apartment where my standing up triggered his aggression. We had already worked with me just sitting there, and the dog was comfortable with approaching me as I sat, even to the point of soliciting my attention and petting (while muzzled). I tried standing up with him ten feet, fifteen feet, and twenty feet away, but that was too much, and it resulted in this 150-pound dog with a damaging bite history lunging at the end of his leash toward me. For his sake, and mine, we moved him further away and changed how I moved. It turned out that he was able to offer replacement behaviors (look away) at the far wall of the apartment if I rose halfway. At that point, however, there was nowhere for him to go so we were unable to use walking away as a functional reward. Remember that he was comfortable with me sitting, so my returning to the sitting position reduced his anxiety. My return to sitting was his functional reward.

So I'd start to get up, he'd look at me for a little bit, and then turn away. His owners verbally marked his choice and I then sat back down and relaxed as his owners told him that he was fabulously brave. He relaxed, too. After a few repetitions, we were able to move him about 5 feet away from the wall, closer to me, with me half-rising as the trigger. Then, I'd return to sitting and he could walk a few feet away within the apartment (a bigger functional reward than before, now that there was room). We gradually moved the choice point closer to my chair, and then we increased the distance and began working on having me stand all the way up. To make it easier, we had him move to the far end of the unit when I stood all the way up as the trigger, and sat back down as his reward. He made great strides in that session. Another way we could have varied this was to have me sitting in a chair in the hallway, outside, or better yet, start in my training center in Seattle, so that he could become comfortable with that trigger at a proper distance away, without the extra stress of me being inside his home.

The last ten feet

The BAT sessions that I do as a set-up with clients usually involve the student dog eventually being able to greet the decoy, or at least sniff from up close. If your dog isn't ready to do a greeting in the first set-up, you can use the same decoy in other sessions until the dog can successfully greet. That usually just takes one or two more sessions. It's important to make sure these greetings are safe, so if you're ever not sure whether you should let the dog greet the decoy, the answer is probably no. One of the most challenging parts of working with reactive dogs is figuring out what to do when they are actually close enough (within about ten feet) to bite another dog, person, animal, or object. I've already given you some safety tips for working up close, but here are some more ideas.

How To Hold The Leash for Dog Greetings

Handlers stay on opposite sides, with dogs in between.
Have a good grip on the leash, but do not attach it to your wrist. Keep the leash loose, if possible, but not so loose that the dogs step over it.

When the dogs change relative positions, handlers should move too. Handlers need to stay opposite each other, with no obstacles between them and their dogs. If one person calls their dog and moves away, the other person should too.

Don't let the leashes tangle. If the leashes tangle, breathe and stay calm. Immediately untangle them, call your dog back and give a treat.

First and foremost, keep things moving. Reactive dogs who are standing still around their triggers are likely to get themselves in trouble. So during these sessions allow only very short greetings, keep walking together in some way, or do something else that lets your dog move his body. If they have to concentrate on where to put their feet, dogs pay a little less attention to the triggers, which can help avoid reactive responses. Greetings should be very short, like a quarter of a second at first. Call the dog away and reward by going further away and giving a treat. I feed a treat here because the dog isn't done gathering information, so leaving is not necessarily a functional reward. Work up to longer greetings and then switch back to Stage 3 BAT (see Chapter 6), where you wait for the dog to be done with the interaction and then walk him away from the trigger.

During an approach, face-to-face greetings are much more challenging than face-to-rear greetings, whether the trigger is another dog or a person. I've listed a general order of difficulty for most greeting approaches below. Keep in mind that every dog is an individual, and your dog may not have read this book about which kind of approach is supposed to be easy or hard. This is also not based on data, but rather on my own observations with clients:

1. Your dog approaching trigger, who is walking away

2. Your dog approaching stationary trigger who is turned sideways. As your dog begins moving, trigger walks away to the left or right (angles can vary)

3. Trigger approaching your dog, who is walking away

4. Your dog approaching trigger, who is stationary, but turned fully away

5. Your dog approaching trigger, who is stationary, but turned sideways

6. Your dog approaching trigger, who is stationary and facing student

7. Trigger approaching your dog, who is stationary, but fully turned away (and possibly being fed)

8. Trigger approaching your dog, who is stationary, but turned sideways

9. Trigger and your dog approaching each other head on (slowly, possibly offset first)

10. Trigger and your dog approaching each other head on (rapidly).

Remember, this is not true for all dogs. For example, sometimes #6 is more challenging than #10, because the dog is stationary as the trigger approaches. Experiment with your dog. You can add more steps in by considering different ways in which your dog and the trigger might approach each other—a straight approach is usually more likely to cause a bad reaction than an arced approach. The tightness of the leash has an effect, too. I like to run through all of the variations at a distance before doing them up close. I recommend trying #9 (dogs moving rapidly toward each other) and stopping at a choice point that's twelve feet away before trying it within striking range.

When you start working within striking range, go back to the easiest ways for the dog to interact with the trigger, and then work up to the challenging ways systematically. This isn't as necessary when you are working at a distance. For example, let's say that I'm the helper and a client has her dog at fifty feet away from me. I might begin with full eye contact with a dog and talking to the handler about what to do. If that is too much for the dog, we just work further away. I'll do some trials without eye contact, some with. When I get up close, I really want to make sure it goes well, because: 1) it's a safety issue and; 2) our training may have missed some aspect of the trigger. To avoid trigger stacking, I take it down to what I think is the easiest for the dog when working within ten feet. So I don't make eye contact, I'm turned or walking away, sitting down, hands in my pockets, etc.

Working up close is dangerous unless you put some safety devices in place. Two ways to reduce the danger is to work with a fence between your dog and the trigger or have your dog muzzled. As I mentioned before, you must take the time to get your dog acclimated to wearing a muzzle before he actually uses it, so the muzzle itself is not a stressful event. Otherwise, you run the risk of your dog associating the stress of the muzzle with the trigger, and instead of learning that the trigger is a good thing, you've made things worse. If you are using a muzzle instead of a fence, have your dog on-leash for the initial up-close sessions, and *be very careful about holding the leash in a useful way.*

What does it mean to hold the leash in a useful way? First of all, make sure you have a good grip on a loose leash. Hold the leash close to your body, close to your center of gravity, so that if the dog suddenly lunges, you can control him. Be ready to step back to get the dog out of the situation. Dogs are much, much faster than humans, but if you're ready, you can do a fairly good job at helping them avoid a bite. That's because dogs usually give some kind of warning, so you have a bit of time to get them out of there. You may not recognize it, but there are usually warnings. If you don't see them, hire a trainer to help you. If a dog truly bites without warning, that's really scary. In that case, you probably shouldn't teach them to be comfortable and interact with their triggers, but teach avoidance, instead.

Have a good grip on the leash for greetings. Make sure it's short enough to avoid tangling, has a few inches of slack so that it feels loose to the dog, and that you're ready to back away if you see any stiffening, staring, holding breath, or other signs of trouble. I also want you to position your body so that your dog's head is directly between you and the trigger and that your leash is perpendicular to your dog's body. That means that you, your leash, your dog's head, and the closest point of the trigger should all be on a straight line. If your dog or the trigger moves, walk around to maintain the right position relative to your dog and the trigger. See illustration on the next page. If the trigger is also a dog, then their head, leash and handler should be in the same line as you and your dog. The reason for this arrangement is that you are now able to get the dog(s) out of there as quickly as possible, because the force of the leash can pull the dog directly away from the trigger. While I don't use the leash for punishments, I do use it for safety. Since I'm not a giant person, and I have slow human reflexes, I want every ounce of force that I put on the leash to help move the dog quickly away from the trigger. Of course, use the least amount of force that you can, to avoid injuring or scaring your dog. See the "Silky Leash" section in Appendix 1 for ways to use the leash without actually yanking on it.

Don't pull the dog out with the leash on a whim, or if you just get nervous. As they say in pre-school, 'use your words.' If you want to interrupt a tense moment, call your dog, yawn, sigh, start to walk away (without tightening the leash), tap the leash, make a kissy noise, or any number of things that I discussed before under the topic of graduated prompting. When you're mountain climbing, you don't just let go because you know you have a safety line—you do your best to avoid falling. It's a big deal to use your safety line. The same goes for pulling the dog out of a conflict with the leash.

As soon as the leash tightens, the tension is likely to go up, so don't just tighten the leash unless you are specifically working on that as a trigger (usually I do that at a distance). Either keep the leash loose or use it to pull the dog away from a scuffle. This goes for any dogs, not just reactive dogs.

After you have gone through all of the various ways to have your dog interact with the trigger on-leash, and that's all going really well, then you might want to start working off-leash, if that's part of your goals. If your dog is just fearful, not likely to bark, growl, bite, or walk up close and put himself over threshold, then you may be able go to off-leash work much sooner as we do in our Reactive Teens class for adolescent dogs. When doing a BAT session, you want to be able to help lower the dog's stress level quickly, by getting the trigger away from them, calling them away, or otherwise diffusing the situation. So before doing off-leash work, it's important to work on your dog's recall cue (see Appendix 1). Your dog should be able to come away from big distractions before working off-leash. Another way to help make that work is to at least have the decoy dog, child, or person able to move away from the student dog. However you do it, you need to be able to reinforce your dog with distance from the trigger from time to time.

It's especially important to know what you're doing when the dog is close enough to do damage. If you are at all unsure how to keep your dog safe at this point, hire a professional trainer!

> Note for Pros: If you are just getting started working with aggression cases, I suggest hiring an experienced trainer or behaviorist as a consultant. This can be done in person, on the phone, or by video chat. Use your imagination!

What success looks like

As I mentioned earlier, many factors will influence the success of your BAT set-up, including keeping the dog below threshold and reinforcing appropriate replacement behaviors with the right functional reward. What does success mean, though?

My clients all have slightly different goals for their dogs, different pictures in their mind about what overall success should look like. If they didn't take reality into account, their goals would all be the same, something like, "I want my dog to be a normal dog." Actually, that's not quite true. What they really want is a dog that's better than normal, and I don't blame them—I think that's what I want, too! They want a bombproof dog, who never shows aggression, no matter what happens. If children pull his tail or fall on him, they want him to wag happily and enjoy himself. If another dog growls in his face, they want him to think it's great. And by the way, could we have that at the end of just one session?

Fortunately, most of my clients (and hopefully you) understand that rehabilitating fear and aggression—like physical therapy, psychotherapy, and learning a new sport—takes time and effort. But there should be some progress in a successful BAT session. Knowing what to look for and having a realistic goal for the training session makes it more likely that you'll get there.

Your dog should be sub-threshold for all or most of a successful session. Collect data on this so you can tell whether this really happens. You should have (at most) a couple of outbursts which should be dealt with calmly and your dog should be given the chance to relax and make better decisions. Your dog should be allowed to take breaks whenever he wants to, and should seem comfortable with the training.

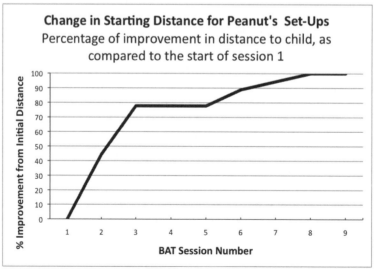

Peanut's progress.

In an ideal session, you have picked a location to work with where there are minimal intrusions, or a location where intrusions still allow your dog to remain sub-threshold. For example, if your dog is reactive to other dogs, and a neighborhood dog comes walking by with their human, you could call your dog away from the sidewalk, cross the street, put her in a car, feed her a bunch of hot dogs, toss a tennis ball, or whatever else it takes to keep her calm.

To consider a session a success, your dog should make progress in one or more dimensions, usually distance to the trigger unless the session is very short. In a lot of my sessions, the dog actually sniffs or meets the helper or decoy dog by the end. I think progress is accelerated when the dog has a chance to learn that the trigger is not scary after all and he leaves the session with a positive feeling. This positive feeling can be created by winding your session down with easier trials, parallel walking at a good distance away from the trigger, or for milder issues, actually letting your dog spend time relaxing around the trigger. Even if you only get to within ten feet of the trigger as your closest approach point during the session, you can spend some time at the end of the session just chatting from fifteen to twenty feet away, a distance at which the dog is more comfortable. Then have your dog move away first, so that the sudden motion of the trigger doesn't startle him.

Ending well is important. I confused a client once by telling her that you would want to get as much use out of a helper as you could, meaning that you could dress them up, have them change their gait, and do all sorts of other things. Once the dog realizes the helper is friendly and not scary, you can't really do BAT with him as the trigger without being creative. So she dutifully did session after session, being careful not to let her dog get to know the person, so she could re-use him as a trigger. Unfortunately, that slowed down her dog's progress. Having her become fully acquainted with one nice person after another would've helped her become comfortable with humans more quickly. Not only does a positive ending to the session help make faster progress, it also helps you see progress more clearly. The number of trials between the beginning of a session and 'first contact' is a good data point to record. You might define first contact as the point where you had to put a muzzle on, a certain distance from the trigger, the first time your dog touched the trigger, or the first time the trigger could touch your dog.

Keep in mind that if your dog starts out a football field away from the trigger, I wouldn't expect them to be able to get close enough to greet in one set-up. Getting to know the trigger can take a while, and you should always take the dog's stress level and stamina into account.

After each successful BAT set-up, the dog can usually begin closer to the trigger than in the previous set-up, even with a different person or dog as the trigger, unless there is something more challenging about the trigger or the set-up.

CHAPTER 7

BAT on Everyday Walks for Fear and Aggression

BAT set-ups can work quickly to rehabilitate dogs (think ten to twenty set-ups for dogs with straightforward issues), but if dogs are rehearsing aggression or panic during their everyday walks they will lose the new skills they have learned in the set-ups. The good news is that I have developed a version of BAT that's split into three stages that works well in unstructured encounters with the trigger. Such encounters happen frequently on walks, so you and your dog can practice the replacement behaviors in a variety of locations.

Bonus rewards

Two of the stages of BAT on walks involve bonus rewards, so let's discuss those first. Bonus rewards are consequences that your dog likes that aren't related to the particular behavior. So unlike a functional reward, this type of reward is more of a bonus than a paycheck. Bonus rewards are given *after* the functional reward, so your dog is allowed the time to appreciate the functional reward first, i.e., to learn that the replacement behavior leads to the same desired consequence as the problem behavior.

I saved the discussion of bonus rewards for this chapter because they are primarily used on walks rather than in set-ups. Formal BAT set-ups don't usually use tangible bonus rewards like food and toys because dogs seem to learn more about the trigger when there is nothing else on which to focus. In other words, there is no distraction due to the presence of treats and no other competing motivation to behave well. Your dog's attention is focused on dealing with the social situation at hand. Dog (and human) brains file away information that they focus on. Background information may not be retained. Dogs seem to miss subtle information in social settings when distracted by the temptation of food or the threat of punishment from their human.

In set-ups, I tend to only use bonus rewards that won't distract the dog during the next trial, like praise or petting, assuming the dog finds them rewarding. Note that not all dogs like petting, especially in the presence of their trigger. If a dog does not really want to move much, or hasn't been trained to walk well on a leash, I might throw in occasional bonus rewards of food or toys to keep things interesting (after the functional reward, of course). I am more likely to use tangible bonus rewards when I do BAT set-ups with inanimate objects, which don't require as much focused attention from the dog (slippery surfaces, scary rooms, getting into cars, etc.). Those situations also don't have the natural magnetism of social situations, so dogs may need bonus rewards to stay engaged with the trigger.

Bonus rewards can be extremely effective to keep the dog non-reactive during walks.

Even though bonus rewards can get in the way during set-ups, they are extremely helpful during walks. The three main effects of bonus rewards are to: 1) help your dog make good choices when close to the trigger; 2) make the training more fun for your dog; and 3) decrease stress.

On a walk, for example, your dog might randomly encounter triggers at ten feet, thirty feet, and then at fifteen feet. This is in contrast to set-ups, when you control the exposure and can make sure your dog is likely to make the choices you like, i.e., do the replacement behaviors. On a walk, however, you may need a little extra help on your side to encourage your dog to avoid aggression or panic. Even though the bonus reward comes *after* you walk your dog away, knowing that their human is carrying freeze-dried liver takes some of their attention off of the triggers and puts it on to you. The presence of treats or toys makes your dog more likely hold herself together around a trigger in such uncontrolled situations.

Dogs have a fabulous sense of smell, and sniffing is a relaxing activity, so the opportunity to do nose work or other scenting activity is another excellent kind of bonus reward. Nose work is a sport where dogs learn to find particular smells on cue, starting with treats or toys and working up to being able to find three essential oils (birch, anise, and clove). The basic Nose work set-up involves hiding treats in boxes. I won't go into the whole sport here, but if you want to try it, start out at home or some quiet place without any triggers. Show your dog a box with a treat in it and set it down, telling her to "Find It." Gradually make it more challenging with more boxes to search through (one box has the treat), hiding the treat further way from her, and doing box work outside.

Nose work is useful for reactive dogs in all sorts of ways (exercise, mental stimulation, confidence booster in new settings, etc.). I first heard of using nose work as a bonus reward for BAT by Donna Savoie, CPDT, on the FunctionalRewards.com discussion group. You can set up boxes for an official K9 Nose Work "hide" at the retreat point, so you basically go toward the trigger, get a good behavior, mark, and the reward is to run back to the boxes and tell your dog to search. Sniffing is a lovely self-soothing behavior and looking for treats puts your dog in a seeking state of mind, which helps relieve any stress that's building up.

A simpler version of using scent work as a bonus reward while on a walk is to toss a treat into the grass at the retreat point and tell your dog to "Find It." If your dog doesn't already know a search cue, you'll need to toss the treat so she sees you doing it. If you have already trained her to know what "Find It" means, then you can get sneaky and toss it just as you head off toward the trigger, so that your dog doesn't see you hide the treat. Then, after you walk away from the trigger, say "Find It" as her bonus reward. With both this and the official Nose Work set-up, it's a good idea to pay attention to the associations your dog makes. If you immediately leave the search area and return to the trigger after your dog finds the treats or odor, then she may see that as a punishment and begin to search more slowly or stop altogether. You can keep your dog from making that connection by waiting a variable amount of time after a successful search, say ten to thirty seconds.

In short, use praise, petting, or other non-distracting bonus rewards with impunity, any time you want to. Use food, toys, scent work and other tangible bonus rewards when the distraction works in your favor. The next section gives some specifics on how and when to use tangible bonus rewards with BAT.

Let's take a look at the main way that BAT can be used on walks and other uncontrolled environments. It should give you a better idea of how exactly to give food or toys as bonus rewards.

Three stages of BAT for use on walks

I split BAT into three stages for use on walks and chance encounters where your dog perceives the trigger in real life, i.e., not part of a set-up. The stages vary the difficulty of your dog's choice and the likelihood that she will be able to make the choice that you want her to make. Advanced stages of BAT put more responsibility on your dog and less responsibility on you.

Stage 1 BAT for walks: Look, go, treat

This is the simplest version of BAT for real life. In Stage 1, you don't stop and wait at a sub-threshold level as you would in a set-up, because on an everyday type walk, the distance to the trigger cannot be controlled, and the dog is likely to just bark and lunge or panic while you wait for a polite cut-off signal as a replacement behavior to reward. *The behavior you reward in Stage 1 is simply noticing the trigger.* As soon as your dog perceives the trigger, click, give the functional reward of guiding your dog away as you praise, and then give your dog a tangible bonus reward. The order matters! The treat is a bonus, not the main reward—the main reward is distance from the trigger. Walk or jog away first, and then surprise your dog with the delicious or fun bonus reward.

dog perceives trigger → click → walk away → treat

For Stage 1 on walks, click when your dog sees the trigger.

The dog usually turns toward the clicker.

Functional reward: walk or jog away from the trigger.

After your dog walks away, feed a treat or play with a toy.

Notice that this means there will be a few seconds of delay between your click and the treat, as you reward your dog first by going away from the trigger. If you're in a tight spot, you can click and then do something else to reduce your dog's stress as a functional reward: go as far away as the space allows and block your dog's view, then treat like mad.

For Stages 1 and 2, which both use tangible bonus rewards, I recommend using a clicker, rather than a verbal marker. The clicker serves two purposes here. It marks the behavior, but it also cues the dog to turn toward you for the bonus reward—away from the trigger—which helps your dog avoid an outburst. If a clicker just makes you feel clumsy or your dog is afraid of the clicker, stick with your regular verbal marker or use your dog's name as a marker.

> Note for Pros: Don't worry about weakening the power of the clicker. A few second's delay, especially when the treat is predictably given in the "click → walk/run away → treat" pattern, is not harmful to the click/treat association. Furthermore, the dog is still getting a reward immediately after the click—the functional reward. If you're still worried, jog or run so that the delay between click and treat is shorter, and praise after the click to bridge the time between your click and the treat.

BAT Stage 1 is very similar to what Leslie McDevitt calls "Look at That" in her excellent book, *Control Unleashed* (see Resources). The basic version of Look at That is to train it as a cued behavior by clicking and treating dogs for looking at a neutral stimulus first, and then reward them for looking at (or listening to) a low-level version triggering stimulus, like another dog or a person. I recently found out that Leslie does use release of social pressure (walking away from the trigger) as part of Look at That in some cases. A lot of the *Control Unleashed* exercises compliment BAT very nicely, and it's worth looking into.

BAT on Walks: STAGE 1

Use STAGE 1 when trigger shows up unexpectedly or when you are in a tight spot and when your dog is most likely to react...

STEP 1: DOG PERCEIVES TRIGGER

* Or ask the dog to LOOK using "Look At That" cue

STEP 2: MARK the instant the dog sees the trigger, using a clicker or verbal marker.

*The CLICK also cues the dog to turn his head away from the trigger and back towards you.

STEP 3: WALK or RUN AWAY ← Functional Reward

* DISTANCE from the trigger reduces stress.

STEP 4: PRAISE & TREAT/TOY! ← Bonus Reward

* The treat or toy comes AFTER the Functional Reward

BAT Stage 1: LOOK, GO, TREAT

Stage 2 BAT for walks: Choose, go, treat

This stage adds in some more responsibility for your dog, but you are still using a tangible bonus reward, usually food. The only difference between Stages 1 and 2 is that you wait for a "good choice." Therefore, in Stage 2, wait for a replacement behavior instead of just clicking when the dog perceives the trigger as you would do in Stage 1. Your dog notices the trigger, then you wait for him to look away or do some other cut-off signal, and that's when you click. The behavior your dog is supposed to do is exactly like in a BAT set-ups (from the previous chapter), but after you walk away as the functional reward, you also give your dog treats, toys, or some other bonus reward. (See the illustration on the next page for a visual explanation of Stage 2.) This is what Stage 2 looks like:

dog perceives trigger → wait for good choice → click → walk away → treat

Use Stage 2 when you would bet money that your dog is able to make a good choice in that situation, given that you have treats or toys. If you aren't willing to make that bet, use Stage 1, instead. If your dog sees a trigger in a particular situation where you think your dog could do the replacement behaviors even without the bonus rewards, you'd advance to Stage 3 of BAT for that encounter.

Stage 3 BAT for walks: Choose and go

Stage 3 is the same process as used in BAT set-ups which I described in the previous chapter. In Stage 3, your dog is responsible for offering a replacement behavior, as with Stage 2, but there is no help from a bonus reward of food or toys. This stage will maximize your dog's attention on the trigger, and therefore, maximize her learning. (See page 99 for an illustration of Stage 3.) Stage 3 looks like this:

dog perceives trigger → wait for good choice → verbally mark → walk away

Use the highest stage that works with your dog, i.e., whatever stage keeps the dog subthreshold. In other words, you don't necessarily start at Stage 1 and work your way up. It all depends on your dog's behavior in set-ups; you'll start right away with using Stage 3 because it is a set-up in a controlled situation. I created the other BAT stages as a way to help dogs behave well on walks. Any time you encounter a trigger, use the highest stage you think your dog can handle, but use a lower stage if you're not sure how your dog will do. Generally, you can use a higher stage as your dog becomes more capable or when triggers are far enough away to help your dog gain social skills faster. The stages that use food or toys as bonus rewards help you and your dog generalize your training to new situations and prevent practicing aggression and panic on walks. At Stage 2, the dog is actually making a choice, which gives the dog more decision-making practice than Stage 1. By Stage 3, your dog is making decisions based on real consequences, which makes it even more effective.

BAT on Walks: STAGE 2

Use **STAGE 2** when you would bet your money that your dog is going to make a **GOOD CHOICE**, knowing that food or toys are around. If you are not sure how he will respond, use **STAGE 1** instead.

STEP 1: DOG PERCEIVES TRIGGER

STEP 2: WAIT FOR A GOOD CHOICE

*Wait for an Engage-Disengage pattern or Cut-Off Signal

STEP 3: MARK the GOOD CHOICE

* Use a CLICKER or a Verbal marker like "Yes!"

EXAMPLE :
LOOKING AWAY

STEP 4: WALK or RUN AWAY ← Functional Reward

*DISTANCE from the trigger reduces stress.

STEP 5: PRAISE & TREAT/TOY! ← Bonus Reward

* The treat or toy comes AFTER the Functional Reward

BAT Stage 2: CHOOSE, GO, TREAT

BAT on Walks: STAGE 3

Use STAGE 3 - the highest stage on walks - for chance encounters where you would bet that the dog would be able to stay below threshold without needing any distractions like food or toys.

STEP 1: DOG PERCEIVES TRIGGER

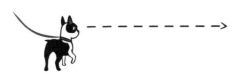

STEP 2: WAIT FOR A GOOD CHOICE

*Wait for an Engage-Disengage pattern or Cut-Off Signal

STEP 3: MARK THE GOOD CHOICE

* Using a Verbal marker

SNIFF
SNIFF

STEP 4: WALK or RUN AWAY & PRAISE! ← Functional Reward

* DISTANCE from the trigger reduces stress.

GOOD BOY!

BAT Stage 3: CHOOSE and GO

This stage is the same as the BASIC BAT SET-UP.

If you use Stage 1 or 2 a lot, you will need to fade (reduce) the use of food at some point, unless you want that as a lifetime management strategy. Use food when you need it, but the less food you use, the less you have to fade. The functional reward of distance can be faded to smaller and smaller retreats by the handler, while still allowing the dog to retreat as much as they need to. The functional reward doesn't necessarily need a formal plan to fade the use of distance because the dog just gradually no longer needs to get away from the former trigger. And she moves herself away, when needed, rather than relying on the handler.

Distraction

Distraction isn't a part of BAT, nor is it necessarily educational, but I'm mentioning it here because sometimes you just get into a situation where you can't do BAT. This would include a situation where you can't walk away and your dog isn't yet ready to just wait until the trigger leaves. In cases like this, feed your dog super-delicious treats, one right after the other—distracting your dog—until the trigger goes away. Stand in between your dog and the trigger, if needed. Ideally, your dog will perceive the trigger and *then* you'll reach for the food. That way, you are doing classical counter-conditioning in the right way and your dog can build some positive association with the appearance of the trigger.

With classical counter-conditioning, the idea is to associate a negatively charged trigger with one that has a positive association, or is inherently positive, like food. If you do present the stimuli in reverse order, i.e., you give your dog a hot dog or rustle with your treat pouch before your dog becomes aware of the trigger, then your dog may become afraid of hot dogs! This is all too easy to do, because people tend to reach inside of their treat bags as soon as they see the trigger, before the dog has perceived it. Using distractions is more like a Band-AID to keep the dog from freaking out when there's no escape. So use food as a distraction to keep the dog from exploding, but do all that you can to avoid a trap like that in the future. If you live in a condo with an elevator and need to use distraction on a daily basis, then watch your timing!

If even stuffing your dog's face full of treats is not enough to prevent an outburst, then sit down after the incident and figure out how you can avoid having your dog encounter the trigger in that way until you have had a chance to do BAT set-ups and get your dog used to that situation. Sometimes, the answer is just to use stinkier, meatier treats or to walk your dog before dinner, when she's hungrier. Sometimes it's better management. You may have to take the stairs instead of the elevator, or put your dog in a back room with a frozen stuffed Kong when company comes over. There is only so much responsibility you can put on your dog at this point. It's like a toddler who keeps falling into a swimming pool. To keep it from happening again, you could yell or explain the concept of death, but neither of those solutions is likely to be effective. For an instant fix, parents put up a barrier around the pool so that they just don't have a problem until the swimming lessons have started working. The same is true for dogs. Sometimes, they just need some environmental engineering to prevent overexposure to the trigger.

To summarize, here is a chart listing the various BAT stages while on walks.

What to Do on Walks						
BAT Stage	**Used For**	**Behavior to Mark / Reward**	**Marker Type**	**Functional Reward**	**Intangible Bonus Reward (praise/ petting)**	**Tangible Bonus Reward (treats/ toys)**
BAT Stage 1: dog perceives trigger → click → walk away → treat						
Stage 1 Look, Go, Treat	Surprises on walks or times when dog would make a 'bad' choice on her own	Looking at or even hearing trigger (see ear movement)	Clicker (can use verbal)	Walk/ run away or some other way to reduce stress	Yes	Yes
BAT Stage 2: dog perceives trigger → wait for good choice → click → walk away → treat						
Stage 2 Choose, Go, Treat	Walks where she can make a good choice with the help of smelling food in your pocket	Engage/ disengage pattern: Looking away from trigger, sniffing ground, shaking off, looking at handler, etc.	Clicker (can use verbal)	Walk/ run away or some other way to reduce stress	Yes	Yes

What to Do on Walks						
BAT Stage 3: dog perceives trigger → wait for good choice → verbal marker → walk away						
Stage 3 Choose and Go	Walks where she can make good choices without interference. BAT set-ups.	Engage/disengage pattern: Looking away from trigger, sniffing ground, shaking off, looking at handler, etc.	Verbal	Walk/run away or some other way to reduce stress	Yes	No
Distraction: See Trigger → Feed/play to distract dog when options are limited						
Not BAT, more like classical counter-conditioning	Tight spots	None or looking at trigger	None	None (no room to escape)	Yes	Yes

More BAT tips and examples for walks

Doing BAT on a walk provides a great opportunity to generalize what the dog is learning from BAT set-ups. Unfortunately, if the dog is put over threshold, walks can also erase some of the gains made in those set-ups. If you follow the safety tips from the management chapter, you should be able to keep your dog below threshold most of the time. That doesn't mean avoiding triggers altogether; that is almost impossible on walks. On the contrary, you'll find that you actually start walking your dog at a more normal time of day and start stalking your dog's trigger—following other dogs from a distance or doing "undercover BAT" in other ways (this has also been called "Stealth BAT" on the Yahoo group). Look for triggers that are relatively stationary or are walking in a predictable way:

- Dogs behind fences
- Gardeners
- People and/or dogs at coffee shops
- Kids at playgrounds

- Dogs tied up at a baseball game
- People or dogs on walking paths
- Dogs in training class or at pet stores.

How exactly would you do BAT on a walk? Let's say your dog is reactive to children. If a child is walking directly at you on a sidewalk, you have a lot of choices. As you're reading these examples, some of them will seem impossible and some will sound reasonable. Do the reasonable ones and keep the other choices in mind for later, as your dog progresses. Remember, the stages are situational—your dog may be doing Stage 1 for one encounter and Stage 2 or 3 for the next one, then back to Stage 1 for the next. *Always do the highest stage that your dog can handle well and use management (muzzles, etc.) to keep everyone safe:*

- **Stage 1 example.** Your dog looks up and notices the child as you are walking. Click as soon as he sees the child, then say "Let's go," jog away, and feed a treat.

- **Stage 1 example.** Your dog looks up and notices the child as you are approaching. Click as soon as he sees the child, then walk away and tell him to "Find it" with several treats tossed on the ground.

- **Stage 1 example.** You want to avoid getting too close. Stop approaching and wait for your dog to notice the child. Click as soon as he sees the child, jog away into a driveway, and then stop to play tug.

- **Stage 1 example.** Walk up to the child and stop as you say "hi." As soon as the dog looks at the child, you click, walk away, and give your dog a treat, praising her bravery.

- **Stage 2 example.** Stop walking and wait for your dog to notice the child and then look at you. Click as soon as he looks at you, jog away into a driveway, and then stop to play tug.

- **Stage 2 example.** Walk up to the child and stop as you say "hi." Your dog looks at the child and then looks away, so you click, walk away, and give your dog a treat, praising her bravery.

- **Stage 2 example.** Walk your dog a little off the sidewalk and wait for the child to pass by. Your dog looks at the child, then sniffs the ground. Mark that choice by clicking, praise as you jog away from the child, and then give your dog a treat.

- **Stage 3 example.** Walk your dog a little off the sidewalk and wait for the child to pass by. Your dog looks at the child, then sniffs the ground. Mark that choice by saying, "Yes" and praise as you jog away from the child.

- **Stage 3 example.** Keep walking toward the child along the sidewalk. As you're walking, the dog looks at the child, and then looks away. Mark that choice by saying, "Yes" and take a step off to the side so that you're arcing around the child (slight increase in distance/decrease in stress as the functional reward).

- **Stage 3 example.** Walk up to the child and allow your dog to greet the child. After a little petting, your dog looks away from the child. You say "Yes, let's go" and continue on your walk, telling your dog he's fabulously brave. Cool, huh?

- **Distraction example.** You are just stuck until they go by, so you shorten the leash (without tightening it, if possible), stand between your dog and the child, and drop treats on the ground, away from the child.

- **Distraction example.** You see the child first and know that if your dog sees the child, he will start barking right away. You do an emergency U-turn to get out of there, and feed your dog a treat for coming with you.

- **Distraction example.** You have to keep going, for some reason, and so you feed your dog a non-stop series of treats as you pass by.

- **Combo example.** As soon as your dog sees the child, you click, walk into a driveway, and treat. The child passes by you. You wait a bit and then you and your dog follow the child down the sidewalk, from a safe distance. As you're walking, he looks at the child, then looks away. You click for the lookaway, then pivot and walk him away from the child, and then give your dog a treat. Successful repetition is the key to progress, so if you can get a few trials in with the triggers you encounter in public, do it!

Your dog may bark and lunge when you misjudge the situation or life happens and suddenly she's too close to the trigger—then even distractions don't always work. Don't yell at your dog for freaking out when you've trapped her with a child (or whatever your dog's trigger is); just get out of there as soon as you can using whatever means possible. See what you can do about avoiding such a situation in the future. If avoiding triggers is really hard, there may be a location that's easier for your dog to walk in without going over threshold. Your dog might benefit from indoor exercise before heading out, stress relief of some kind (medical and/or training), or may need more BAT setups before the real world is not overwhelming.

BAT can almost always be done on walks, in one form or another. Any time your dog is exposed to the trigger, you should be aware of his body language so that you can reinforce good choices with a functional reward. Be aware of your location, so that you know how best to retreat. When you walk away, you can turn around entirely and head in the opposite direction or turn at a right angle and cross the street or walk into a driveway. Remember that you, not your dog, choose whether to put your dog into a given situation. Doing BAT on walks can help your dog learn that he has choices about how to reduce the stress of living in a world orchestrated by humans.

CHAPTER 8

BAT for Frustrated Greeters

A lot of the barking and lunging on-leash dogs do when they 'greet' other dogs from a distance is not the result of fear or aggression. They are simply frustrated and the more we hold them back, the more desperately they want to go see their own species! It's important to deal with frustration in a way that teaches dogs that there is nothing to fear or get mad about. Use BAT to help your dog understand that polite on-leash is the only way to get what they want. For many of my fearful dog clients, their reactivity may have started with frustration, but a lifetime of leash corrections and disastrous on-leash greetings has led to a fear of what happens when they are on-leash around other dogs. For those dogs, the path is clear—being able to get away from the other dogs is a functional reward. This chapter, however, is for the other category of dogs, the frustrated greeters who just want to go say hi.

Replacement behaviors for frustrated greeters

The most effective replacement behaviors for frustrated greeters are similar to the ones you would reward with other kinds of reactive dogs, but not exactly the same. With a shy dog, I might reward pro-social approach behaviors, but since those behaviors taken to extremes would be problematic with frustrated greeters, I prefer to reward any sign of self-control. When you do BAT set-ups with frustrated greeters, look for polite cut-off signals such as these to reinforce:

- Looking away from other dog
- Turning head away
- Turning body away
- Backing away
- Sniffing the ground
- Sitting

- Lying down

- Looking at you

- Slowly stretching.

Some of these may actually be problem behaviors in certain dogs, so choose wisely! For example, a Border Collie might lie down just before pouncing on the other dog, so that's actually a problem behavior, not a replacement behavior. But in an English Mastiff, lying down might indicate a relaxed state, because getting up from a Down is a big deal.

Just as with the other kinds of reactive dogs, you'll need to work at a distance to help your frustrated greeter be able to offer these replacement behaviors on her own. If you get lunging, barking, or another negative reaction instead, move further away and wait for your dog to offer an acceptable replacement behavior.

Functional rewards for frustrated greeters

There is a bit of a paradox with frustrated greeters—dogs who are not fearful or aggressive, but just want to greet. I have done BAT with frustrated greeters using walking away as a reward and also with walking toward the other dog as a reward. In both cases, I waited for the student dog to disengage from the other dog before rewarding with either walking away or walking toward the other dog. The retreat as a reward was about fifteen feet. Forward progress as a reward was about one foot. Paradoxically, both seem to work!

I have some theories as to why this might be. For one thing, simply walking or running anywhere, versus standing around, might function as a reward. All of the rewards in BAT are usually accompanied by praise, so that's another reward. The greeting process is a stressful thing, even if your dog just wants to greet. So after the dog has disengaged from the other dog, walking away may be preferable to just standing there, because it reduces stress. However, if your dog is dying to go say hello to the other dog, it makes perfect sense that moving closer to the other dog would be reinforcing.

While both approaching and walking away seem to work as functional rewards for frustrated greeters, one or the other may end up being better for a particular dog, so try it both ways. If the dog is really not good at greeting, I prefer to use walking away as a reward, possibly also adding in bonus rewards to strengthen the effect and help teach your dog that walking away is fun! If greetings go well, then walking forward is ideal to use, particularly during set-ups. I have clients who use forward progress in set-ups and Stage 2 BAT (with retreat and bonus reward) on walks, and that seems to go well. Using BAT to teach frustrated dogs how to get closer to another dog is great, because it teaches them that in order to get close to their friends (new or old), they have to be polite. They are building a repertoire of great social behaviors that decrease tension, which most dogs do without human intervention. They look at the other dogs, then look away (replacement behavior), get closer (functional reward); look at them, sniff the ground, get closer; look at them, shake off, get closer.

Tarzan greetings

Many frustrated greeters act crazy from a distance but can actually greet just fine once they actually reach another dog. For dogs who can greet well, all you need to work on is a calm approach, and the problem is solved. Just practice several polite approaches with different dogs and let the dogs greet whenever they are close enough to do so.

Other frustrated greeters tend to be like the "Tarzan" dogs that Jean Donaldson mentions in her book *Fight!* (see Resources). Tarzan dogs really love other dogs, but lack the little negotiation skills that dogs use to avoid conflict. They want to interact, but they just aren't good at it. For example, instead of approaching in an arc and sniffing the rear first, a Tarzan dog might try to start a play session with a new dog by running straight at the new dog and tackling him, which can then start a scuffle or a real fight. I like the techniques that Donaldson mentions in her book, including using a group of well-socialized dogs to facilitate learning. If you have a Tarzan dog, that's a great book to add to your library. I especially like her use of warnings followed by time outs for rude behavior.

For those dogs who don't greet well, review the information I gave in Chapter 6 about "the last ten feet." Even though they have good intentions, Tarzan dogs come on pretty strong and can irritate even patient decoy dogs. Teaching Tarzan dogs to greet in short bits can be helpful. For example, you may need to call your dog back and jog away after a very short greeting (like one second). Because you called your dog away before she was done, give a toy or food reward, then do another BAT trial.

Because frustrated greeters don't necessarily know how to cool off greetings, you'll need to keep the greetings short, just as you would with other reactive dogs. Call your dog after a short greeting (about a quarter of a second), walk away, reward, and return to the other dog. Use the information on clicker training in Appendix 1 to learn how to get started on coming when called and also how to teach the play bow as a default behavior. A side-effect of rewarding a lot of play bows in your dog's interactions with you is that it becomes a part of his repertoire, and he's more likely to offer it to other dogs, too. When he does that, he signals his peaceful intent, which most dogs will understand naturally, and the interaction will go more smoothly.

Part of your dog's frustration is that she might not know when you will allow her to interact with other dogs and when you won't. One way to make that really clear is to never allow your dog to greet another dog when you are out for a walk. I have to admit that I don't have the heart for that, but I trust the trainers who say that it works, like Pia Silvani (see Resources). Another way is to have a cue that signals that the dogs will be allowed to greet, like "Go say hi" and a cue that signals you are not going to allow greetings, like "Leave it." Any time we can be really clear with dogs, they have a better chance of success.

The same basic process is used with a frustrated greeter who gets overly excited approaching a person. The following set of six photos shows BAT principles being used in this type of situation.

Problem behavior: jumping. Functional reward: attention.

1. Waiting for calm look away.

2. Dog turns head, so mark with "Yes!"

3. Functional reward: one step closer!

4. Waiting again...

5. Another look away, mark with "Yes!"

6. Functional reward: attention. Dog also gets a bonus reward—food!

Lack of self-control

Many of the frustrated greeters lack self-control in other areas of their lives. For example, Yo-Yo is a female Black Lab who barked and lunged whenever she saw other dogs. But she also barked and lunged when her (human) Dad held the leash and prevented her from getting to Mom. It's hard to find decoy dogs, but relatively easy for a couple to work together with their own dog.

I had Yo-yo's owners do several set-ups for their homework, with Dad holding Yo-Yo on-leash and Mom standing fifty feet holding visible treats in her hands. Dad walked Yo-Yo toward Mom, turning around and going ten feet away from her if Yo-Yo barked or lunged. Every time Yo-Yo looked at Mom and then looked away, Dad allowed Yo-Yo to walk two feet closer to Mom and her treats. The first session took a while, but Yo-Yo caught on pretty quickly, after that. They practiced in several locations, to help generalize the behavior. They noticed progress the next time they worked on the polite behavior with dogs on the sidewalk. The number of outbursts was drastically reduced and he was able to be calm around the other dog much sooner.

This is an example of using functional rewards and it's called the **Premack Principle.** The Premack Principle states that the opportunity to perform a high probability behavior reinforces a low probability behavior. That is, the chance to do something that the dog is likely to do can be used as a reinforcement for something the dog is unlikely to do. Even a frustrated greeter is likely to offer head turns. So the chance to go greet can be used to reinforce the replacement behavior of turning her head. There are other behaviors that are very likely, but they aren't ideal as a reinforcement in this situation, because they don't meet the dog's needs in that moment, i.e., they aren't functional rewards. Greeting is a perfect reinforcement because it is both a functional reward and a high probability behavior.

If your dog is a frustrated greeter, you should also use clicker training (see Appendix 1) with food/toys and functional rewards to teach her to wait at curbs, wait at doors, wait for you to throw the ball, sit down to ask permission to get up on the couch, lie down while you eat dinner, sit down to greet you, leave food/toys/squirrels when asked, walk politely on-leash, etc. Any bit of self-control that your dog learns can extend to the realm of frustrated greeting.

In summary, you may need to experiment with different functional rewards or add more bonus rewards for frustrated greeters. Walking away after your dog gathers information may be a functional reward, but walking closer may also work. As with any other kind of interaction with reactive dogs, safety should be a primary concern. Having a fence between the dogs can minimize the chances of the leashes tangling and can also help everybody relax. It can allow you to work your dog off-leash without any risk, too. On the other hand, fences can be part of the problem for frustrated greeters and others. That leads us to the next topic: Fence Fighting.

CHAPTER 9

Love Thy Neighbor:

Fence Fighting

Dogs are great at alerting their pack that an intruder has entered their territory. That's part of why humans have dogs. Knowing that my dogs will sound the alarm if someone were to break into my home comforts me. Several years ago, a man opened our door at 2 a.m. and two hundred pounds of barking dogs kept him outside. Even the friendliest dog takes this job very seriously. Unfortunately, *a lot* of dogs also consider it imperative to keep other dogs and people away from their fence line, even if that 'intruder' happens to live in the house next door.

To work on fence fighting issues, I always recommend management, because environmental changes can quickly reduce stress. Environmental changes combine well with passive training, active training, or both. Let's look at each of these three approaches in turn.

Environmental changes

If a dog is fence fighting, he is probably getting a fair amount of reinforcement for the behavior, especially if he is reacting to dogs who are on the sidewalk, on the other side of the fence. Look at it from your dog's perspective. A stranger appears, he charges out to bark and growl, and the other dog or person leaves in defeat. It doesn't matter that they were leaving anyway. He still feels that he has successfully guarded his territory. As I mentioned before, this system of automatic reinforcement for barking needs to be removed and a lot of this can be handled by the management techniques discussed below.

If your dog fence fights with neighbors or neighboring dogs, one simple technique is to work out a schedule where the dogs are out at different times. You should also do all of the steps I mentioned above in the "out of sight, out of mind" section of Chapter 3.

Even if you have a fenced-in yard, you may need to walk your dog on a leash in the backyard for a while, so he can avoid getting sucked into a conflict at the fence. You can also tether your dog with a long leash that doesn't allow him to reach the fence—the further away he is from the fence, the less likely he is to bark. Always supervise a tethered dog—go outside with him. The safest way that I've found to tether a dog is to

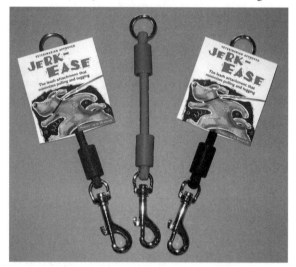

have a bungee attachment at the end that secures the leash to the stake, house, or other solid object. Use a long lead that is not likely to get tangled, like plastic-coated wire or climber's webbing. Clip that lead to the back of a harness on your dog. That way, if your dog does decide to charge out and hits the end of the leash, there's a bungee to absorb the shock and the harness distributes the remaining force instead of choking your dog on a collar.

Bungee shock absorbers make long lines safer when the dog is tethered. Use a back-attachment harness, rather than the collar pictured here.

You can also landscape the yard so that your dog can't get right up to the fence. Plant something thick and/or prickly next to the fence. In addition to reducing visibility, plants can absorb more of the noise that the 'intruders' make, which keeps your dog calmer. If you are on good terms with the neighbor, suggest that they consider some landscaping that might keep their dog away from the fence, too. If it's possible, plant something like arbor vitae between your fence and the sidewalk, as well. It will keep passersby further away from your fence. If you need some more ideas, Cheryl Smith has a book on creating gardens and landscaping that are both beautiful and dog-friendly (see Resources).

Use your creative human brain to look at the situation and see if there are any other changes that can be made to reduce the chance of barking in the backyard. Environmental changes can be quicker and easier than training, so think long and hard about what you can do. Question your assumptions, too. Does your dog need the whole yard? Are you giving your dog front-yard access when the backyard will do? Is your dog's life improved by having your dog door open all day, or is that really causing more stress? Thinking this through can help everybody relax.

Passive training: Lazy Bones BAT

With passive training, the human does a lot less work. You just arrange the situation so that your dog can succeed and be reinforced by the environment. **Lazy Bones BAT** is a form of passive training. It gives your dog some entertainment to focus on, which can help to minimize exposure levels of various real life triggers. One example of a simple way to do this is to stuff an easy, but long-lasting food puzzle and give it to your dog out in the yard. This, combined with attaching a harness and long leash to keep your dog away from the fence, should help keep your dog calmer (remember to still supervise).

In a situation like this, the stuffed food puzzle acts as a magnet for your dog's attention. As other dogs pass by, you'll see your dog look up, think about barking, and then go back to work. Yay! He ignores the other dog and the other dog leaves (they were going to, anyway), so your dog gets his functional reward for behavior you like. Magic. If you're still getting barking, then do Lazy Bones BAT with the food puzzle and your dog closer to the house or even inside with the door open (as in a formal set-up, you are increasing the distance to the trigger). You can also train your dog to "Get your toy" and if you think he's about to bark, cue him to get the food puzzle that he was just eating. That worked well for my dog, Peanut.

We are all busy, and I know from experience that if preparing a food puzzle takes too much time out of people's day, they won't do it. Here's how I made the preparation process efficient and quick at my house. Get some kind of food that comes out as a paste, without chunks, so that you can easily get it into the food puzzles. If you're really into food prep, you can grind your own meat. I'm busy and lazy, so I buy canned dog food or dehydrated raw dog food to which I can just add water to rehydrate. You can buy a pastry tube or scoop the wet dog food into a baggie, close it, and cut off one of the bottom corners of the baggie, so you have a hole about half an inch wide. Now you have a homemade version of a pastry tube, so you can squeeze just the right amount in each toy. The toys can then go into baggies or a reusable container in the freezer. As your dog empties the toys, just put them back into a big container in the freezer. You can stuff a bunch all at once, which saves you time. Putting the used puzzle toys back into the freezer ensures that any leftover food doesn't mold. I have a portion of my freezer dedicated to the dogs, so we have about a dozen stuffed Kongs and other food puzzles. For the very busy dog owner, don't worry, you don't have to wash the toys; simply put them in the dishwasher.

For fastest learning, feed your dog all his meals this way while working on his fence fighting issues. If you do need to feed the rest in a bowl, do the food puzzle outside first, and the bowl second. Make sure to take into account how many calories your dog gets from the food puzzle each day. Remember that treats are often more calorie-dense than dog food. The last thing we want to do is make your dog chunky. Overweight dogs have more health problems and shorter lives, so don't overstuff your dog! Overfed dogs are also generally less food motivated, so Lazy Bones BAT doesn't work as well for them. How can you tell if your dog is the right weight? About sixty percent of dogs in this country are overweight, so you can't just compare to other dogs that you see. You should be able to feel your dog's ribs without having to really press in your hands to search for them, and if you look at your wet dog from above, you should see that he has a waist.

Back to Lazy Bones BAT. As your dog completes the food puzzle, she is more likely to react to triggers again, so stay out there with her so that you can see when she's done with the food puzzle. You don't have to just concentrate on the dog while you're outside. You can read a book, do yard work, talk on the phone, etc., as your dog plays with the toy. Be ready to either bring her in or give her another food puzzle (or set multiple puzzles out from the beginning). While you do Lazy Bones BAT, only allow her to be out in the yard for potty time or when she has a food puzzle. It may take several months for her to learn to ignore the background noise—less time if she's new to fence fighting. Once she's doing well, you can start to remove the long leash and harness. You can even gradually shorten the long leash and have her drag it around so that there's not such a big contrast between being tethered and being free in the yard. Again, make sure you supervise when your dog is on a leash.

Continue doing the food puzzles for every non-potty trip outside until your dog is not reacting badly to any of the passersby or the neighbor's dog. Once that's gone well for a month or two, then start having more gaps in between the food puzzles, so that your dog has more time out in the yard without distractions. Gradually have the puzzle less and less full. You might still want to leave some kind of toys out in the yard, so your dog can self-soothe as people or dogs pass by.

Active training
If you're willing to take a more active role, there are some other exercises that you can do to reduce or eliminate fence fighting using BAT. The first active training that you can do to work on fence fighting with a neighbor is to do a regular BAT set-up with both of the dogs involved, so they can become friends or at least friendly

acquaintances. When dogs actually know and like each other, they don't usually fence fight. If there are multiple dogs in each yard, start with the pair that fights most intensely, and work your way down.

Doing BAT with the dogs 'on location' in their own yards may pose some difficulties: 1) there may not be enough room to maneuver (although opening the door to retreat inside the house can help); 2) it's an emotionally charged area; and 3) the fence between the dogs may be part of the trigger. Most of the time, I have neighbors do set-ups on the sidewalk first, with the dogs on-leash and no fence between them. Get them to the point where they can go on walks and ignore each other or interact well. If they can play safely off-leash in a neutral area, like a park or someone else's yard, that can help. Try to find a 'neutral' fence in between, i.e., not their own fence, where you can do set-ups. However, if their fence fighting is based on frustration relating on not being able to play together, seeing each other as playmates may do more harm than good, so you might want to keep things fairly mellow, rather than letting them play.

After they have gotten used to each other on the sidewalk, then you can do a BAT set-up with each dog in their own yard with the fence in between, on-leash. Remember to do this with just the pair you have been working with, without adding in extra dogs. It's a big enough criteria leap to go to the backyard, without adding in the stress of a third dog. Once you have success with the most challenging pair, work all of the pairs of dogs, then work all of the triplets, quadruplets, and so on until you have worked with all of your dogs and all of the neighbors' dogs. The people on the other side of the fence may not be willing to work their dogs, but may allow you and a friend or trainer to do so.

If your neighbor is unwilling or unable to help you, then the task is a lot harder, because you won't be able to take the dogs out of the high-stress area or keep your neighbor's dog away from the fence. You may still be able to do BAT with the off-leash neighbor dog in the yard as the unwilling decoy. If you have multiple dogs, work with each of your own dogs individually, then in pairs, and so on, using the neighbor's dog(s) as the trigger each time. This will be most successful if you first do some landscaping and make the neighbors less visible/audible/sniffable by putting up a solid privacy fence and some strong-smelling bushes in front of it. One of my dogs really hates the smell of ladybugs. I've always wanted to plant marigolds and other plants that attract ladybugs near the fence, to see if she'd avoid sniffing in that direction. Get creative!

What if it's not the neighbor's dog? If your dog barks at random people or dogs walking by, recruit helpers and decoy dogs for several BAT set-ups, including some work on Sudden Environmental Contrast (see Chapter 6 for more info on SEC). If there is no place within the yard that your dog can see the helper without barking, then you'll need to do set-ups outside on the street, so that she gets used to people, generally near her house first. This kind of barking is usually part SEC and part territoriality, so you will probably need to do basic BAT set-ups as well as SEC set-ups. If the problem is just SEC, or the territoriality is mild, you can just go right to having decoys walk up to and away from the fence. When the student dog is off-leash, expect that she will be standing at the fence for most of the session. If there is some distance from the fence at which the helper can walk without your dog barking, then your dog can be off-leash. If not, start with your dog on-leash and away from the fence.

The helper should walk all of the various routes by the house that pedestrians normally take. The only difference is that the helper should walk up, stop or move slowly and then time his exits so that they serve as functional rewards for your dog's behavior. You can watch your dog and mark with "Yes" for an acceptable replacement behavior and signal the helper to walk away as a functional reward. So the helper walks or wheels parallel to the fence, stops at some approach point, waits for you to say "Yes," and then goes back the way he came or leaves in some other way. Don't forget that there are all sorts of passersby—so try this out with kids, bikes, people with walkers or wheel chairs, people in cars stopping by to say hi, and pedestrians with and without dogs. Try to get some of each at some point in your training. A person jingling his keys can make your dog think that the person is walking a dog, so you may be able to get away with using fewer decoy dogs using that trick.

You can also do BAT Stages 1 and 2 from inside the yard. I like to use the Manners Minder, a remote control treat dispenser, to deliver bonus rewards. The remote works from about one hundred feet away, even with walls in between the remote and the dispenser. When you press the remote, the machine beeps and then dispenses food, so your dog knows that they've earned a treat. A remote control treat dispenser allows you to watch good behavior in the backyard and click the remote to signal your dog to run away from the fence to the Manners Minder for her treat. Because she's got to run away from the trigger to get her treat, she's getting a functional reward of distance as well as a bonus reward. You can train while your dog is outside and you are inside the house, or you could also be handling the neighbor's dog, remote in hand, while you reward your own dog for good behavior. I find it best to place the Manners Minder by your own back door so that your dog must run toward the house and away from the trigger for her treat.

Treats from the Manners Minder make good bonus rewards, as the dog must run to the machine for the reward.

Teaching dogs to react well around their triggers, even while off-leash and inside their own fences, can be a challenge, but the peace and quiet that you get at the end is worth it! Whether you are doing active or passive training, be patient with the process and make changes to the yard in order to keep outbursts to a minimum.

CHAPTER 10

BAT for Puppy Socialization

Don't' skip this chapter. You may not have a puppy now, but you probably will either have a puppy or an older dog that's new to you some day. You can use much of what you have learned so far about Behavior Adjustment Training to keep that puppy or dog from developing problem behaviors during the socialization process. Getting things right the first time is a whole lot easier than rehabilitation! If you are a trainer teaching puppy classes or working with rescue dogs, please pay special attention to this chapter. If you have a puppy, you can use the information in this chapter to help your puppy avoid reactivity problems. You can also use it as a litmus test when choosing puppy kindergarten class for your puppy.

Raising a puppy is like launching a space shuttle—you have a tight schedule and fixing things after the deadline is a whole lot harder than the initial assembly. I wish I could do Peanut's puppyhood over. I would have tried to get him before he landed in the shelter, or made his family wait just two more weeks until his fear period was over before they gave him up. Most importantly, I would have integrated BAT into his everyday life, which means that I would have watched his responses more closely and honored his requests for space so that he could have become brave.

You can weave BAT into a puppy's socialization process by watching her behavior. When she goes to check something out on a walk, let her go investigate on a loose leash. When she decides that she has investigated enough, say "Yes" or give your Let's Go cue, walk her away, and praise and/or treat her for coming with you.

Socialization with people

People love petting dogs. I do, too, and I have to admit that's a huge reason why I have a dog and why I love my career working with dogs. Unfortunately, most people are rude to dogs. They walk straight up and put their 'paws' on a dog's head and shoulders. Kids hug and kiss dogs, and do all sorts of other things that primates find soothing, but which are rude from the dog's perspective. People cause them pain sometimes—kids pull their tails, vets poke them with needles, groomers clip their nails. I think nail clipping probably feels like a bite to a dog.

One key element of socialization is for a puppy to be able to meet and greet humans, despite their unintentional rudeness, and you can use some of what you have learned about BAT to make this process a success. As children or adults come up to your puppy, you can tell her to "Go say hi," and then allow an interaction to occur based on the puppy's behavior. If the puppy walks up to say hello, then let the person greet your puppy. The instant that the puppy turns away from the person, happily call the puppy back so that she is out of reach of whoever she just met. Praise the puppy for coming back to you, and if she wants to go say "hi" again, let her. It's also fine if she doesn't want to walk back to the person. You just keep things upbeat and walk away with her. Better yet, if the person has time and your puppy is not in a panic, you can also just stay there and chat until the puppy decides to go check the person out again, and repeat the recall process when she turns away from the person, sniffs the ground, or offers other behaviors that indicate she is through investigating. If she's jumping up to greet, just kneel down and hold the leash near the ground, so she can't jump up, or grab the chest strap of her harness.

Help the children in your life learn to respect your puppy's requests for space. This is a great chance to educate kids on dog body language. The cut-off signals that can be reinforced in a reactive dog—like lookaways, head turns, body turns, ground sniffing, shaking off—can and should be rewarded in puppies, too. Very young puppies learn cut-off signals during play fights in the litter and with other dogs. We can help continue their normal development by reinforcing those behaviors in their new homes. Kids should learn to calmly step back and/or turn to the side in response to puppies who do cut-off signals. This is for the child's own safety and for the puppy's socialization. Puppies have short attention spans and when they give a cut-off signal to 'ask' for distance, they don't mean that they want to be alone forever. They just need a little relief from the social pressure. When a child steps back after seeing a cut-off signal, the puppy will pause only briefly before following the child, and the game will be on again. Doing this kind of exercise can help make children aware of what a dog's body language says about the dog's emotional state and willingness to engage in petting or play. Children can use their own cut-off signals to calm down boisterous puppies.

Once a puppy's requests for distance are being consistently rewarded, she can learn to be more patient with humans and persistent with their polite requests for distance as opposed to barking or biting. One way to do this is to start systematically skipping chances to reward such requests for distance (intermittent reinforcement). For example, you might have your puppy greet a person and reward the second head turn away from the person by calling the puppy to you. After you do that about every other time for a week or so, switch to every third time, then every fourth time, and so on.

As you work with a puppy, she should gradually be getting braver. At some point, there may be a fear period—usually at about eight to ten weeks of age and then later in adolescence for a few weeks when they're about six to twelve months old. If you see your puppy suddenly get stressed about something that's minor, she's probably in a fear period. In that case, just be patient and tone down your puppy's experiences so that she doesn't accidentally become sensitized. *Always help your puppy stay below threshold, and be aware that the threshold changes as the puppy develops.* Go back to reinforcing every request for distance for a little while.

For a really shy puppy, make sure people don't accidentally punish her tentative explorations by trying to pet her (if she's afraid of people, she may perceive their petting as punishment, something to avoid). As the puppy goes up to the person, have them back away. If it's a stranger that you can't boss around, just call your puppy away before the stranger can pet her. Give her a treat and let her go investigate again.

Socialization with dogs and other non-human animals

Dog-dog interaction is another important element of the socialization process. Puppies need to get used to dogs of all breeds and sizes and also the various other animals that they might encounter in their lives. I discussed socialization with people separately because dogs definitely view humans as being in a different category—some dogs are only reactive to people, some only to dogs, and some to both. So puppies need to be socialized to people and dogs, as well as other species of animals.

Many puppies get their first major exposure to other puppies outside of their family in puppy kindergarten classes. Owners need to consider their own puppy's socialization as well as the experience of the other puppies in a class. As discussed earlier in the book, most dogs already do a form of BAT naturally—if another dog turns away, sits facing away or shakes off, for example, then most dogs will pause for a bit or play bow or do something else to decrease the stress of the situation. While some puppies learn these body language skills from their mother and littermates, some are not adept at reading other dogs, or are clumsy, so humans often need to step in during puppy play.

If you have a puppy, it's important to recognize when your own puppy is giving cut-off signals to request distance from another dog. Let's say that your puppy is in a play time and you see him turn his back on a female puppy and start to slowly walk away from her. The other puppy follows, pouncing. Help honor your puppy's request for safety by going in to distract the other puppy: pet her, call her away, or even pick her up and set her down somewhere else in the room.

It's equally important to learn to understand that your puppy may fail to recognize another dog's cut-off signals. Puppies are still learning, after all. Watch the other dogs and puppies that your puppy greets. If you recognize the other dog giving cut-off signals, wait for your dog to respond to them appropriately. But, if she doesn't, call your puppy to redirect her or go pick her up and give your puppy a time out (fifteen to thirty seconds of boring time in your arms).

Expose your puppy to cats and other animals in a way that won't make them run. For example, have the cat up on a surface, like a couch or in a carrier (taking the cat's own mental state into account), with the puppy on-leash and in a harness. When your puppy investigates this new animal and then turns away, happpily run away and reward. Repeat! This should sound familiar by now, since it's basically a BAT trial. If your own cat is timid, you can do BAT with her. Start with the puppy in the carrier with a stuffed Kong, and let the cat approach and calmly retreat. Or see if a friend has the type of cat that will stand her ground. There's a pet supply store near me that has three cats who are very dog savvy. They make excellent puppy socializers.

Exposure to surfaces, crates, noises, and other experiences

In addition to socialization with humans, dogs, and other species, puppies need positive exposure to inanimate objects, noises and all sorts of things beyond people and other dogs. As with reactive dogs, I tend to use more treats with puppies in situations that don't require them to be aware of social cues. When socializing with dogs and people, I want the puppy to pay a lot of attention to the dogs and people so I use treats carefully. When I'm just trying to get her to walk on a slippery floor or get into a crate, I use treats much more freely, but I still use the return to a safe spot as a functional reward.

For example, a puppy named Lulu was afraid of slippery floors. She loved the clicker, so I used it to mark her good behavior of approaching the kitchen. I worked with her off-leash, starting in the carpeted hallway. I tossed a treat at the edge of the kitchen tile to make it interesting, and then walked with her in the hallway toward the kitchen. When she sniffed toward the treat, I clicked and walked her away from the kitchen down the hall a few feet and fed her a treat. I turned around and we approached the kitchen again. This time she snatched up the treat, I clicked, and called her away from the tile kitchen, and gave her another treat. I tossed another treat into the kitchen, this time about six inches into the tile floor. As she headed in for the treat, I clicked, walked back away from the kitchen, and fed her. Then I tossed a treat into the center of the kitchen and clicked/retreated/treated about ten more times, each time trying to click while she was still headed into the kitchen, but further and further into the room. On our next approach, I clicked as her nose headed toward the floor, as she snatched up the treat from the middle of the room. We retreated and I treated again. After that, I repeated without food on the floor for a few more trials, still clicking for the same behavior of kitchen-ward motion.

After about a total of fifteen trials, I started just clicking for having four paws on the tile floor, treating in the kitchen, and then walking away as the reward, for another thirteen trials. The relief of leaving the kitchen was weakening, and the joy of getting treats in the kitchen was getting stronger. Remember that she wasn't on-leash, and after those thirteen trials, she didn't want to leave the kitchen any more. I came back and jackpotted her with a handful of treats all over the kitchen floor.

This kind of training can apply to any room that the dog doesn't want to be in, whether it's a crate, a car, a surface the dog doesn't feel comfortable being on, or a location with a scary noise. The key is that the dog can leave whenever she wants, but you actually call her away before she's uncomfortable and gradually increase the value of being in the scary place or on the scary surface. You can actually do the same sort of thing with socialization with humans, too, if the dog is very shy.

With sounds, like thunder, fireworks, or babies crying, the functional reward is a decrease in volume or moving away from the sound. You can use a recording and adjust the volume based on the puppy's behavior. Terry Ryan has a CD series called *Sound Socialization* designed to acclimate dogs to such types of sounds and the Company of Animals has a CD called *CLIX Noises & Sounds* (see Resources). Play it at low volume—just high enough so that the puppy becomes interested. When he stops being interested, turn the volume down for about thirty seconds to a minute. Turn it back up a decibel or two higher than before, and wait again for the puppy to lose interest. Repeat until you can eventually have it quite loud. If the puppy ever leaves the room as a way to get away from the sound, let her, and play the sound more quietly the next time.

CLIX Noises and Sounds CD

The point of socialization is not only to expose the puppy to various stimuli that he might encounter as an adult, but also to teach him how to cope with novelty. BAT allows for a puppy to learn this kind of skill, rather than just what my dog Peanut initially learned via our classical counter-conditioning phase, which is that "people give me food, other dogs make mom give me food, and skateboards make mom give me food." That was helpful in getting him over a lot of fears, but I felt like he didn't really take the time to check things out without my interference. Looking back, it was like I was trying to make up his mind for him by treating him whenever something potentially scary came along. He didn't really learn to trust the world on its own merit or to accurately determine the safety of a situation, but he made many positive associations. In contrast, a puppy socialized with BAT learns to gather information about his environment, trust what he learns, and to diffuse tension when he needs to. He knows how to cope with the world as it is, because his handler gave him time to check things out.

CHAPTER 11

For Trainers and Behaviorists:

Using BAT with Clients

Clients want to know how to help their dog become safer and less reactive as soon as possible. Trainers need to assess their canine clients' reactivity and then guide their clients through a treatment plan. In this chapter, I'll discuss how we explain BAT in private lessons for dog-reactive or human-reactive dogs and in Growly Dog classes for dog-reactive dogs at Ahimsa Dog Training. Our puppy class students also learn a little about BAT, which I covered in Chapter 10 on socialization.

What's your dog's problem? Get a good history

Our clients go online to fill out a form in advance for private lessons and Growly Dog class. A written history gives clients a chance to efficiently share their dog's history, problem behaviors, and goals. This includes the dog's major medical history, how and why the dog was acquired, the dog's daily lifestyle, training history, and more. The other trainers and I can quickly read through this form and then ask other questions in person during the session. Keep in mind that people are not always honest or detailed enough in a written form, so you may need to pry a bit to get all of the details of a dog's situation.

Here are some of the topics that we ask about on the form and in the interview for an accurate functional assessment of the problems:

- Contact information
- Names and ages of humans in home
- Names, ages, species, weight, and breeds of non-human animals in home, including the student dog
- How and why dog was acquired
- Primary trainer in the home

- Whether someone has given up on the dog and do they have authority to euthanize/rehome
- Detailed description of dog's problem behaviors
- Ranking of dog's primary problem behaviors
- Goals for what they want the dog to do
- Other professional trainers or behaviorists with whom they have worked. Are they still with them? If not, why not? (Indicates compliance, how much convincing it will take to work without force, etc. Keep in mind that it's not always the previous trainers' mistakes that keep the training from working!)
- What they have done to work on the problem in the past / how that worked
- Books, TV shows, etc. about dogs that they like
- What type of training they have done—clicker / choke chain / treats / shock
- Medications / last vet check / have they done a thorough vet check
- Bite history including puppy biting
- Does the dog have any dog friends (more is better)
- Response to various stimuli and situations—men, women, children, being picked up, having food taken away, grooming, etc.
- Behaviors that the dog knows, including tricks. How well does the dog know those behaviors (gives indication of their interest in training)?
- Is the dog accustomed to a muzzle? If so, why and how? If not, why not?
- What type of building does the dog live in?
- Is there a fence? Real or invisible?

Knowing the dog's full history will help give you an idea of what needs to be done. BAT is a part of most of the treatment plans I come up with, but it's never the only thing. There is always some management and some behavior modification for the dog's other issues that may not involve BAT. I might add in tools from *Control Unleashed,* classical counter-conditioning, or other dog-friendly training methods.

Private lessons

In emergency room triage, the idea is to stop the bleeding and save the patient. My first advice to new clients in private lessons is almost always along the lines of environmental changes that can be made to make the situation safer and improve everyone's quality of life. That's why this book starts out with Safety and Management Essentials (Chapter 3). Look at the whole picture of the daily life of the dog and the family. Step one is to prevent dangerous situations. Step two is to reduce the dog's overall stress, so that the training you develop has a chance to kick in.

My private lessons are ninety minutes. Some cases are cut-and-dried and I whip through the history and management pieces and am able to talk about training for most of the session. In others, I find out that there is something dangerous going on and see that the family needs a lot of help with management. I need every last detail of what's going on so that we can have a twenty-four hour management plan for the dog. In cases like that, we spend most of the first session going over muzzle training and ways to keep doors and gates shut. This is usually what happens when there are kids in the family that are in danger from the dog or who might let the dog out. It's also the case when there is fighting with the dogs in the home. Successful management of fighting or biting within the home takes a lot of planning.

Safety and management is also important within the session itself. Most of my private clients have issues with humans, including me, so I meet them at my training center to reduce their stress and ensure my safety. I am seated when they walk in, so the dog is less likely to be reactive to me. Our chairs are stationed further away than chairs would normally be for human conversation, but it works. I have treats and give them to the dog if he comes up to me. I read the dog's history in advance, so that if I feel it's necessary, I can take other safety measures like putting an exercise pen around my chair or requiring the clients to use the wall tethers for their dog. Most of my clients' dogs are not already used to the muzzle, so I use the fence and leashes and do not muzzle during the first session.

When I meet clients at their homes, we have usually already had an appointment at the training center, so I've already met the dog. Whether or not their dog liked me during our first meeting at my facility, I assume that reactive dogs won't love me coming into their home. They may only be barky, but that stress sets them up to have more trouble during our session, so I usually start in-home sessions with a short walk. I call when I arrive and the clients meet me outside with their dog, in a carefully orchestrated introduction. I wait at least twenty feet away from their door, and start walking away when they come out. When the dog sees me, his first impression is of a person with treats in her hand, walking away from him. That's not a huge threat. We just keep walking and they gradually catch up to me. If it's a safe enough situation, I allow the dog to eat the treats from my hand.

If the dog has a history of damaging bites, I usually have them condition a muzzle before I go to their house, have a fence between us, or have the client keep the dog out of reach throughout the session. It's really important to me that the dog does not feel forced to bite me. I haven't had any bites from my reactive clients, but a puppy in puppy class really nailed me one time and I was bitten on my forehead and scalp as a child. So I know that dog bites hurt, but my biggest concern is for the dog—I can heal, but the real damage is that the dog now has a bigger bite history. In my opinion, a trainer should never risk causing a dog to bite him or her. Whatever you do, set up your session to be safe. For me, that includes escorting my dog-reactive clients to their car at the end.

Here's how I explain BAT to clients in private lessons. I start with a discussion of what they think is motivating the dog to bark, lunge, flee, or offer other 'bad' behaviors. Then we explore the concept of distance as a functional reward. I describe how to do BAT set-ups and animate a simple sketch by hand as I talk. One of my trainers uses the BAT set-up illustration drawn by Lili Chin (see Chapter 6).

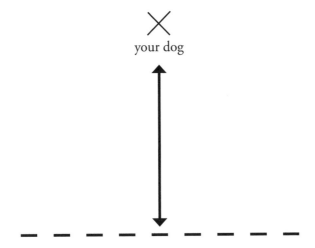

your dog

trigger

I face the paper so that their dog is on the end closest to them and the trigger is on the end closest to me, since I'm usually the helper or I'm animating the fake decoy dog. Going over Lili's "good choices" illustration from Chapter 5 helps clients understand which behaviors we are looking for. I also go through what they would do if their dog started to aggress at me: call the dog back and start again about five feet further than they were when the dog barked/growled/or otherwise reacted. If he barks again, go another five feet back. If he still barks, step back an additional five feet. I talk about why I don't want them to correct their dog if he does one of those behaviors, because it shuts down the warning system and we end up with a silent biter. That's the scariest kind of dog for me—one that looks ok, but then bites me. This is an important point to get across.

Clients receive a handout on BAT to help the students fully get the concept (online at http://functionalrewards.com). They can share this handout with people doing set-ups with them, so that the helpers have a general idea of the BAT process before they start. Trainers from the FunctionalReward.com discussion group on Yahoo! say that they have shown clips from the BAT DVDs to their clients to help them get the concept before doing a set-up. *The Organic Socialization* DVD set is a good choice for that because it has a disk of all of the demonstrations in that presentation (see Resources).

After a verbal and visual explanation of BAT, the clients and I do a set-up with a fake dog or me as the helper. If their dog is wearing a prong collar or choke chain, I talk about why I prefer harnesses and usually loan them a front-attachment freedom harness before we get started. They have to put the harness on their dog. I can only supervise as they fit it because I can't move without starting their dog into reactivity.

I explain their roles in the set-up before we do anything else. I tell them that my first task during the BAT set-up will be to tell them when to stop walking toward me. My second task will be to say, "Yes," to signal when the dog does a good behavior. Their tasks are to: 1) watch their dog and walk forward until told to stop; 2) when I say, "Yes," call their dog and happily walk away from me, then praise and pet when they get about fifteen to twenty feet away; and 3) they are also supposed to listen for me to say, "Call your dog" when it looks like things are going badly. That's it. Keep it simple and shape the client's behavior.

With human-reactive dogs, I've been seated the whole time at this point and tell them that when I stand up, the dog is likely to bark at me. So I have them walk away first and then I stand up and walk to the far wall, so that the dog can be maximally distant from me in the room. For some dogs, that's not enough and we need to go work outside. Most dogs see the room as "my house," so their normal reactivity distance is less than usual and they can work inside.

Next we start doing BAT trials, as I described in Chapter 6, without treats. Along the way, I point out the good behaviors that the dog or the handlers are doing. They start to catch on to which dog behaviors I'm marking, and begin to say, "Yes," on their own. I point out their success when the leash is loose as they walk away or direct them to work on keeping it loose in the next trial if they have the other bits but they are still accidentally popping the dog as they turn to walk away from me. I mention that if I say "Yes" and the dog doesn't want to walk away, then it was my mistake, and walking away was not a functional reward at that instant. I tell them to just turn back around toward me (playing the helper role) and wait until the dog's next good choice.

Once clients are able to approach, mark, and retreat on their own, I talk about the different stages of BAT that they can use on walks. As you go down in stage number (3, 2, 1), it's easier on the dog, but harder on the person, so that's why I teach them in that order. I also want the people to focus on the functional reward part, and training without treats helps them realize that the functional reward is truly important to the dog.

Since the set-up version of BAT is the same as Stage 3 for walks, we work on Stage 2 after the set-ups. I tell them that the version without treats is perfect for set-ups, but can be harder on walks. The treats help the dog focus on the human, so they're less likely to react badly to their triggers on walks. Now, we start to add the clicker and treats. If the clients aren't already clicker-savy, I click the clicker for them, so their only new task is to feed after they've walked away from me. Most of my clients are couples, so I usually do the clicker myself first, then have one of the clients do it as the other one continues to do the dog handling and treating. Then they switch who is clicking and who is handling the dog. Finally, each of the clients practices clicking and treating on their own.

If clients have any trouble with feeding too soon, I have the treats placed at the re-treat point, on a table or chair, or held by the dog's other owner. So the dog walks up toward me, I click, and they run back to the food to get a treat. This helps them get the concept of giving the bonus reward after the functional reward of walking away.

After the clients and their dogs have done well with Stage 2, we move on to BAT Stage 1. The only change now is that they need to click sooner: right when the dog sees the trigger. If they mess up and click late, it's still ok, it's just BAT Stage 2! I usually practice their timing by jumping out from behind some barrier, at a distance so they can click the instant the dog focuses on me. Then, they walk away and reward.

All in all, my clients and I usually do about twenty to thirty minutes of BAT together in the first session. I explain that the way we did things was different from most BAT set-ups, because we tend to just do it 'the first way' with set-ups—no treats, unless it looks like the dog needs them. Regular set-ups are longer, and usually end with the dog being more comfortable at close range.

I teach the BAT stages to clients this way because it's easier to build up their handling skills by adding in one new thing at a time. I also teach it this way because the retreat is the main reward in BAT, and just like dogs, if you add in treats, people focus on that as the reward. Besides, humans tend to default back to whatever they learned first, and I want them to do BAT Stage 3 whenever they can, and use the other stages if they need to.

In private lessons at Ahimsa, we gradually put the students more in charge of running the session as time goes on, because they will eventually be doing many of these sessions on their own. For example, I always run the first BAT set-up with a fake dog or me as the decoy. In our second private lesson, I often coordinate a BAT set-up with a real dog as the decoy or myself as the helper at their house. After that, I observe and give feedback as they run their own sessions with other decoys. I usually work with clients for about three to five sessions, but I'm always available for follow-ups if they feel they are plateauing. If they have a dog walker, I try to get them involved in at least one of the sessions.

In the Growly Dog class, where we focus on reactivity toward dogs rather than the dog's other issues, BAT is the main method we cover. Classes are six weeks long and we have six canine students who are reactive to dogs, but not people. We have them fill out a comprehensive questionnaire online after they register. Our first lesson in Growly Dog is without dogs. After getting a short verbal history on their dog's issues and discussing management, we demonstrate BAT with two fake dogs and they get a DVD of BAT to take home and watch. In weeks two through four, we have dogs come in pairs to work on BAT together outside. For weeks five and six, all of the dogs come to class and they do BAT set-ups in pairs outside.

Our Growly Dog students get the verbal and visual demo that I mentioned in week one, and then they observe or participate in several set-ups in the remaining five sessions. The clients usually coordinate their own set-ups on weeks five and six. The instructor and assistant are there to help out as they move between the working pairs. Students are encouraged to do their own BAT set-ups outside of class when they feel ready to do so.

Both male and female clients seem to understand the idea of BAT and really like using this natural way to reinforce better choices. I feel like I'm getting less resistance than I did with the use of classical counter-conditioning for reactivity, but it does take a little more time to explain. The key in presenting BAT to clients is to keep them from feeling like they have to do too many new things at once, and to show them the progress that their dog can make in a short time.

Finding decoy dogs and helpers

Getting enough decoys is one of the hard parts of any rehabilitation program that relies on the dogs being sub-threshold. The good thing about BAT is that it can be done on walks and in real life, not just in set-ups. That said, dogs definitely make the fastest progress when we are able to expose them to their triggers in a systematic way, i.e., set-ups.

We have a Google group for our Growly Dog students and private clients so that they can set up sessions with each other. BAT sessions can be done with both dogs working at the same time, so they are approaching and retreating from one another, but staying in sight. Owners of human-reactive dogs can volunteer themselves as helpers for each others' dogs.

It is easier to get decoy dogs if you have something to trade. The table on the next page shows who the family can offer to serve as a decoy or helper for another reactive dog. The first column assumes the other dog is reactive to dogs and the second column assumes the other dog is only reactive to people.

	Can be a decoy/ helper for a dog-reactive dog	Can be a decoy/ helper for a human-reactive dog
Your reactive dog	Yes	
Another dog in your household	Yes	Yes
Humans in household	Yes	Yes
Friends	Yes	Yes

Life-sized plush dogs also make great volunteers for distance work. Once they get up close, the dog usually figures it out within a few minutes, but I often use the fake dogs for assessment purposes. I do a lot of risky things with the fake dogs that I can't do with real decoys, like allowing the reactive dog to walk right up to the fake dog on a tight leash. I usually kneel down to animate the fake dog, so it bounces or puts its head over the dog's neck. Always check with the client to see if the reaction you're seeing is normal for that dog. For example, sometimes my students' assertive dogs are a little scared by the fake dog, when their normal reaction doesn't look fearful at all. Sometimes dogs will ignore the fake dog because they have experience with a fake dog or a big stuffed toy somewhere else.

I don't tend to use my own dogs as decoys unless I'm also doing BAT work with them as well; I usually do Stage 2 with 'veteran' decoy dogs. By that I mean that the decoy dog's handler is used to marking good choices, retreating, and giving a bonus reward while the reactive dog is working on Stage 3 BAT. Being a stationary decoy from time to time is fine, but it's the sort of thing that can burn a dog out after a while, and honoring the decoy dog's own needs by doing BAT is helpful. Make sure clients understand that, so that if they're loaning out their other 'good' dog over and over, they should consider still doing BAT with that dog, so that they continue to be reinforced for their good choices, or make sure to encounter non-reactive dogs on-leash during their daily life, to help them unwind. This advice goes for dogs used as decoys for classical counter-conditioning, too. You can time the decoy's appearances and disappearances based on the behaviors of the decoy dog.

Hopefully this chapter has given you some ways to successfully integrate BAT into your training toolbox. BAT is not meant to replace the techniques that already work well for you, but rather to add another tool to help make your behavior modification more efficient. My human clients seem to have grasped the concepts behind BAT and their dogs have more thorough progress than ever before. Trainers and behaviorists around the world have reported similar success, so it's definitely worth trying out. Your turn!

CONCLUSION

I hope you've enjoyed our foray into BAT. I have to warn you that when you look around, you're going to start seeing opportunities for BAT and functional rewards everywhere. There are a lot of changes that we all can make in how we work with our dogs, and I hope that this book will make you see more of their behavior from a functional perspective than you did before.

If you haven't tried BAT with a dog yet, now is the time! Find a friend to help you, film the session, and consider that an additional part of your education. If you are a trainer, I recommend working pro bono on some cases, or doing BAT first with your own dog. The FunctionalRewards discussion group on Yahoo! is a great way to continue your education. If you are a visual learner, check out some of the BAT videos on YouTube via my website or purchase one or more of the DVDs on BAT.

Above all, it's important to just try BAT out. The proof is in the pudding, as they say. As long as you keep your dog below threshold, or do something to help your dog calm down when they have trouble, you can't really mess things up. Of course, getting the details of BAT right will speed up your progress! That's why it's a great idea to work through this with a friend and/or a video camera, so that you can get another perspective on the training sessions. Good luck!

APPENDIX 1

Clicker Training Foundations

If you haven't seen a clicker or tried clicker training yet, now is the perfect time to learn! Clicker training uses a marker signal to tell the animal that his behavior has earned a reward. Clicker training is used with all sorts of animals, from tuberculosis-detecting rats in South Africa to service dogs to killer whales. The marker signal pinpoints the specific moment in the dog's mind. The most common marker signals in dog training are clickers and verbal markers. A clicker is a tiny handheld box that makes a clicking noise. A verbal marker is a word that serves the same purpose as the clicker; it's a sound from our mouths, like "Yes" or "Yip."

The key to a good reward marker is that it's something the dog will pay attention to, and that it always predicts a reward is coming soon.

You can hide some treats in your clicker hand for easy access.

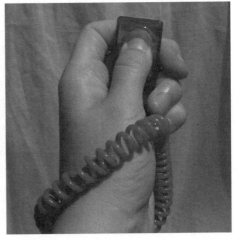

Training clicker with a wrist coil. Push on the metal and release to make a click-click sound.

The following are some behaviors that are great for the dog to learn before or between BAT sessions. I don't require my clients to finish these exercises first, because they are chomping at the bit to work on their dog's aggression. I also don't require a specific time of pre-training, because just practicing BAT helps the dog learn these skills. But having these foundation skills in their toolbox makes our BAT work even more successful.

Attention

Attention does not mean that the dog is constantly staring at their human. By attention, I just mean that you can get your dog's attention, and that your dog always has some connection with you during a walk. I like to train automatic check-ins as well as teaching the dog to respond quickly to their name.

The Lassie Protocol

The Lassie Protocol (Lassie was always very attentive!) jump-starts dog training in seven days and is a simple way to train a dog to automatically check in. The Lassie Protocol is the first assignment in all of our basic training classes, and our most successful students do their Lassie work before their class even starts.

I recommend trying this technique with any dog that needs a little more focus. Try it on your dog after reading the rest of this section, especially if you've never tried clicker training before. Because every dog learns at a different pace, the days listed are just a suggestion. If you have an attentive Border Collie, you can fast-forward through the process in a few quick sessions. If you have a new rescue dog that doesn't even know who you are, you might need to stretch the training out to a few weeks.

Days 1-2: Mark and reward every time the dog pays attention to you on his own
Use the clicker or a verbal marker to pinpoint any glances your way, and pay handsomely. Try to mark the exact instant he turns his head toward you, so that you are rewarding the choice of turning his head.

1. If you're not going to train for a while, tell him "All done." When you're ready to train again, say his name and click/treat the turn toward you. I recommend not doing this while you're eating your own dinner. That's a perfect time to say "All done," meaning there is no chance for rewards until further notice.

2. Reward with your dog's food in quiet places, like in the living room, and offer better rewards when your dog looks at you around distractions. Dogs deserve 'hazard pay.'

3. When you are using a clicker as the marker, attach a keychain wrist coil to it so that the clicker is always at hand. You can swap back and forth between the clicker and the verbal marker, so use whichever one is avail-

Clicker Training Foundations

1. THE LASSIE PROTOCOL

* Training your dog to automatically check in
* Encouraging more focus & attention
* Mark & Reward every time your dog pays attention to you on his own.

2. THE NAME GAME

* Teaching your dog that his name = Pay attention, the next thing I say is for you.
* Use this cue wisely. Never just ignore a dog after saying his name.
* Mark & Reward eye contact or whiplash head turn.

3. EMERGENCY U-TURN

* Training your dog to turn around and walk away
* Make your walk safer because you can quickly get your dog out of a stressful situation
* Back away from your dog. Mark as your dog turns and have her catch up to get the treat.

4. LOOSE LEASH WALKING

* Golden rule: Never let your dog move forward if the leash is tight
* Different methods to train this: Click in position, Be A Tree, Silky Leash etc.
* Mark and Reward when the leash is loosened, or when dog is in correct position

5. EMERGENCY RECALL

* Useful in emergency situations when a reliable recall is needed
* This is a special cue always followed by loads of fabulous treats.

6. PLAY BOW

* A fun alternative way for a dog to get attention (vs jumping or barking or sitting)
* A very obviously friendly signal to teach dogs who lack social skills

able first. The clicker is more memorable to the dog, so use that when you can.

4. Don't forget to praise your dog after you mark her glance!

Days 3-4: Mark and reward about every other time your dog looks toward you
We are now weaning off the treats a little. Continue to use praise for most head turns or eye contact.

1. Every time you mark, you still reward; you just won't be marking as much.

2. Get a little picky—click for the faster head turns, longer glances, or whatever is somehow 'above average.'

Days 5-7: Wean off of the treats
Mark and reward on a random schedule, for about one-third of the responses. Try to reward the best responses. Reward by just paying attention and/or praising the rest of the time. Gradually shift to a one in four schedule, then one in five. Change the reward schedule slowly, so that your dog won't suspect the odds are getting longer. Vary the type of reward and where it comes from. Mark and then pull a hidden toy out of a tree or off a shelf. Mark and pick up a stick to toss. Mark and play a game of chase (dog chasing human). Mark and run to the kitchen together and grab a treat for the dog from your refrigerator. It helps to match the type of distraction the dog was looking away from, so that looking away from food gets them food, looking away from a toy gets them a toy, etc.

The Lassie Protocol is great to do during the first week of training, in combination with BAT Stage 1 on walks, which you read about in Chapter 7. Do it again whenever the dog needs a refresher, like when you have a baby or move to a new home.

The Name Game

The Name Game teaches a dog to turn when she hears her name, so that she catches the next bit of information from the human.

Let's say your dog's name is Riley. If you have said his name a lot in an angry voice, use a nickname, instead—either a brand new one or one already in use. Use a name that you don't mind saying in public. Start off with the dog in a quiet setting. It helps to do the Lassie Protocol first.

1. Say his name one time, and then give him a treat. He doesn't have to look at you at this point, but he probably will look if you're in a quiet setting. Do several pairings of "Riley" → treat. Start to say it when he's not looking, then follow up with a treat.

2. Repeat step one in several locations, inside and out.

3. Start to require that Riley actually make eye contact for his treat. Start with the 5-second rule: if he looks within 5 seconds of your saying his name once, he can have the treat. You can click to mark the moment or mark with your word, "Yes!" Otherwise, you say "Too bad!" in a sad, regretful tone, show the treat he lost, and then put it away. If the treat is 'human food,' eat it! You can even get creative and leave the house or start playing with his toys while he watches. Just make him feel like he's missed out on something. Wait several minutes before playing the Name Game again. If he fails the 5-Second Rule several times in a row, you're pushing too quickly. Go back to step one or work in a less distracting environment.

4. Move on to the 3-Second Rule, then 2, then 1, then the Whiplash Rule—only instant looks get treats.

I learned of this game from Leslie Nelson in the *Really Reliable Recall* (see Resources). She gives three reasons for the Name Game to fail:

1. **Icky treats.** So use great treats!! The dog gets to decide what that means.

2. **Not enough practice.** Do fifteen name-food pairings each day. Surprise your dog.

3. **Repeating the name.** Say the name only once, and then apply whatever rule you were using. Eat the treat, make a smoochy noise if you really must, but don't repeat the name.

I think it's fair to repeat the name after ten to twenty seconds if the environment has changed, the dog looks ready to pay attention, or you know some other reason that it's going to work if you try again. And remember, your dog is always learning from you, whether you think you're training or not. Every time you say the dog's name, he's learning what it means.

Speaking of meaning, make sure that *you* really know what the name means. To me, the name means, "pay attention, the next thing I say is for you." The dog's name should be followed by a cue for what to do next, either a release cue or some other cue. Saying "Freddie," followed by praise for looking, is fine. Saying "Freddie," followed by "Sit," and then a release cue is also fine. Saying "Freddie," followed by nothing is not fine, unless you want the name to mean "leave me alone." That's specifically how I teach the "All done" cue that I mentioned above, which tells the dog that their request has been denied and to stop begging at the table, bringing me toys, or offering cute tricks. I just say, "All done" at the end of a training session and then ignore the dog! Use that name cue wisely, and never just ignore a dog after saying her name.

"Let's Go" / Emergency U-turn

I mentioned the U-turn above as a way to get out of a jam. Two of my favorite verbal cues for emergency U-turns are "Oh Sh%@!" (because it is something the client can easily remember to say in case of emergency) and "Call your dog!" (because it is a multi-purpose cue). Using "Call your dog" to signal the emergency U-turn communicates to the oncoming dog, the student dog, and the other owner, all at once.

That one signal 1) tells the other owner to call their dog, 2) cues your dog to turn around, away from trouble, and 3) slows down the oncoming dog because of the tone. It's also easy to remember, but not quite as gratifying as shouting profanity when faced with yet another off-leash Golden Retriever. ☺ Most clients choose to teach two cues for the same behavior: "Let's go" and "Call your dog."

I first heard of the emergency U-turn in Patricia McConnell's great book, *Feisty Fido* (see Resources). Here's how I teach it now. Starting indoors, with your dog off-leash beside you, facing the same direction that you are:

1. Say the cue, "Call your dog," back up (causing your dog to U-turn to face you), and toss the treat or a toy so that your dog runs past you. Repeat fifty times in different locations.

2. Repeat the above and click at the instant your dog turns when hearing "Call your dog," then toss the reinforcement, as before. Repeat exercise in various locations until dog is able to turn instantly in every room of your home (including the garage, basement, or outbuildings), with the TV on, and around distractions on sidewalks, at the park, etc. Work off-leash in a safe place, on-leash in public.

3. Over the course of multiple sessions, escalate the volume and tone until it sounds like what you'd really say on walks.

4. Rehearse simultaneously giving the traffic cop signal and saying (or shouting), "Call your dog."

Note that you can start right away with using the cue in the training session that I just described, because you're working in a quiet location and you are using a prompt that will already work to get the behavior—backing away from the dog. I love using a toy as the reward, because you can practice this training any time you play fetch with your dog. Non-fetching dogs still usually love the chance to chase treats, and you can feed your dog's meals this way. Whenever possible, training should be part of your daily routine. U-turns should be repeatedly rehearsed on regular walks, so that you and your dog have it fresh in your minds.

If your dog already has another positively trained cue for the U-turn, such as, "Let's go," you can use a cue transfer instead of starting from scratch. To transfer the meaning of a cue, start with the second step, above, and have the old cue follow the new cue, over and over, as in "Call your dog" → 1 second pause →"Let's go!" followed by backing up a few steps, clicking, and tossing the treat so that the dog runs past you. Even though backing up may get in the way of the verbal cue acquisition, it's important because it's good for you to rehearse your own role for real situations.

Just to make sure that the cue transfer is clear, let's reverse it. If you teach "Call your dog" as the first cue and want to add "Let's go" as a cue, then the order would be opposite of what we had above. That means you'd practice this way: "Let's go" (new cue) → 1 second pause →"Call your dog" (old cue as a translation) followed by backing up a few steps, clicking, and tossing the treat so that the dog runs past you.

The emergency U-turn makes walks safer because you can quickly get the dog out of stressful situations. Learning to walk politely on-leash the rest of the time is also helpful.

> I love rehearsing the emergency U-turn with squirrels as the distraction and a tug or a tossed toy as the reward. Many reactive dogs also love to chase prey, and eliminating this opportunity to pull on-leash makes walks more pleasant.)

Leash walking

I think I can count on one hand the number of reactive dogs I've seen that walked perfectly on a leash. Even though clients come to me for their dog's aggression or fear issues, one of the presentations of that reactivity is that the dog pulls and lunges toward the trigger or panics and pulls home. A tight leash can cause reactive dogs to get into fights, so I like to teach both the client and the dog to keep the leash loose, as well as teaching the dog that a tight leash is just a cue for where to walk.

When I say to keep the leash loose, I mean that the leash is loose between you and your dog. You still have a good grip on the leash, but the leash doesn't feel tight to the dog. I'm looking for a natural solid grip, which is not so tight that you get white knuckles, but not so loose that the leash can come out. If the dog is on the left, hold the leash in the right hand, so that you can grab with both hands, if needed. Holding the leash on the right side also makes you stronger, because the dog has to pull your whole body if he wants to go off to the left. If the leash were in your left hand, then it's easy to be thrown off balance by a lunging dog. Do the reverse if the dog is on the right. Try it and compare!

Be very aware of how you hold the handle and how you take up extra slack. If the dog were to lunge, would it hurt your hand? Would it pull the extra leash right out of your hands? Experiment to see what really works best.

Sometimes it's helpful to attach the leash to your waist or around your shoulder like a sash, using a carabiner (mountain climbing clip), though you should be careful if you have a big dog. Don't just hook it to your belt loop, though, unless you don't mind ripped pants! Until they catch on, expect some walks where you just don't get anywhere. For times when you must move forward, use treats to reinforce your dog for being in the right position, or if it's a small dog, scoop him up and carry him to your destination.

Forward motion is very rewarding to a dog, so the primary rule for leash walking is to *never let your dog move forward if the leash is tight*. If you do allow him to move forward on a tight leash, you are rewarding him for pulling, so trying to teach him to come up with something else is like trying to convince a fish not to swim. Pulling is bad for a dog's neck and it isn't much fun for us, either.

Think about which side you want the dog to be on. It's harder for dogs to learn to walk on both sides, but I think it's easier on their spines, and ours. The standard side for competition is the left, but you can teach them to stay on a particular side until you give them the Switch cue.

There are lots of different techniques for leash walking. I like using a combination. The Lassie Protocol from above is a great start. Here are some of the other methods that you can use:

- Click for Position
- Turn and Click
- Focused Walking
- Being a Tree or Backing Up (a.k.a. the ♫ Canine Cha Cha ♫)
- Speed Training
- Penalty Yards
- Silky Leash.

Click for position

1. Click any move your dog makes toward your left side. Imagine a big square on the floor at your left side and any time the dog steps into it or looks at it, click and treat. Try to definitely catch the times when she is on the left side *and* looking at you. If you are in a quiet place, let your dog find the side, don't try to help her. If you just need to get going, then you can set your dog up to be successful here by moving around to get your dog on the left. Be sure to give her more responsibility for finding your left side, or you may create a dog that just sits there as *you* do all the moving. Be patient! Keep the session short, about one minute long. Keep the rate of reinforcement high; don't be stingy! Click often. Think of your dog as a teenager and yourself as a movie producer that has to keep her attention. After the click, give her the treat and praise her lavishly for focusing on you.

2. After your dog has mastered the left side idea, then only click when she is on the left side *and* looking at you.

3. Take it on the road! Repeat the two steps above on a walk. If you have trouble getting focus at all, you may want to practice the Lassie Protocol in the backyard or in front of your house first. Keep doing that until you're getting good focus, then move into the three steps described above. After that, gradually extend how many times your dog must look at you for one click.

Remember: *The click is a promise of a reward!* You can toss the treat or feed in a particular location. The standard heeling position is on the left side, so I feed the treat about at my pants seam, on my left, when working on teaching that position.

Click and treat any time your dog is directly next to you or looking at you. This exercise and the Lassie Protocol are essential pieces of the training, because you're showing your dog what you *want* him to do. Over time, you'll be clicking less and frequently, but don't just make it harder and harder for the dog. You might have this pattern (the numbers are the number of feet the dog walks next to you before you click and treat): 1, 5, 10, 1, 2, 15, 5, 20, 10, 1, 25, … The distance is increasing, but the dog doesn't always have to go forever between treats. This keeps the dog from getting a treat and then giving up and pulling because he knows it'll be a while before the next treat arrives.

This behavior can be called "Heel," (although it's not an official Heel) or "Close" or "With me," or any other name you choose. Just like with everything else, you'll be saying the cue just before you know the dog will be walking nicely next to you.

Turn and click

Start your dog's training by doing the click mentioned above. Outside on a leash, though, your dog is probably still going to be likely to pull. For this exercise, grab a bunch of the leash in one hand so the leash is short.

Let's say your dog is on the left. When your dog speeds up or begins pulling, make a kissing noise and rotate to your right. Give your dog some slack so that he's not being pulled and walk away from him. Click when he follows at your side. Give the treat to your dog at the side seam of your pants. He will then probably head off again, so be ready to rotate right away. The idea is not to have your dog come with you because he feels pain or pressure, but rather because he sees you turning. So I like starting this activity off-leash, using a bungee leash, and/or being sure not to "pop" the dog.

Focused walking (touch and you're heeled!)

In the early stages of training, you can use Focused Walking to get past big distractions rather than just hoping the dog will do something worth clicking. This is especially helpful for reactive dogs.

This technique will help you teach your dog to focus on you instead of distractions. In particular, she'll be looking at your finger as you walk along (also known as "finger targeting" or "hand targeting"). This is great for getting past a distraction. Once your dog knows this behavior well, you can use it to walk past things that might otherwise ruin your lovely walk.

The idea is for this to be a fun, fantastic game for your dog, something you occasionally play on walks. I build up excitement first by asking, "Reaaaady?" to tell my dog we're about to play this or other fun games.

The behavior here is that your dog touches her nose to a human's hand, but you can also apply this to a target of some sort. I'll use "Touch" as the cue in this example. You can use it to move the dog around in space. You can also teach them to Heel nicely beside you.

Let's say the dog is on your left. Start out with a treat and the clicker in your right hand. You can have your target hand a flat hand or whatever you want, but I like to do it the following way. Make a fist with your left hand, except put your pointer and middle fingers out. Present that hand to your dog. Your dog will then probably go toward your hand, expecting a treat. Ignore any pawing.

When she touches the target hand with her nose, click and treat. While she's eating, put your target hand behind your back and then present it again when you're ready to click and treat again. For some reason, it makes your hand "brand-new" and interesting again.

Do this several times before beginning to teach a cue. Once she's got the hang of it, and you're relatively sure she will touch your hand, do the same activity, but start saying "Touch" right before you put your target hand out.

Target fist (left hand). Note treats and clicker are in the right hand.

Click when your dog touches the target.

Pass a treat to your target hand.

Your dog eats the treat from your target hand.

If your dog stares at you and doesn't touch the hand, then either wait her out or put your hand behind your back and bring it back out again. Don't lean into her or stare (that's a bit scary). Your hand may also look like a hand signal you've already been giving her. If that's the case, change this to a new signal—hand flat, only one finger, or other signal of your choice. If she is biting your hand rather than gently touching with her nose, make sure you aren't clicking for the bite. Click sooner to reward her before her mouth opens, or click later, waiting for her mouth to close before clicking. Changing where you put your hand may help.

Next, begin to move the target a bit, so the dog has to walk a step or two to touch your hand. Test to see if your dog will touch the target hand even if it's right beside you, instead of being in front of him. After this step, you're ready to use it for Heeling.

Next, be a moving target. After you have practiced "Touch" for a while and your dog is readily touching your hand, next you will present your hand and when your dog moves to touch it, back up so your dog has to follow you a few steps in order to touch the target. Click and treat when the dog touches the target. You can also move in a semi-circle while offering the target. The key is to get your dog following the target to touch it.

Now we'll start getting your dog to follow the target hand when it's beside you. Now it's going to start looking like Heel. If you want your dog to walk on your left, your target hand is your left hand, and vice versa if they're on the right. You might work both sides, but work only one during a particular session.

Start practicing this off-leash in your house. Say "Touch" and present the target hand with your arm straight down, against your leg, and walk a few steps away from your dog. Wait for your dog to catch up to your hand and touch it. Click and deliver the treat slightly behind or precisely at the outside seam of your pants (never ahead of you). This ensures your dog doesn't surge past you and out of Heel position.

After your dog gets a treat, say "Touch" again and continue to walk forward. As the dog catches up to you and touches your hand again, click and treat. You're Heeling!

After the dog is doing well at this, you can begin to say "Heel" instead of "Touch," or say, "Heel," and then "Touch," if the dog gets confused.

Next, it's time to start "random treating." Put Heel on a variable reward schedule by gradually spacing out the amount of time or number of steps between clicks and treats. Increase every other interval. The numbers below can be seconds or number of steps.

Ex. 3, 5, 3, 7, 4, 9, 4, 11, 5, 13, 5, 15, 6, 17, 6, 19,….

(easy, hard, easy, harder, not quite so easy, harder still…)

Heel for a short time after each long stretch, so the dog doesn't notice the long pauses between treats are getting longer. You want to keep the dog thinking, "Maybe it's only two more steps before the next treat!" Note that even the short pauses are getting longer. Random treating works for "Stay," too!

If you encounter a bigger distraction, go back to rewarding more frequently or rewarding continuously.

Once it's working at home, try it for a few blocks at a time out on your walks, when there aren't big distractions around. When there *are* big distractions like one of your dog's triggers, you can use the same technique, but put some extra-tasty food in your target hand, and make it easy for the dog by putting it to their nose and then moving it toward you.

Being a tree or backing up

It's important that your dog not move forward when the leash is tight. This includes walking next to you on a tight leash. Forward motion reinforces pulling. Period. Unless you like pulling, you must never, ever, ever let your dog walk forward on a tight leash. Okay, maybe not ever: if you're escaping a fire, being chased by a pack of wild dogs, your dog is panicking, or you're doing Silky Leash training, described below, you can make an exception!

If the dog is pulling in a direction that you want to go, you can do Turn and Click and then turn back around again. But you can also just stop and wait for the leash to get loose, then immediately walk forward. The forward motion itself is the functional reward, so you can skip the food. Alternatively, you can back up and make a kissing noise or call the dog to cause the dog to follow you and make the leash loose, then walk forward (canine Cha Cha). If you see your dog running ahead, about to hit the end of the leash, put the brakes on gradually by holding a bit onto the leash and letting it slide through your fingers, until they hit the end and then you stop moving. Both of these options are negative punishment (taking away forward motion). It can help to say "eeeeeeeasy" or slap your thigh a few times so that your dog doesn't find himself suddenly stopped. Eventually, the word warns the dog that the leash is about to run out, so he slows down.

Speed training

This is a functional reward approach that uses positive reinforcement (when dog walks beside the human, he gets to walk faster) instead of negative punishment (when dog pulls, he gets stopped). We just discussed the Be a Tree method if the dog gets to the end of the leash. I have extended that technique into what I call Speed Training.

Walk fastest when the dog is next to you in Heel position (speed = 1) and slower as he gets farther away (speed =.75, .25, etc.). Slightly before they arrive at the end of the leash, you have the option of slapping your thigh or saying something like "Easy" and if he reaches the end, either stop (speed = 0) or do the Cha-Cha (speed = -1). At first, the maximum speed might be running—whatever pace your dog wants to go.

As the weeks go by, it's gradually slower and slower to match our boring human pace. By inserting the word "Run!" or "Quickly!" just before you speed up, you can also teach your dog to walk fast on cue, which is useful for crossing the street or avoiding triggers.

I used this method with Peanut and I lost ten pounds. Seriously! He became my personal trainer. I still sometimes run when he's beside me and walk if he's up ahead. He doesn't pull much anymore, but on hills, I always hope that he does, so I can use that as an excuse to slow down!

Penalty yards

This is a great technique for all dogs, but an essential one for dogs that are too distracted to eat in public. It's meant for dogs that pull toward something in particular, like into the dog park or up to a person.

The Penalty Yards technique is similar to the Cha Cha, in that you are reversing course when the dog is about to pull. But you would do Penalty Yards more as a set-up, when you have time to really focus on the dog's pulling issues. After doing several Penalty Yards set-ups, the Cha-Cha becomes a quick reminder to get your dog out of a pulling mood on walks.

Set up a course that's about twenty to thirty feet long. On one end is your start line. On the other end is the finish line, which has something wonderful, like a helper with a baggie full of fresh chicken that the dog has just smelled. The helper can rile up the dog, but don't say any cues, like Come or the dog's name, because the dog is on a leash with you at the start line. The finish line can also be a squirrel in a tree that your dog wants to go chase.

Get your dog's focus, either by waiting or saying his name. Say your walking cue, like "Easy" or "Let's go." Start to walk forward. If the dog pulls off to the side, you need to make the end game more enticing. If he is just about to pull forward, say a no reward marker, like "Too bad" (in a sad or regular voice, not angry) and return to the start line. You can use kissy noises or whatever to encourage them to come with you. The point is to reverse course, not to give a leash correction. The punishment is to walk away from the fun stuff.

Repeat. A lot.

Make sure you are giving the no reward marker ("Too bad") before you turn, otherwise you're punishing the dog for coming with you! If you don't say it in time, don't say it at all.

Eventually, the dog will walk all the way from the start line to six feet from the distraction on a loose leash. This may take only a few minutes or it may take twenty minutes or more. While the dog is still being good, say your release word, like "Free!" and let him run up to the distraction and have a bite of chicken or sniff the tree where the squirrel was hiding. That's his functional reward.

Gradually require the dog to go all the way up to the finish line on a loose leash before giving his release cue.

Silky Leash technique

Silky Leash uses positive reinforcement to teach a dog to pay attention to the feeling of light pressure on the collar or harness. It's really useful for dogs who spark into reactivity when their leashes get tight. Silky Leash is the exact opposite of being a tree, almost. Use the techniques like Backing Up or Be a Tree for when the dog is on a harness on your real walks. Practice Silky Leash at home on a collar, until the dog is great, and then combine techniques. If you have a strong dog who is a lunger, you may want to use the front attachment harness for your Silky Leash work. That way, if your dog ever does lunge, you still have control. This method is hard to explain in words, so I highly recommend you watch one of the Silky Leash videos on my website at http://DoggieZen.com/silkyleash.

So what is Silky Leash? That's the name I use with my students for a technique from Shirley Chong's website (see Resources). Think of it as guiding your dog along with a single strand of silk. It has several steps, and you want to really follow this technique to the letter so that you teach the dog to notice the lightest flutter of your leash. Until things are going really well using the Silky Leash method, use something like a front attachment harness for walks on which your dog may pull or lunge.

As your dog gets better at this, you'll start to practice on real walks, but at first, you will set up the whole situation so you have full control just like you would do with BAT.

There are two students here—you are learning to give instructions by leash very softly, and your dog is learning to listen to them. If things aren't working, examine both students! *Stay at each step below until your dog is responding quickly.*

Step 1: Sitting in a tiny room—the basics. With a hungry dog in a tiny, nondistracting area, like a bathroom or exercise pen, set up a chair for you and have the clicker in your hand and treats accessible. I usually have treats in a pouch and the clicker and leash in the same hand (my right). Clip the leash to the dog's collar or whatever you eventually want to walk your dog with. The room should be small enough that when you sit in the chair, your dog cannot pull—the walls are closer than the length of the leash.

If a friend had a collar around your neck and had no way to communicate to you that she wanted your attention, you'd want her to pull lightly on the leash. Your dog agrees! Pretend that you have a raw egg in your palm, with the leash wrapped around it. Say the amount of force your normally put on your dog to stop him is one hundred pounds. What we're looking for here is about one quarter of a pound.

Put a tiny bit of pressure on the leash, just enough to have the leash make a straight line from you to your dog. Keep the pressure low and wait. If your dog pulls away from the pressure, let your hand go with him, so that the pressure stays constant. If you are tired of waiting, you may vibrate the leash, just a tiny "chick's heart" flutter. Eventually, as your dog is not a frozen statue, and the room is small, he will move in the direction of the pull and the pressure will lower.

At that point, the clasp of the leash (by the collar) will probably dip down. Click for that and feed a treat. After each click/treat, give your dog a few seconds to pause and then put pressure on the leash again. I hesitate to use the word pull, because that sounds a lot more forceful than what you should be doing. Repeat, repeat, repeat.

Step 2: Sitting in a tiny room—raise criteria. Now you raise your criteria. Instead of just one step to ease off the pressure, we want more, about twice as far as your dog moved before! Remember that you are not trying to drag the dog around, but rather saying to the dog, "Move this way until I signal you to stop." You aren't putting enough pressure on the leash to *make* the dog move, just enough to signal that you'd *like* him to.

What you'll do is just apply pressure a little longer than before. So you pull lightly on the leash (no harder than before, remember, this is your friend!) and when the dog moves toward the pressure, move slightly away from him, so the pressure stays constant. As he takes the second step, stop pulling away. The leash pressure will become zero again and you'll click/treat. Repeat many times.

On her site, Shirley Chong wrote, "At this stage, it may well take the dog awhile to notice the cue and respond. That is perfectly okay. For dogs who have been pulling for a period of time (*years* for some of them!), it is going to take them awhile to recalibrate what it is that they pay attention to." Be patient with your dog!

Remember, we're teaching your hands to be gentler, too. How are you doing?

Step 3: Sitting in a tiny room—walk in a circle. If your dog is tall, you may have to stand for this step, but sit, if you can. The goal for this step is to get your dog to move in a full circle, cued only by leash pressure.

Repeat Step 2, but now just wait longer and longer before clicking—ease off on the pressure later and later. Try both directions.

Step 4: Sitting in a tiny room—figure 8. Now we make the dog (and you!) work a bit harder by trying for a figure 8. Remember, you still want to have the finish be that the dog successfully got the pressure to go away and you click/treat for that. The main lesson here for the dog is that the *pressure means something:* "go in the direction of the pull until it stops." *Dogs have a natural reflex to go the opposite direction of pulling,* so we're fighting against that reflex.

Step 5: Walking in a slightly bigger room—follow the leader. You'll take turns playing follow the leader. Remember, we still don't want a sudden jolt of pressure, so you may need to follow your dog during this time. This is the one situation where I allow dogs to pull on a collar. The room should still be fairly boring, so they don't want to pull a lot, and small enough that you can follow them with constant pressure. If things go awry at this stage, you probably didn't practice the earlier steps enough times.

Start by following your dog for a bit (no pressure) and then put a tiny pressure on your dog. Click/treat when he eases up on the pressure (right away—no figure 8s yet). If he walks into the pressure (i.e., pulls), follow him so that the pressure stays constant. Remember, this is supposed to be a smallish, boring room. Alternate back and forth between following him and then using a feather-light pressure to cue him to follow you. Gradually extend the number of steps your dog has to do before you allow the leash to go slack and then click and treat.

Step 6: Walking in a slightly bigger area—follow the leader continues. This is where you head out to the yard. If you don't have a yard, you might use an exercise pen that you've set up at a park, or someone else's house, for the distractions. Work in an area where you can still keep up with your dog, so that may require cardboard boxes or ex-pens or something to make the area smaller. You can get fairly cheap temporary construction fencing from hardware stores.

Now you'll be practicing having your dog do turns, zig zags, serpentines and circles while you walk relatively straight within the confines of your area. You are still clicking and treating your dog, as we've raised the criteria. If this setting is too distracting, practice more of this on Step 5 first. Don't worry if your dog is distracted some of the time; that gives you a chance to flutter the leash and click/treat for him heading in your direction.

Remember that we're imagining the leash to be a silken thread. It takes two to pull! You'll still need to follow your dog if he heads off, so you can keep the pressure constant and occasionally flutter.

At this point, you should still be walking your dog in his harness or other temporary gear for most of his regular walks. If he is tired at the end of a walk and is not likely to pull, go ahead and attach the leash to his collar.

Step 7: The real world. Now you're ready for the big time. Continue to have soft hands and flutter your silky leash, and click, then treat whenever your dog follows that cue. I would start with adding a few more distractions at a time, and walk in a place where it's easy to go in any direction, rather than only two. In the best of all worlds, with a typical dog, you'd be able to walk right past any distraction. At first, though, you may have to do a lot of what Shirley calls "transitions." Transitions are turns and speed changes.

If there's a big distraction up ahead on your walk, flutter the leash and take a right turn, then take a wide arc around the distraction, or gradually turn away and retreat. Click and treat your dog for following each cue. Super-big distractions like one of your dog's triggers? If you've been using a flat collar, you probably should clip the leash to the harness again for that.

Over time, you'll need to make fewer transitions, and you'll be clicking less and less as your dog gains confidence and skill. You'll also be using more "real world" rewards, like permission to go sniff or chase squirrels up into trees. The less your dog has practiced pulling before you started, the faster this process of weaning off of the treats will be.

Keep it up, wean off of the treats, and don't let your dog practice pulling in between sessions. Remember, your dog is always learning. Shirley writes, "And then everyone will tell you 'well, it's easy for you, your dog just never pulls!' You can just smile and mentally add the truth: your dog never pulls because you never pull."

Coming when called

Coming when called, directly and without hesitation, can save a dog's life. When a dog is likely to get into fights with other dogs or bite people, it's also an important way to keep others safe. If all of the physical safeguards fail—the leash, the fence, or whatever else—then the recall is there to get the dog back. Many dogs have no dangerous bite history and the goal is to get them to play well with others, off-leash; to be around other dogs off-leash, they definitely need a reliable recall. There are bound to be times when your dog gets in over his head, and the only way to get him out, from a distance, is to call him.

I've actually already covered a sneaky way of getting a dog to come when called. The Touch cue is great because in order to touch their nose to your hand, the dog has to come over to you. She's also close enough to grab. Other training books have various great ways to create a solid recall for everyday use (see Resources), but the Touch cue can be enough if you practice in lots of different places.

I like to teach a separate cue for an emergency recall. This cue is not eroded by everyday use, but remains strong because you practice it with amazing rewards, in several situations. I teach the dog to come to a special cue using an adapted version of Leslie Nelson's *Really Reliable Recall* (see Resources). My students usually use the cue, "Treat party." At my house, the cue is a high-pitched, "Boop," because that's not something the dogs ever hear, except when they are about to get a load of fabulous treats. This is straightforward classical conditioning. Here's how it works.

1. (Optional) Say your regular recall cue. Starting with this helps the joy of the treat party rub off on your regular cue, so you get twice the training.

2. Say the cue, "Treat party."

3. One after the other, hand out about twenty small, extraordinarily fabulous treats; bits of meat or leftover macaroni and cheese work great for this. Set them on the ground near the dog so he scarfs them up. Just before you hand out each treat, say, "Treat party!" That way, within about twenty seconds, you've conditioned the phrase, "Treat party" twenty times, plus you have the cumulative effect of an overwhelming number of great treats. The phrase begins to have the same magnetic pull as the slot machine bells ringing for gambling in Vegas. It doesn't always have to be a party of treats; if you have a toy-loving dog, announce that a treat party is coming before a game of tug, and repeat the phrase as you play. If you're doing it right, you should be out of breath by the end of each treat party.

4. Practice three times a day, gradually announcing the party when farther away from the dog or out of sight. If you have non-spicy leftover foods, put them in the refrigerator as you wash dishes and then pull them out for a Treat Party after the meal. Practice indoors, outdoors, in front of the house, with distractions, and anywhere else you can think of.

Leslie Nelson's way of doing the Really Reliable Recall is to give a jackpot of rewards for the recall, presented one at a time. She calls that "fine dining." What I added to her protocol was the cue of Treat Party, instead of just praising during the party, so that you get an emergency recall cue for free while you train your regular recall. I've had clients tell me that after only a few weeks, they've been able to use the "Treat Party" cue to rescue their dog from traffic, and that even then, they remembered to celebrate with a Treat Party for their dog.

I love using that goofy cue, because it reminds the students to keep the behavior strong by keeping up a fabulous rate of reinforcement. They don't say "Treat Party" unless they mean it. Saying "Treat Party" without handing out a lot of treats seems more like lying to their dog than not providing reinforcement for other cues. They also don't overuse the cue for everyday recalls, because it's sort of an embarrassing thing to shout. They even remember to avoid saying the cue at other times. My clients refer to it as a "T.P." or a "celebration" when talking about the cue, to make sure their dog isn't disappointed.

Play bow

This is a fun addition to the dog's repertoire, but it's also really useful. I mostly teach it to dogs as a default way to get their human's attention. Play bowing is a lot better than jumping up or barking at us for attention, and it's a lot more fun than sitting. It's also a nice way to stretch a dog before agility or other dog sports. Finally, Play Bow is also great for dogs that lack social skills. See the "Frustrated Greeters" chapter for more information. Special thanks to trainer Joey Iversen for letting me steal her idea of teaching play bows for attention.

Author and researcher Alexandra Horowitz observed that in the dog world, a dog tends to only do a Play Bow if the other dog is paying attention first (see Resources). So, the Play Bow is not exactly the first thing a dog does as an attention-getter, but it's a very obvious signal and it's a dog's way of signaling "Hey, I'm talking to you! Let's do something together" in a peaceful way.

I use the cue Yoga for the Play Bow, because it is a fun play on the "downward facing dog" pose and because Bow sounds too much like Down.

Teaching Yoga using capturing is ideal, because it gives the dogs a very natural stretch. Simply use a verbal marker like "Yes" or a clicker to mark the instant that the dog is in a deep, Play Bow stretch and then give a treat. This deep stretch often happens when they first wake up, so be ready to capture it then. Many dogs will bow if you stretch in your own version of a Play Bow, so you can try that too. If you can feed while they're still bowing, do that! Be sure to give your regular release cue like OK or Free, so she knows that she can get up.

Once a dog catches on that you like the Play Bow, she should begin to offer it more and more. Reward using treats, attention, or whatever the dog seems to want in the moment. You can either just leave it like that, or you can add the verbal cue, Yoga. Simply say, "Yoga," when you first notice that the bowing has begun. Mark the behavior when the dog is fully bowing, and then reward.

Appendix 2

Other Techniques that Use
Functional Rewards

This appendix is helpful if you are a training geek, like me, or if you know a lot of other techniques and want to fit BAT into the scheme of things. If you are new to training, this section may be overwhelming.

As an overall package, BAT is a new way of training, but it was influenced by a variety of training tools that use functional rewards. Several of those methods even use the functional reward of distance from the trigger. I'll discuss those methods below.

Premack principle

The Premack principle isn't a technique, but it's the basis of a lot of common training techniques (see Resources). Discovered in 1959 by David Premack, the Premack principle states that the opportunity to perform a more likely behavior will reinforce a less likely behavior. Your mom used the Premack principle if she ever told you, "After you do your homework, you can go play with your friends." If the functional reward of the behavior you're teaching is permission to do a particular behavior, like polite walking leading to squirrel chasing, you're using the Premack principle. Functional rewards aren't always permission to do more likely behaviors, though. Walking away from a trigger isn't necessarily more likely than barking/lunging, etc., but it is reinforcing. Functional rewards can also be something that happens around or to them, like the trigger walking away or a person walking back to a crated dog.

Retreat n' Treat was developed by Ian Dunbar in 1982, and Ian says that the term itself was coined by Suzanne Clothier (see Resources). The idea is to treat the dog and then walk away or toss the treat behind the dog, playing hard to get. The dog will then follow you when you leave; repeat. The functional reward is the relief that the dog feels when he goes away from you to get the treat or when you back away from him. Dunbar says he used this to get himself out of a sticky situation with a big Akita who had bitten four men. Suzanne Clothier has extended this method, which she now calls "Treat and Retreat." She elegantly explains how tossing treats to where the dog feels comfortable approaching, and then leaving, is infinitely better than luring a dog forward to you with treats, because it takes the social pressure off of the dog. I use Treat and Retreat frequently with fearful dogs in puppy class.

Two-Reward method

John Fisher developed the Two-Reward method to work with dog aggression, especially for Velcro dogs who are quite attached to their owners (see Resources). It appeared in print in his posthumous work *Diaries of a "Dotty Dog" Doctor* in 1997, but he had been using it for a while. The Two-Reward method used different rewards to teach dogs to offer calm behaviors, instead of barking and lunging. Fisher would tether a human-reactive dog with the owner standing or sitting beside the dog. Then he would walk toward the dog until she barked at him. At that point, the owner would walk away, as negative punishment. When the dog relaxed fully, she would obtain two rewards: the return of the owner (who may also feed treats) and the exit of the stranger. He also mentioned that the dog could be rewarded for smaller amounts of relaxation, rather than waiting for her to lie down. The Two-Reward method was one of the precursors of Trish King's Abandonment Training and also Constructional Aggression Treatment (see Resources).

Constructional Aggression Treatment

Constructional Aggression Treatment (or CAT) was developed from a series of research projects at University of North Texas under the supervision of Behavior Analyst Jesús Rosales-Ruiz. Eddie Fernandez researched the effectiveness of using the retreat of the person as a reward for sheep holding still in 2000, Melissa Morehead studied something similar for cows in 2005, and Kellie Snider studied the use of negative reinforcement in treating aggression in dogs in 2007 (see Resources). In the CAT protocol, the dogs are usually tethered, and the decoy approaches and retreats, as in the Two-Reward method, but they try to keep the dog from barking, lunging, or growling by having the decoy approach to a distance that does not cause the dog to react with aggression. When the dog starts barking, lunging, or growling then the result is similar to the Two-Reward method, in that the decoy stays in place as the dog barks themselves out, i.e., until the aggression stops and the dog displays an acceptable alternative behavior. In the original research, the dogs went through quite a few extinction bursts. CAT practitioners have begun to work to create set-ups that cause fewer outbursts, but this extinction process is considered to be an essential aspect of CAT. The owner remains with the dog during the entire protocol and does not feed treats during the process or talk to the dog during the approach phase, but may interact with him between trials.

Horse training

Horse trainers, including Monty Roberts and Alexandra Kurland, have used walking away from the animal as their reward for decades, and Kurland also used a clicker and treats at the same time (see Resources). Besides Karen Pryor, I think Kurland is the only trainer to write about training with a marker signal along with the functional reward of increased distance (see Resources). As a clicker trainer, I think Alexandra Kurland made a great decision when she used a marker signal. BAT always uses a marker signal; it may be a verbal marker or a clicker, depending on whether we are using treats or not.

The theory behind using walking away from a horse as a reward for them holding still or acting friendly is that they are prey animals, and that they would especially appreciate distance. I think that in any species, most aggressive displays are about proximity in some way—whether they are protecting their territory, themselves, or something else. Resource guarding can be interpreted to be about distance, too, as in, "Get away from my bone/bed/house/mom!"

The evolution of BAT

In all but Dunbar's Retreat n' Treat method (and Suzanne Clothier's version as well), the subject dog is stationary as the decoy approaches. In all of the other methods I am familiar with, it is the decoy that usually retreats, or the subject dog may be tossed a treat to prompt a retreat. I think there is great power in teaching the animal to retreat and self-reward throughout this process, whether he is walking toward the trigger or is the one being approached. BAT reduces the dog's stress by allowing her to approach the trigger for most trials, and to retreat whenever she wants.

Until 2008, I had been using functional rewards as "real life rewards" for a range of behavior problems, but not systematically for aggression. For aggressive dogs, I used classical counter-conditioning, along with methods similar to Control Unleashed and other reward-based methods. Hearing about CAT got me started in using functional rewards to work with aggression and fear instead of the classical counter-conditioning and systematic desensitization methods I had been using. I watched the CAT DVD and saw a lot of promise in it, although, like many other positive trainers, I was concerned that it would be too stressful for the dogs. I filmed my CAT sessions. Looking back on them, I can see that I began making changes within the first session, but I definitely should have gotten rid of the extinction aspect sooner. For example, I used a verbal marker. CAT does not use an event marker, and I'm a clicker trainer, so I know that has a lot of benefit without any side effects. I know that it's a myth that you have to fade the event marker. I took out unnecessary stressors, like tethering and marathon sessions. I added in some of my own ideas, plus powerful techniques and tools from other methods, all with the goal of rehabilitating a dog as quickly as possible, reducing stress, and making it practical for clients.

By 2009, I had read on the CAT Yahoo group that the techniques of CAT were beginning to evolve to reduce stress. I defended CAT to fellow dog-friendly trainers who said that CAT was inhumane by giving examples of how I was training. I even talked my wife into using her dog as a demo for a CAT seminar with Kellie Snider and Jesús Rosales-Ruiz, and talked my trainer friends into attending, thinking it would be an eye-opening experience for them. Kellie and Jesús had a lot of good scientific information on how dogs learn, and I enjoyed most of the seminar. But it was during the demo that I realized what I was doing was no longer CAT—not from the trainer's perspective and definitely not from the dog's perspective. Our poor dog was so stressed out from barking for three hours straight that she continued to bark at all stimuli on the way home, including triggers to which she hadn't been reactive to before. I was mortified and had a lot of apologizing to do (to my parnter and her dog, as well as my friends) as well as some retraining for the dog.

I suggested changes to the CAT protocol online and jokingly used the term "BAT" as a shorthand way to refer to what I was doing. Those changes and my discussion of it were rejected by supporters of CAT, so I began discussing BAT with others as an independent method. At that point, I read up more on functional analysis and other methods that use functional rewards, and ran my ideas for even more changes in BAT by my friend Lori Stevens, a TTouch practitioner. She asked insightful questions of the form "why do you do such and such" that were excellent food for thought!

Because it was informed by many different methods, BAT is more of a cousin of CAT, not CAT 2.0, even though CAT was my original inspiration. BAT uses some of the shaping from CAT that was suggested in Fisher's explanation of the Two-Reward method, but eliminates the extinction aspect from both of them. I think that waiting for extinction with such emotionally laden behaviors causes too much stress on the dog you are working with, the decoy, and even the owner. Besides, in real life, the triggers are constantly in motion; standing still while the dog barks himself out is impractical and embarrassing for walks. Furthermore, I don't want to turn off the dog's built-in warning system by getting rid of growling or barking through extinction or punishment. Rather than punishing or extinguishing growling and barking episodes, BAT practitioners prompt the dog to make a better choice at the first sign of panic or aggression. That makes life less stressful for the decoys, the neighbors, the dog, and his handler!

In conclusion, the other methods that use functional rewards for reactivity are all forms of **operant counter-conditioning,** because they change the dog's emotional responses by first teaching new behaviors. These methods teach the dog to offer appropriate behaviors without prompting from the human, and *can* teach dogs to be comfortable and even begin to like interacting with former triggers. But in BAT, the dog is kept below threshold and the dog and his human both have an active role in training. These factors, and others, create a positive and trusting relationship and make BAT a humane and low-stress process for all involved (dogs, decoys, humans, etc.). As I mentioned before, BAT teaches the animal to self-soothe (retreat when needed) versus teaching alternate ways to repel the intruder. I think that's a subtle, but important difference between BAT and its many predecessors.

APPENDIX 3

For Trainers and Behaviorists: Geek Speak on Terms and Quadrants

If you read this book and questions like, "Which quadrant does this use?" or "Isn't this just an application of behavior analysis?" pop into your head, then this chapter is for you. Or if you want to be one of those people, then you can read this chapter too. I think it's important that as dog trainers and behaviorists, we understand the science behind our training techniques. I also think that if we can get our students to understand the principles, their dogs will benefit. But I don't think it's important to overwhelm our students with terms and technical arguments, so I saved that for this appendix.

Behavior analysis: Functional behavior assessments

Applied Behavior Analysis assumes that all behavior has a function (i.e., it serves some sort of purpose) for the person or animal doing the behavior. A **functional behavior assessment** determines the relationship between behaviors and environmental events to determine the function of the behavior. It's the sort of thing that trainers look at when we consider antecedents, behaviors, and consequences. A functional behavior assessment can be done in different ways including indirect functional behavior assessment, descriptive functional behavior assessment, and functional analysis. I'll explain each of those below in terms of a functional assessment of reactive dog behavior, but of course this applies to all species and behaviors.

Indirect functional behavior assessment. The behaviorist gathers information about what happens from people who have observed the dog's behavior in his regular environment. Interview the dog's guardians (live or via a history questionnaire) on what happens before the dog reacts (**setting events** and triggers), how the dog reacts, what happens next, etc. This is very common for work with pet dogs.

Descriptive Functional Behavior Assessment. The trainer collects data by observing the dog's behavior and situation directly without manipulating consequences, then analyzes that to determine the function of the behavior. For example, the trainer watches the dog and owner as they walk by a fake or real dog, looking for what triggers the reaction, what the specific behaviors are when the dog reacts, and what the consequences are from the environment and the owner. Another example is that the client brings in a video recording of the dog in a situation in which the reactivity occurs. Dog professionals tend to rarely actually collect and analyze data in a technical way, but rather make informal assessments.

Functional Analysis. The behaviorist sets up scenarios to measure whether changing the consequences of the reactivity has any effect on it. For example, collecting data to analyze whether the treatment decreases the reactivity is a functional analysis. Formally measuring whether BAT reduces barking would be one way of doing a functional analysis. Another way to test whether achieving Consequence A is the function of the reactivity is to see whether the reactivity can be made worse by having Consequence A follow the reactivity. The ethics on this route are questionable, because if it is "successful" then the dog is *more* reactive. If the relief that the subject dog feels when walking away from the triggering stimulus is hypothesized to be the function of the reactivity, then the trainer would test that hypothesis by setting up a situation where the subject dog would be over threshold and react, followed by the subject dog walking away from the triggering stimulus.

The answer to the question of "Isn't BAT just an application of behavior analysis?" is yes and no, because it uses the function of the problem behavior to reinforce replacement behaviors, but it uses additional reinforcements as well. And even if it were "just" an application of functional analysis, since when is there a problem with using science to develop treatment protocols? ☺

The quadrant quandary: Should quadrants determine our ethics?

I've had several people ask me which **quadrant** BAT is in, i.e., which theoretical learning quadrant the consequences used in BAT lie in. I've heard arguments for every quadrant by now, some of which are more believable than others. I'll give a brief description of the quadrants so that you can decide for yourself.

Here's how the quadrant model of **operant conditioning** works. If a certain consequence follows a behavior, that behavior can have no change (no learning in terms of the behavior), or it can be more or less likely to occur in the future. The consequence is reinforcement or a punishment of the behavior, depending on what happens next:

- Reinforcement: the behavior is more likely to occur in the future.

- Punishment: the behavior is less likely to occur in the future.

Using the definitions of these two types of learning, BAT clearly is a reinforcement protocol, as it makes the replacement behaviors *more* likely. The consequence of doing replacement behaviors is a functional reward, which serves a purpose for the dog and reinforces the behavior.

I have to insert here that it should technically not be termed a "functional reward," but rather a "functional reinforcement" because it reinforces behavior. A reward is technically a stimulus that is appetitive to a dog, something that draws the dog toward it. So moving away from the trigger couldn't technically be a "reward," but in the vernacular, reward basically means the same thing as reinforcement, and reward has only two syllables instead of four. Even B.F. Skinner wrote, in his 1953 textbook, *Science and Human Behavior,* "Insofar as scientific definition corresponds to lay usage, they [positive and negative reinforcement] are both rewards." It's not ideal to use a scientific term in its everyday sense, but there you have it. If you feel uncomfortable with saying "functional reward,'" then you can use "functional reinforcement," instead. I will just be able to say more words during the same amount of time, because I have saved two syllables. ☺

Ok, so now we know for sure that BAT uses reinforcement. But does BAT have a punishment component? Does it suppress behavior? No. At least, I can't see how it would.[1] To decide whether this is a protocol involving punishment, you'd first need to figure out which behavior or behaviors are being punished. BAT decreases reactivity, so maybe the reactive behaviors of barking, lunging, growling are being punished. I believe that reactivity decreases because the dog becomes more comfortable with the trigger and has more efficient ways to create safety than relying on the old reactive behaviors. But let's look at the hypothesis that there might also be some punishment going on, using growling as the problem behavior.

Remember that growling should rarely, if ever, happen during BAT, because we set the dog up to do only the replacement behaviors. But sometimes humans make mistakes and the dog does growl. Does BAT punish that behavior? In order for this to be punishment for growling, there must be a consequence that follows growling that makes the growling less likely in the future. When a dog growls with BAT, the consequence is that you interrupt using the least invasive way that works. Examples including calling your dog, snapping your fingers, getting into your dog's peripheral vision, moving away so that the dog follows, etc. Occasionally, the dog must be physically moved further from the trigger in order to settle. If I could just beam the dog a bit further away from the triggering stimulus, like in Star Trek, I would do that. But we can't, so sometimes there is pressure on the harness.

---

[1]There could be accidental reinforcement, because exposure to the other dog or person is potentially aversive, but that exposure doesn't follow a consistent set of behaviors, except for a behavior we actually like: a calm approach to the trigger. The approach behavior increases during the protocol, so if there is any punishment at all, it's trumped by reinforcement.

But that's probably not punishment. Here's why. The dogs do not seem less likely to growl in the future because of the consequence of being moved farther from the triggering stimulus. If that worked, the clients probably wouldn't need to see a trainer in the first place. One could collect data on this, but it's possible that the growling is reinforced by this action. Walking away is, after all, the hypothesized reinforcement. At any rate, this scenario only happens when the training situation fails. It is a brief, minimally aversive experience for the dog and happens rarely during training.

So that rules out half of the quadrants. *BAT is a protocol based purely on reinforcement (building behavior up), not punishment (suppressing behavior).* Many behavioral scientists would stop there and say that going into the quadrants from here is pointless, because the division between positive and negative depends on which stimulus you look at and other factors (see Resources). But let's continue this quadrant discussion anyway because it comes up a lot and I want to address it.

There are two kinds of reinforcement in the quadrant model: positive and negative, based on whether something is being brought into or removed from the situation.

- Positive: a stimulus or activity is presented
- Negative: a stimulus or activity is taken away.

Here's where the confusion comes in. If you reinforce a behavior by feeding a dog a treat, are you adding a treat (positive reinforcement) or removing the aversive state of hunger (negative reinforcement)? As Jack Michael wrote in 1975 (republished in 2005, see Resources),

> ...the critical distinction between positive and negative reinforcement depends upon being able to distinguish stimulus changes which are presentations from those which are removals or withdrawals, and these latter terms are not very satisfactory descriptions of changes. The circumstances under which we have a tendency to say 'present' certainly seem to differ from those where we say 'remove' in much vernacular usage, but some of these differences are irrelevant to a science of behavior, and there are a number of circumstances where the distinction is not easily made.

Jack Michael concludes that the more important distinction is the reinforcement and punishment part, not whether it is positive or negative, since that is unclear (and therefore not rigorously scientific enough):

> As we find ourselves applying behavioral analysis to more and more complex human situations we find it increasingly difficult to distinguish between presenting and removing, or we find an increasing number of situations that seem to involve both. A fairly common response to this situation is to avoid making the distinction, and simply refer to the relevant environmental change as "reinforcement,"

without attempting to determine whether a positive reinforcer is being presented or a negative removed. One might well ask, then, why we bother making the distinction even in those cases where it can easily be made.

He then summarily dismisses the various reasons one might have for maintaining the positive/negative distinction. The arguments are that it might be helpful to know what kind of procedure one used, for replication, that there may be different biological processes at work, and that it's helpful as an ethical distinction.

It is quite clear that for someone to replicate some particular behavioral manipulation it is not much more helpful to know that it involved negative reinforcement than to know, simply, that it involved reinforcement. The details must still be provided and without them the situation remains quite unclear.... Our past efforts to develop behavioral terminology on the basis of supposed or real physiological entities, this is not a very attractive strategy...To maintain a distinction at the level of basic science because of its possible social implications seems a risky practice, and one that is usually avoided in other sciences when possible.

I do think that it's helpful to have some concept of whether the training or behavior modification uses aversives, and to what extent, but I am not sure that the dichotomy of positive or negative reinforcement fully captures that concept. Another possible use of this split into removal/addition of stimuli is to see whether learning in those two quadrants occurs in some better way in one versus the other, has different extinction curves, or is processed differently by the brain. As brain research gets more and more precise, it's interesting to see whether there is a physiological difference in positive versus negative reinforcement, although there are differences within the quadrants, too.

You may still want to know which quadrant BAT lives in, so let's look at a BAT trial and see what is being presented or removed to reinforce the replacement behaviors. After the dog looks at the triggering stimulus and does a head turn, you would mark the behavior, walk or jog away with the dog, praise as you go, and possibly give a bonus reward of food, toys, petting, etc.

Consequence	What is Presented (Positive Reinforcement)	What is Taken Away (Negative Reinforcement)
Mark the behavior	Sound ("Yes" or click) or visual stimulus for deaf dogs	Sound ("Yes" or click) or visual stimulus for deaf dogs
Walk/jog away	Opportunity to move	Triggering stimulus
Praise	Sound (praise words) and visual (human expression of happiness)	—
Bonus reward	Food, toys, petting, etc.	—

For some dogs, the triggering stimulus may be the most important aspect and for others, the chance to move at all is the more important event. The clicker or marker signal could serve as a prediction of positive reinforcement, but it could also serve as a conditioned negative reinforcer, a safety cue, predicting that the dog is about to move away from the trigger (see Resources). Note that, either way, the click must come after the behavior, which is after the exposure to the trigger. If you accidentally click or the dog consistently notices the clicker before seeing the trigger, the clicker could become a conditioned punisher.

Looking at this, you can see that there are consequences that indicate BAT can use both positive reinforcement and negative reinforcement. Even given the UNT study about combining positive and negative reinforcement, I think that there is no problem with this particular combination of reinforcements, except that some people use the quadrants to decide which methods are ethical and which are not.

Using the quadrants as an ethical guide is not entirely bad, because negative reinforcement can involve a lot of icky aversives. Aversives are stimuli or experiences that the dog will work to avoid. I find most methods that rely on the negative reinforcement and positive punishment quadrants to be too intrusive (containing unnecessary aversives). Most methods in the positive reinforcement quadrant are pleasant for the dog, and since dogs can't give consent on which kind of training they would like to have, I prefer to use positive reinforcement. But depending on certain factors, like how you set criteria and whether you rely on extinction bursts for shaping, and how the dog handles the excitement of training, positive reinforcement isn't necessarily all rosy, either. Furthermore, rehabilitation without environmental aversives is not always possible. I'll comment more on that below.

Given that not all positive reinforcement training is fun for the dog and not all negative reinforcement is overly intrusive, *we can't decide whether a method is ethical or not based purely on the quadrants.* Frankly, I think doing so is the lazy way out. As intelligent, empathetic beings, we have to put more thought into it than that. Here are some factors that I propose you consider when deciding whether a training method that uses aversives is humane.

1. Will the aversive stimulus remain aversive after treatment?

2. Do any other effective treatments avoid the aversive altogether?

3. If no, is the level of exposure to the aversive at the lowest amount possible for efficient learning?

4. Is exposure to the aversive active or passive?

5. Is the dog able to remove himself from the aversive at any time?

I'll address these questions one at a time with regard to BAT. If you use other kinds of training methods that involve any aversives (like leash walking, reactivity protocols, etc.), I suggest you walk through the list for those methods, too, even if you are 100% certain that what you are doing is humane. It's a good activity to repeat periodically, as new training methods are developed that can change your answers to the questions above.

1. No. The aversive stimulus does not remain aversive after BAT is finished. The whole point of BAT is to get the dog comfortable around the trigger. This is not the use of artificial aversives for the sake of changing unrelated behavior, like training a recall using a shock collar or using a head collar to lift a reactive dog's head and close his mouth until he calms down. BAT uses an aversive stimulus only in order to acclimate the dog to the stimulus, i.e. teach him that that particular environmental aversive stimulus is actually benign or pleasant. BAT and other reactivity rehabilitation methods like Control Unleashed and Counter-conditioning with systematic desensitization all pass this test. I consider all of these methods to be "dog-friendly" and criterion #1 is essential for that.

2. No. All methods that I know of to rehabilitate or prevent dog reactivity involve having the dog perceive the aversive triggering stimulus. Being nonverbal creatures, we can't have them lie on a therapy couch to discuss their relationship with other dogs or people. We have to train experientially.

3. Yes. In a BAT session, the level of arousal caused by the triggering stimulus should be just at the level of noticing and definitely not past the reactivity threshold. This is similar to other dog-friendly reactivity rehabilitation methods. However, since BAT doesn't usually use food or toys during set-ups, more of the dog's attention is on the helper. In order to achieve the same level of non-reactivity without distractions present, the helper is usually further away at the beginning of a BAT session than with other dog-friendly methods.

4. Exposure is active in BAT, except when specifically using passive exposure as the trigger that the trainer is getting the dog used to. The subject dog is usually walked toward the triggering stimulus, rather than having the stimulus presented to the dog. The handler's role is often to keep the dog from over-exposing herself to the trigger, i.e., walking too close to the trigger. In scenarios to specifically work on Sudden Environmental Contrast, the exposure is passive (e.g. a dog appears from behind a corner), but the exposure is active whenever possible. I think this is a strength of BAT over the way many other dog-friendly methods are practiced.

5. Yes! Allowing the dog to remove himself from the trigger at any time is essential for BAT. The dog is always allowed to avoid the triggering stimulus. This is a huge benefit of having the dog walking on a leash versus being tethered or stationary with passive exposure. The handler is responsible for noticing when the dog is uncomfortable. Since the dog doesn't speak a human language, the communication is imperfect, but certainly the goal is to allow the dog to avoid anything she wants to avoid. Note: if a dog will not look at the helper or refuses to walk forward, you are working too close! The beauty of BAT is that the dog learns to make her own choices under your supervision, whether she is creating a buffer of extra space from the stimulus, or curiously moving closer to the stimulus while remaining below threshold.

In my opinion, giving the dog the opportunity to control her exposure to the trigger is essential for a technique to be dog-friendly or humane. Having control over the level of stress is empowering and should be part of any protocol for reactivity, whether it's BAT or any of the other techniques. Having control over one's own safety creates learned optimism, the opposite of learned helplessness. Be aware that there is more than one way to force a dog into an uncomfortable situation. The obvious way would be to tether the dog or to pull him toward the aversive on a leash. But even if you use treats and never pull on the dog, be cautious and check in frequently with the dog's comfort level: even though you are not physically forcing the dog to be too close to the trigger, the value of the food may cause her to be conflicted, and stay too close even though she really wants to go away.

The quadrant issue is important to me. I hope that we can have a conversation in our community to see whether we, as a profession, have taken the easy way out and allowed learning theory quadrants, a construct, to replace our ability to decide whether a technique is humane. Fortunately, I see a shift in the way people are thinking about this. I think it's important to have criteria by which we judge the use of a training method in a particular situation, so that things like cognitive dissonance don't convince us that the training we do is humane (see below). However, I think it's also important to make sure those criteria are up to date, so that when we use them to judge a method, the result is consistent with our ethics.

Try Again: More Thoughts on What to Do When the Dog Goes Over Threshold

I wrote above that you should use graduated prompting when the dog looks like he is about to go over threshold, and that if that isn't enough and he reacts, you would call or pull him away and go several feet further away from the trigger to start a new trial. Because we can't use punishment (risk of fallout and also it eliminates communication, which we like better than silent biting), we need the least reinforcing stimulus to interrupt the behavior. As I mentioned, this has the possible repercussion of reinforcing the reactivity, because the dog does get to go away from the trigger. Since it happens infrequently, this is not a huge risk, but it's technically still a risk.

The "Try Again" cue, which means do something different, is one way to interrupt mild reactivity that I didn't discuss earlier. Now, the Try Again cue may still be reinforcing in that it signals reinforcement is possible if the dog does the next behavior right. But it puts more of the onus on the dog and does serve as a bit of a No Reward Marker for the behavior that just happened. I skipped this before because it's a bit technical to use with clients and they tend to use it wrong and cause stress, but I did use it with Peanut. I first taught him Try Again during the "101 Things to Do With a Box" creativity game that Karen Pryor mentioned in *Don't Shoot the Dog*. (See Resources.)

In the normal version of this game, you do nothing until the dog offers a behavior that you haven't clicked before during the session. To use this activity to teach Try Again, still click only for behaviors that haven't been done before during that session, but add in the "Try Again" cue at certain points. So for example, click for a nose touch to the box, treat, and then say, "Try Again," meaning "give me something I haven't seen." If your dog does another nose touch in the same way, don't click, but rather repeat, "Try Again." When the new behavior is offered, click and treat that. Repeat. As an aside, you can use a similar strategy to teach Try Again meaning "do what you just did." You can work on both cues simultaneously to teach them as opposite concepts. The cue could also mean, "do that again and repeat until I click."

While there is debate in the clicker training community over whether it's necessary or a good idea to use a no reward marker, (I don't think it's usually necessary), the Try Again turned out to be quite useful for reactivity in Peanut. First Peanut learned to offer something different during creativity training sessions, and eventually I could use Try Again for reactivity as well. During a BAT session or a walk, if he barked, particularly if it was a mild sort of bark or a bark at me, I would often cue Try Again so that he would offer a different behavior. I'd then mark with, "Yes," and then walk away from the trigger with him. Note that on most of the trials, I just reset him as described above. I'd love to collect data on the virtues of one way versus the other, but I wanted to share both ways here. As I said, with clients, I just do the reset so that we can quickly cut our losses.

Some useful ideas from social psychology

Social psychologists do research on how our species behaves as a whole. They look at general trends of what we do relative to one another, rather than looking at your childhood or personal situation like a therapist might do.

Social psychology studies how other humans (real or imagined) influence human behavior. I am including some concepts here that I think are relevant to this book because they might help you understand why clients or other trainers might be resistant to change.

Cognitive Dissonance. This is the feeling we get when we simultaneously believe two ideas that can't both be true. It is an uncomfortable feeling to hold onto conflicting opinions and the theories on cognitive dissonance in social psychology is that humans work hard to avoid this state of being. Here are some examples of conflicting ideas:

1. "I love animals," "I love cheese," and "Using animals for cheese production is inhumane."

2. "I have trained with choke chains," and "Training with choke chains is inhumane," and "I am a good person."

3. "Using aversives in your training is bad" and "I use classical counter-conditioning to help dogs get over their fears."

4. "All negative reinforcement training is inhumane" and "I love BAT!"

The theory of cognitive dissonance proposes that people have an innate motivational drive to reduce dissonance. People get rid of cognitive dissonance in different ways. Some just simply ignore the question. So the cheese-loving animal rights activist may just avoid thinking about this issue. Or he may do something so that he believes one of the ideas no longer is true, so there is no conflict, after all. Perhaps he justifies the cheese eating with the idea that animals don't actually die during cheese production, and he eats only organic cheese made in local farms that he has personally inspected for safety and the humane treatment of the animals, so using animals for cheese production is not necessarily inhumane. Or he decides, "actually, I don't love cows" or "I will stop eating cheese."

Taking a look at the second line, you'll see an example of the quandary that a trainer may have after her first exposure to positive training. Seeing that positive reinforcement training produces reliable results may have made her realize that choke chains are unnecessary. If they are not necessary and they are aversive, the trainer has been using inhumane training. But only bad people do inhumane things, and she is a good person! Her head threatens to spin off of her neck unless she can get rid of the cognitive dissonance. At this point, she has at least three choices in order to continue to believe she is a good person: become a "crossover trainer" and decide to stop using choke chains, become a "balanced trainer" by eliminating the belief that choke chains are unnecessary, or discount her learning of positive training altogether and go back to her old way of training. (If you're in this boat, I hope you choose the first option!)

Let's move on to the third set of inconsistent beliefs. At first glance, you might think that those are consistent, but as I discussed above, any kind of rehabilitation requires exposure to the trigger in some way. A trainer with this set of beliefs could decide that the first belief needs to be changed so that using low-stress exposure to environmental aversives in order to change the dog's emotional response to those stimuli is necessary and humane (my personal preference if this is you). Another way to get rid of the cognitive dissonance is to for the trainer to assert that she only does classical counter-conditioning (CCC) with a fearful dog at a sub-aversive level, i.e., that she always works at a distance at which the dog is not only behaviorally sub-threshold, but also the dog's internal emotional reaction to the stimulus is completely neutral. Unfortunately, I think that this just isn't possible. I could be wrong, of course, but I just don't see the evidence to support it.

For CCC to work, the dog has to actually notice the stimulus. The strengths of emotional reactions to stimuli are probably on a continuum. So if the stimulus is 10% aversive at a certain distance, and you move away, it probably goes down to 5% or 1% or .0001%, but the only way to get it to 0% at the beginning of training with a fearful dog is for the dog not to notice it at all. I don't think it is possible to work with a non-verbal animal on reactivity toward a triggering stimulus without some sort exposure to that stimulus. If the triggering stimulus is salient, then it is either aversive to some small degree, or you are done training.

This question would make a great research study, I think, testing whether CCC (or BAT) would work if the trigger were at such a distance that it didn't bring up any fear at all in the dog. Heart rate and rectal temperature would be good indicators of a stress response to the trigger, as they can be more sensitive than behavioral responses (the dog can look "fine" but the heart rate and/or temperature are elevated. However, the heart rate changes more quickly than rectal temperature. In a 2006 study by Niwako Ogata, Takefumi Kikusui, Yukari Takeuchi, and Yuji Mori on the autonomic responses of dogs to a conditioned fear-eliciting stimulus, namely a buzzer predicting the spray of a citronella collar (see Resources), Ogata, et al. found that after the buzz became a conditioned punisher, the buzz caused the dogs' heart rates to spike immediately and remains up for only about 5 minutes, while the temperature peaked at 20 minutes after the buzz of the spray collar and continued to be high for about an hour. The control group showed no such response. There is a wash of other chemical responses, of course, and one could test salivary cortisol levels via cheek swabs, for example. I mention this study to illustrate the fact that there are many ways for researchers to measure stress objectively, with a more sensitive tool than observation.

Ogata et al. summarized their results on measuring autonomic fear-responses this way:

> *Fear-related autonomic responses, such as increased heart rate and increased body temperature, rose consistently in response to a conditioned stimulus, but behavioral changes did not consistently correlate with the physiological responses. Our findings show that dogs clearly respond to conditioned stimuli and that their autonomic reactions assessed in objective indices can be more reliable and consistent measures than some behavioral measures. Based on these results, we propose that associative learning between fear-inducing conditioned and unconditioned stimuli can be assessed accurately in dogs.*

Until it's proven that there is any way around exposing a dog to the trigger at some minute level of aversiveness, the person with the third set of beliefs will just have to accept that it's not evil if the dog does happen to still be a tiny bit afraid when the stimulus is presented far, far away, or stop doing CCC, BAT, and other dog-friendly methods.

The cognitive dissonance in the fourth set of beliefs could be alleviated by asserting that BAT does not use negative reinforcement. It's always *possible* that BAT set-ups don't use negative reinforcement at all, i.e., that BAT is just a good way to do desensitization. I think replacement behaviors increase more than they would with desensitization, but that's something that needs research. Another way to relieve dissonance is to assert that walking away is only adding to the dog's experience and so BAT is all positive reinforcement. A third way, which I have personally done (confession of a former Quadrant Ethicist) is to look at the first statement and decide that it is not true that all negative reinforcement training is inhumane. My argument for that, and my revised way to test whether the use of aversives is humane, is in the section above. Even though CCC and other dog-friendly techniques don't always remove the stimulus to reinforce particular behaviors, they are still adding and removing the same stimulus as we use in BAT. Because it's using the same stimulus level as other dog-friendly methods, but just gives the dog more control over their ability to get away from the other dogs or people, BAT couldn't possibly be inhumane, even though it does use negative reinforcement. It was easier when I could just have the kneejerk argument that if it's in the wrong quadrant, it's inhumane, but life just isn't that simple.

If your head is spinning, now might be a good time to take a break, although you're almost done with this book! Here's some food for thought, as I think out loud. Is it possible to be glad that you are finished with a task, even if you enjoyed it? Does something really have to be aversive for its removal to be reinforcing? Or is it reinforcing just to end a task that takes effort? Maybe what is really behind the learning in BAT is that the dog is glad to be done greeting, which is a task that takes effort.

Fundamental Attribution Error. When we do something, people who aren't depressed tend to think of it as being justified by something that happened, even if it turned out to be a mistake. For example, let's say you're on a walk and your dog poops in someone's yard. Suddenly, you realize you have no bags, so you make a mental note to come back later to get the poo. You know everything that happened and you know that your decision to walk away was based on what just happened. But the neighbor sees you walking away without scooping and calls you a lazy, inconsiderate dog walker. You knew the behavior happened for a reason, but the other guy assumed it was a character flaw.

According to the research of social psychologists, people have a tendency to look for character flaws to explain bad behavior, rather than looking for a situational explanation. It's the reason why it's so common to see dogs as being "dominant" or "stubborn" rather than "under-socialized" or "under-motivated." In ourselves and those close to us, we tend to create situational explanations of behavior (unless we are in a conflict with them over the behavior in question). With others, we tend to just write them off entirely as being fundamentally flawed. As another example, you probably have some explanation for why your dog my lunge on a walk, but if another dog does that, you might think of that dog as a bad dog.

The fundamental attribution error also comes out when we think of "aggressive dogs," versus "dogs who have shown aggressive behaviors in response to certain triggers." The former is a personality assessment and the latter is a more helpful description, which is behavioral and situational. I am just as guilty as the next person of using the phrase "reactive dogs," "aggressive dogs," "fearful dogs," etc., because those phrases are a whole lot shorter and easier to say. Be aware of what it means when you use this kind of shorthand.

I'm writing about this here for two reasons. First, make sure that you remember to look for situational justifications of your dog's behavior (and then use those to train alternative behaviors). Second, this principle applies to other trainers, too. "Positive" trainers tend to see a character flaw in "traditional" trainers who use physical punishment, thinking of them as inhumane or cruel, too stupid to learn good, modern training. Conversely, traditional trainers tend to see character flaws in "cookie pushers," thinking that we are weak people who don't have the stomach for real training. Both sides think that the other does harm and that their own behavior is justified. While I don't always agree with the justifications that other people have, it helps to remember that they do not necessarily have character flaws, but that they have some justification that may be hard to overcome, due to the cognitive dissonance problem that I mentioned before.

APPENDIX 4

Trainers and Clients Share Their Experiences with BAT

I'm leaving the last paragraphs to some of the forward-thinking trainers and devoted dog lovers who have used BAT in the last few years. I think it is only fitting, because without the interest of early-adopters like the people below, I wouldn't have been inspired to write this book! The articles are different interpretations of my deliberately vague call for short write-ups on their experiences with BAT. These letters came in from all over the world, so you'll note British English as well as our Americanized form.

I am very grateful that so many people took time out of their busy lives to share their experiences of BAT for this book. As far as I know, the people who submitted articles for this appendix are great trainers. However, since I haven't vetted them 100% or seen them work with clients personally, this is not necessarily a list of referrals. Think of this appendix as feedback on the BAT method itself and an example of the many ways people have used BAT successfully. There is a database of trainers on the Yahoo group as well, and there may eventually be one on the functionalrewards.com website.

Walking on clouds
Laura Monaco Torelli CPDT-KA, KPACTP
Director of Training at Animal Behavior Training Concepts
Chicago, Illinois, USA
www.abtconcepts.com
Posted to the FunctionalRewards.com Yahoo group and reprinted with permission.

Today marked one of those many wonderful days that remind me of why we love what we do to help families and their pups be successful.

I am walking on clouds, and want to share the significance of what today's training session means to me and one of my dog teams here in Chicago. This team is a member of this list, and she gave permission for me to post. Out of confidentiality, I will not disclose her or her dog's name. But she can choose to introduce herself should she like.

We met 1.5 years ago after she rescued a male Ridgeback mix from an abusive home. There was the calm before the storm: the period that occurs after a dog has been placed into a safe home, can sleep soundly, eat healthy food, have access to clean water, receive gentle affection, patience and kind interactions in the presence of a new family. Not living in an unpredictable and volatile environment that has put him into survival mode for who knows how long. As time went by, his behavioral concerns became more evident, and they were referred to me for additional help.

The baseline video of his developing reactivity toward other people was heart breaking. He has (until today) always been wearing equipment and carefully managed due to his quick arousal time and lunging in my presence. More about today in a bit!

The owner is, for lack of better verbiage, one of the most magnificent natural teachers. Her patience and dedication toward her rescued dog are beyond admirable, and the patience and empathy that she has for herself and this journey has me at a loss for words at times. She is the reason her pup is where he is today with our progress.

My initial assessment referred her to our Veterinary Behaviorist here in Chicago, Dr. John Ciribassi. He immediately came on board to help build our collaboration. With his expertise, the support of her referring veterinarian, and myself, we moved forward with the slow and steady process to help her and her dog.

After some trials, my client shared a critical thread of information about her dog and what seems to make him more comfortable in the presence of a new person—if that person is walking one of his favorite dog friends around the neighborhood. So in complement with medication management, clicker training, foundation training and the help of a sweet female black mix, I was able to get closer to her dog than I ever had before.

The process of having this female dog help me help her dog was also slow going. I am a very conservative trainer based on my zoo and aquarium background and working with large animals that require extensive safety protocols. And I am truly grateful that my client respected and understood why we were focused on keeping him below threshold in my presence as much as we could. We would set up our trials in controlled settings outside at a local park, have "pre-session" and "post-session" meetings, arrange for a friend of my client's to videotape the process that her dog was relaxed and felt safe with, and would ensure that we were all safe.

Combining and integrating Behavior Adjustment Training into our overall treatment plan proved critical toward this client and dog's success, and toward our success as a collaborative team helping them move forward.

This post could go on and on, but we are where we are today because of so many critical and appreciated variables.

Today (after ~3 months of not seeing each other) we set up another session and trials. We met at the local park (no black lab mix friend needed!) and started our sessions. It was magnificent to watch. My client has approached our plan like an art form. She has been teaching him how to offer excellent canine communication below his threshold, how to make relaxed choices that he can now control, and how to offer beautiful default behaviors that keep him from escalating up the canine communication pyramid.

So at the end of our session, he allowed me to come into his home, while he was off leash, and decided that playing with his favorite ball while lying on his couch was just the ticket for him. He made the choice to let me into his home. He made the choice to walk away from me and play with a favorite toy. He made excellent choices with minimal social pressure from me. He was relaxed.

I always share with my puppy and dog teams that our goals need to be fun so we are having a good time so we repeat the behaviors of teaching and positively managing our dogs. Some families are emotionally exhausted because their attempts to walk their dog have been effectively punishing them due to their dog's behavioral concerns. So they stop trying and nothing changes to swing the pendulum in a positive direction.

Today was a great session for me, our client, and her dog on so many levels. The beauty of the basics, foundation training, and veterinary collaborations all came together.

Thanks to Grisha and this group for being such a valuable educational resource.

Use of BAT
Teoti Anderson, CPDT-KA, KPA-CTP
Trainer and Owner of Pawsitive Results, LLC, APDT Past President, author of *Your Outta Control Puppy, Quick and Easy Guide to Crate Training, Super Simple Guide to Housetraining and Puppy Care and Training*
Lexington, South Carolina, USA
www.getpawsitiveresults.com

I had been hearing about BAT and reading about other trainers having success with it for reactive dogs. I got Grisha's DVD and really enjoyed learning more about the program. I also immediately thought of an excellent candidate for me to try this technique with—an adolescent, insecure Doberman client of mine.

This dog had gone through several of my Family Manners classes and did very well with obedience, but he was insecure at heart. His triggers were strangers, exacerbated by new environments. He also reacted to other dogs but would warm up to them and play with them once introduced. When the Doberman saw a stranger he would growl and lunge at the end of the leash, but then retreat. He often would put his owner in between him and the stranger. He also growled at the family's young daughters and had nipped one.

Detailed interviews revealed the dog had been fearful as a puppy, and that the girls would often corner him in an attempt to engage him in play. I also learned the dog had, time after time, made great choices in trying to avoid confrontations, but the owners had not recognized this. It seemed the dog had a low threshold for close contact and when it was breached, he would growl a warning and try to get away. If escape was not possible, that's when he would lunge and nip.

While the owner was embarrassed and frustrated by the dog's behavior, he was one of those clients you just love to work with —he truly loved his dog and was willing to work! I thought this combination was a great opportunity to try BAT.

For our first session, I gave my client instruction on how to use the clicker. We warmed up with clicking for the dog giving eye contact. Then for our first scenario, we had my assistant come down the family's stairs in the house. This had proven to be a trigger in the past with guests and visiting family. Once the dog noticed the assistant and looked at his owner, the owner clicked and walked briskly with the dog down the hall, away from the stairs into the kitchen. In just a few minutes, the dog was able to approach my assistant without reacting.

This was repeated over several different sessions, with different assistants serving as "scary strangers," some scenarios inside the house and some outside. With each session the dog improved faster and faster. In between our sessions the client worked with his dog at home and in the neighborhood, and reported considerable improvement. Our last session was at a park, with considerable distractions. While we did cross threshold a few times due to an inability to completely control the environment, each episode was brief, with a quick recovery. I was extremely proud of this team's progress! While the owner realized that this was still a work in progress, he was very pleased with the results.

BAT proved to be an excellent program for this team:

- I really liked the use of the clicker as a marker to specifically identify to the dog what behavior we wanted. It made it much easier for my client to identify desired behavior, and helped redirect his focus from his frustration at the dog's aggressive behaviors.
- By allowing the dog to move away from the "scary strangers" it offered the dog an additional reward for desired behavior, as the distance was more of a comfort than proximity to "danger."

- By moving briskly, sometimes even running, it also allowed this athletic, adolescent bundle of nerves to expend his energy in a more desirable manner. He was happy to run away! He began to look forward to the running, and as a result his body language considerably relaxed and he sometimes even offered play behaviors. We did use treats at the beginning of the program, but found that the running was a more desired reward for this particular dog.

- While I understand the science behind this program, my client didn't have to in order to practice at home and see results. This is critical to me—it doesn't do the client any good if I'm the only one who can perform the treatment. It's true that as a professional I am more aware of environments and able to set scenarios up more efficiently, but this is still a very practical program for the pet owner.

Before we began BAT, the owner was considering possibly rehoming this dog. After our sessions the owner realized his dog's aggression was based in fear, he learned how to recognize when his dog was uncomfortable, and BAT gave him a way to teach his dog more desirable behaviors. They continue to be a great team!

Primary protocol for reactivity
Trainer and Owner of When Hounds Fly
Toronto, Ontario, Canada
www.whenhoundsfly.com

I first learned about Behavior Adjustment Training in the fall of 2009. At that point, I had been working on Duke's (my rescue Beagle) on-leash reactivity for over three years.

Prior to being introduced to Behavior Adjustment Training, I had primarily been using operant methods with food reinforcement—exercises like "Watch me" and "Look at that," and reinforcing Duke for polite greetings with dogs. These methods had produced good results over those three years for Duke. During that period, Duke even attended group classes at busy indoor training halls and he was fine, although he was heavily managed.

As I started up own my training business, I taught others with reactive dogs the same exercises that I was taught—operant methods with food reinforcement. For most dogs, the owners were thrilled with the results they saw. Some dogs improved miraculously in a matter of weeks – so much so that their owners could take them anywhere again and no longer worry about their reactivity. While I was thrilled for them, it left me wondering why I had been unable to achieve that sort of change with Duke. So, my quest for an answer continued.

That quest led me serendipitously to Behavior Adjustment Training. It was on a lunch break at a Karen Pryor Academy workshop that I was introduced to it briefly. Searching for it online took me to Grisha's resource page, and the rest is history. Since incorporating Behavior Adjustment Training into my toolbox, I have found it to be the primary protocol I use and prescribe for treating reactivity. I've achieved the greatest breakthroughs in helping reactive dogs through its use. I believe that those dogs that struggle with pure classical counter-conditioning, or operant methods using food reinforcement find their salvation in Behavior Adjustment Training.

What I find most compelling about Behavior Adjustment Training is it allows a dog to relearn natural distance increasing behaviors. After years of training with food reinforcement, a reactive dog can end up heeling past rows and rows of triggers. Certainly that is incredibly liberating for the owner, but to me, it always seemed kind of mechanical for the dog. In contrast, in just one or two sessions of Behavior Adjustment Training, we see dogs offer an amazing array of behaviors – head turns, lip kicks, sniffs, yawns, scratches, sits, downs, and many more. Also, the absence of food forces handlers to be honest about what a dog's true threshold is, and begin work at that point, instead of starting at an artificial threshold that can be supported by the presence of food.

In the last year, my clients and I have celebrated a lot of successes thanks to Behavior Adjustment Training—one Mini Schnauzer that had not met another dog in over two years, that can now visit the nearby dog run and make friends, a Maltese-cross that used to spin in the air at the sight of another dog that can now walk right past another barking, snarling dog, to my boy Duke, who can happily resume sniffing the ground as dogs that used to bother him pass by.

BAT creates an atmosphere of trust between the dog and the handler
Casey Lomonaco, KPA CTP, APDT
Trainer and Owner of Rewarding Behaviors Dog Training
www.rewardingbehaviors.com
Endicott, New York, USA

Why exactly do I like Behavior Adjustment Training so much? I thought about this question when Grisha informed me she was releasing a new book. There are a number of reasons I really enjoy using this technique both with my own dogs and my client dogs. These include:

- It gives dog owners incentive to learn to read their dog's body language. Any trainer will tell you that this critical skill is the foundation of creating both empathy toward and a relationship with an animal of any other species. While many of my clients have said, "I wish my dog would just talk to me," BAT teaches them that dogs actually do talk to them in a language they can learn to understand and use to their training advantage.

- It creates a relationship and atmosphere of trust between the dog and handler. Like other dog-friendly behavior modification techniques, it removes the oppositional barriers created by traditional training while empowering both the dog and the owner. The owner is empowered by having tangible skills to immediately reduce her dog's stress, arousal, and frustration levels. The dog is empowered because she learns that she has the ability to control her environment through communicating her needs to her owner. It's a win/win!

- No more waiting to start on critical behavior modification. It's not uncommon for me to get a severely obese and very reactive dog in my practice. Often, it is extremely difficult to motivate these dogs with food initially, and I never want to tell a handler, "We can start work once you get the weight off your dog." BAT allows us to begin training right away, using the rewards the dog is already receiving or desiring from the environment. This is helpful to the dog's emotional health (through stress reduction), and physical health (once the owner has the tools needed to walk/live with the dog successfully, the dog will get more exercise and the weight will begin coming off)!

- It provides handlers with a tangible, effective, and thorough introduction to the critical concept of the Premack Principle. Many novice handlers have a hard time identifying environmental reinforcers and using them effectively along with primary reinforcement (often, food) in the development and maintenance of behaviors. BAT helps dog owners become better dog handlers—the lessons learned in BAT apply directly toward other aspects of living with dogs, including refining manners and other behaviors in "every day" life situations.

- BAT is flexible. I've used BAT with both reactive dogs who would like to increase distance from their triggers as well as with frustrated dogs that want to decrease the distance to the trigger but don't yet know how to retain their composure to earn that opportunity.

- BAT plays well with others! BAT is not exclusive—I have a number of clients who use BAT techniques in conjunction with Look at That and other Control Unleashed games in addition to simple "Open Bar, Closed Bar" classical conditioning techniques—sometimes all of these techniques will be used within a single session!

- It's fun! Last of all, Behavior Adjustment Training is fun for dogs and their people. Above and beyond anything else, trainers know that the only way owners follow through with training protocols consistently and reliably is if doing so is enjoyable for them and gives them results. BAT offers both to harried clients and owners of reactive dogs!

Shelter dog trainer BAT experience
Alice Tong, LCSW
Shelter Dog Trainer
Oakland, California, USA
http://tiny.cc/alicetongdogs

As a Shelter Dog Trainer, I see a lot of dogs with reactivity to and fear of other dogs, children, or men. With limited space and time in a shelter environment and high noise and stress levels, shelter dogs need to gain progress with these issues and become more adoptable as quickly as possible. Using Grisha's BAT I have not only seen dogs gain progress with these issues quickly and effectively, they have simultaneously become more confident and sociable by using (and sometimes re-learning) their calming signals. In the shelter environment we are able to have access to multiple "neutral dogs" to use for BAT sessions, and thus can have some consistency to work with a dog more than just once a week. I have worked with many shelter dogs that tended to become immediately over-stimulated when exiting their confined living spaces, and yet were still able to respond well to BAT sessions, often coming back more relaxed. This is not a surprise when I think about how in a BAT session, a shelter dog is given hope again that he/she can actually have an effect on their environment through instinctive calming signals, rather than needing to resort to barking, lunging, or biting.

BAT has also strengthened my ability as a shelter dog trainer to build a more healing relationship with individual dogs by becoming even more adept at observing the subtleties of their body and facial movements. Even the slightest turn of the head, an eyebrow muscle lifting a bit, or an increase in rate of respiration, could be an important signal for the trainer to read, and may determine how fast or slow the dog progresses. With so many dogs in the shelter who need help and attention, it is a wonderful way to naturally get to know each dog's personality by "listening" to their body language through their preferred calming signals. If I am reading the dog well enough, the dog can begin to work his/her own program without the micro-management that often occurs with on-cue handler work. BAT succeeds in increasing a reactive shelter dog's confidence and decreasing feelings of fear and insecurity, resulting in a dog that no longer needs to act out through reactive/aggressive behaviors. I am excited for BAT to reach not only more trainers and shelter workers, but the average owner as well. By learning BAT, owners can learn to "hear" what their dogs are saying, their dogs can feel understood and empowered, and the relationship between them can reach new depths they never knew they could have.

More aware, more creative trainers
Elizabeth Haysom
Dog Handler at FCCW

I have been learning to train dogs full-time for about 15 months and my training partner, Teresa Mullins, a year longer than that. We are cellmates, with our shelter rescue dog, in a maximum-security prison where we participate in a dog program called Pixie's Pen Pals. Virginia Broitman is our outside trainer who encourages us to understand the science of operant conditioning and to master a range of behavioral techniques.

The first dog Teresa and I used BAT on was an 8-month old male border collie mix who was aloof and very fearful. Unfortunately, he looked like a cuddly panda bear so officers wanted to touch and hug him. Consequently, our top priority was to teach him to enjoy people.

One mistake we made with our BAT technique was that we frequently did the approach and retreat with officers who had their backs turned to us. We decided to do it this way because frontal approaches always resulted in the officer moving towards us and reaching for Zephyr, which would in turn put him over threshold. (As inmates it can be awkward to ask an officer not to do something. Nonetheless, a year later, the officers have become interested in the work we are doing and are now often eager to assist with training. They ask good questions and will stand still!)

Zephyr

After daily BAT sessions over several weeks, Zephyr's confidence grew and he began to choose to interact with people. Then he started to nip them in the butt whenever he thought he could get away with it. Not good for officer-inmate relations! Not good for the program! We realized that Zephyr had developed a false confidence from his rear approaches, and we had to start all over from the front—now with the learned nipping behavior.

Another incidental problem was that his new owners were not willing or interested in continuing his BAT training, which was not complete when he was adopted. Zephyr therefore had a difficult transition to his new home, where he gave a level 3 bite to a person's leg.

After that rocky start, we have become much more adept at reading the dog and refining the functional reward, and BAT has seeped into many aspects of our training. For example, our current dog, Enzo, a 4-year old male beagle mix, would put his teeth on us if we tried to clip his front toe nails. We desensitized him to front paw handling and the clippers, but it was elements of BAT that have really made an impact.

Enzo didn't like to be held in a person's lap. We trained him to "snuggle" but it was obvious he was still uneasy and we wanted him to be completely relaxed about the experience. So every time he was in our lap and showed the slightest relaxation, we encouraged him to get down. Quickly he was coming and going. After several weeks he began to ask to get in our laps. We then added the toe nail clipping elements – handling his paws, nails, touching him with clippers and rewarding him with treats.

Enzo

It took six weeks before we cut a nail, but Enzo allowed every moment of the experience. At any time, he could choose to leave my lap. He offered his paw when he was ready. Now he frequently leaves after a toe or two and then returns a few minutes later to finish the rest.

Sometimes I think he is exploring the contract we have established—if I'm uncomfortable, I don't have to. I also think he is exploring his relationship with us.

This, I believe, is the most significant lesson for me. Reinforcements such as food and toy play are marvelously effective, but many of our rescue dogs won't eat under stress and have no interest in toy play. They also frequently have poor or little experience with appropriate relationships with people. Because BAT teaches the dog he can retreat, he can choose, he doesn't have to endure or submit to "horrible" things, BAT has helped many of our dogs find appropriate ways to cope with the humans in their lives. Because BAT teaches us to watch (and learn) the dog's body language (to respect that information!), to stay under threshold, to discover what motivates—interests—the dog beyond food, to use the environment—distance, sniffing, rolling, digging—to reinforce desired replacement behaviors, we are much better trainers. We are more aware, more creative.

Ironically because of BAT, Teresa and I have been less focused on obedience and more focused on fundamental behavioral issues, which has resulted in more efficient obedience training. With BAT we work towards a cooperative trust with the dogs in our care. With Enzo that trust has transformed a withdrawn animal into a relaxed, friendly, bright-eyed companion.

Fearful of riding mowers
Lauren O'Dell
Dog Handler at FCCW

I work as a dog handler for Pixie's Pen Pals, which places shelter dogs with inmates for obedience training prior to adoption, and I'd like to share a BAT success story.

Sidney

Sidney was very sweet, but she was also fearful of large, moving objects, especially riding mowers. One morning, I saw the mowers entering the compound and I brought her to the fenced play area where she could play with other dogs. But as the mowers went back and forth around us, Sidney's anxiety level increased, so I leashed her back up and began doing BAT exercises.

As the mowers came near the fence, we'd approach them at a normal pace, and I made sure to stop before Sidney tensed up. Then we'd quickly turn and run back to our starting point, while I praised and treated her. Sidney loved the idea of running away and it quickly became a fun game for her. We did several more approaches, always staying sub-threshold. In a short while (about 20 minutes), she was able to calmly walk right up to the fence as the mowers passed by.

Grass is mown here once a week, so we did BAT sessions again for a total of three sessions. By that point, when Sidney saw the mower, she'd become excited and look to me for a treat. Her "monster" had turned into an object she looked forward to seeing.

Waltzing through the grass with glee
Jennifer Kszepka
Dog Handler at FCCW

The successful application of BAT with my current dog, Nadia, astounded me. It was easy to use and I'm thrilled with Nadia's joyful emotional response.

Nadia

What began as her reluctance to walk in tall, wet grass turned into a full-blown fear when I decided to pull her into the grassy area she had been using for elimination. Occasionally, I've done this with other dogs in my care when they've 'put on the brakes' and the issue resolved quickly. But after 2-3 weeks of using leash pressure to guide Nadia into the grassy area, it was pretty clear this technique was the wrong choice for her. She developed a negative association with that particular area of grass, even if it was freshly mowed and dry.

My next idea was to wait her out, and treat her when she made even the slightest step. I did see minute progress after doing this repeatedly over two days. And then things took a dramatic, downward turn. As she was eliminating there one morning, loud thunder suddenly roared from the sky. In that instant, Nadia became afraid of all grassy areas. (Where we live, there are 12 large sections of grass divided by sidewalks.)

Feeling very defeated, I sat for a few hours and tried to formulate an elaborate desensitization plan. Then I remembered having watched the BAT DVD and figured we'd give that a try.

I began using BAT in a section she had seldom been to, and within 3-4 minutes, she was walking through the grass beautifully. I moved from one grassy area to another, using BAT each time, and having the same level of success. Nadia became more enthusiastic with each session, and I was overjoyed!

The real test came when I finally made my way to the original section of grass where the drama began. In this area, I had to increase my distance and take much smaller steps. I also had to use BAT entering this grassy area from all directions. After several sessions, over a 2-day period, Nadia and I began waltzing through the grass with glee.

BAT is amazing. Thanks, Grisha, for sharing your brilliant ideas. It has made the work I do with dogs much simpler.

On the BATwagon!
Nancy Yamin, CPDT-KA
Guild Certified Tellington TTouch Practitioner
www.MuttsBetter.com

When I read the premises that BAT is based on I knew immediately that it was brilliant, and the results I have witnessed are amazing. As a positive dog trainer and a Tellington TTouch Practitioner, BAT was the missing link for me. It is a great combination of teaching a dog to use better signals and empowering them to remain calm. My initial use of BAT was with a dog who reacted by barking, lunging, and spinning at any and all noises and movements, especially on walks. This included cars, strollers, bicycles, deer, people, trees, you name it.

I had already started using other positive methods in our first session, and the going was slow with very mixed results. At the second session we used BAT with a stroller starting at a distance of around 120 feet as anything closer caused the dog to react. Within twenty minutes this dog remained calm as the stroller with a person pushing it went right by him. A few minutes later when a car drove up the street and there was no reaction whatsoever, the dog's owner looked at me and I looked at her and we were both amazed and thrilled. In that moment I knew that what I was seeing was just the beginning of many more BAT successes to come.

Since then I have used BAT with dog reactive dogs, for teaching an older dog not to be bothered by the younger dog in the house, with aggressive dogs, with a dog who guarded her owner and one who guarded the car, a dog that alert barked at any human in sight, and in many other situations as well. The program is clear, concise, science based and easy to implement. I am glad to have BAT as a great addition to my toolbox, one that I know I will be using frequently.

Breakthrough
Kiki Yablon with Pigeon
USA

I think of BAT as a way for my dog-reactive Shepherd mix, Pigeon, to negotiate with me. "If I turn away, we don't have to go over there, right?" I do my best to make sure she is right, and as a result she's learned that she can control our distance from another dog with smaller, less dramatic gestures.

But the "magic" (or really, the science) is that BAT doesn't just help a dog communicate her preferred distance. It can actually decrease the preferred distance. Gaining control over her environment can make a dog feel better about her environment.

A big BAT breakthrough came for us in August. I confess that I do pretty much all my BAT on walks; for semiformal setups, I use the many dogs left out all day behind fences in my Chicago neighborhood. On this particular day we approached a house where there's often a Malamute behind the fence. The Malamute usually runs to the fence when he hears another dog; when he gets there he sometimes stands, sometimes lies down, sometimes play bows. Still, Pigeon had always acted as though he were the most offensive dog in the world.

This day I stopped about ten feet from the corner of the yard on the sidewalk to let Pigeon get a look and make a decision. She looked at the dog, then looked at me. I marked, and we retreated. We came back and did it again. On the third approach, as we walked back toward the fence, she didn't look at the dog at all. She kept trotting forward down the sidewalk. I decided to follow her lead. She trotted purposefully all the way past the yard without glancing at, much less reacting to, the Malamute. We have had many more walk-by moments since.

Thomas: A cautionary tale
Dani Weinberg, Ph.D.
Certified Dog Behavior Consultant at Dogs & Their People, Karen Pryor Academy Faculty, Author of "Teaching People Teaching Dogs"
Albuquerque, New Mexico, USA
http://home.earthlink.net/~hardpretzel/DaniDogPage.html

Note: All names of dogs and people have been changed.

This is the story of Thomas, a neutered Pit Bull/Blue Heeler mix, owned by a busy professional woman. More importantly, it's the story of how a successful BAT intervention can go wrong—not for lack of skill on the part of the trainer, nor for poor response on the part of the dog, but because the owners are not committed to the process. I have used BAT with other dogs and their supportive and grateful owners. It has always helped the dog to learn better coping strategies to deal with Scary Things, and it's easy to teach to owners as well so that they can use it immediately. That's why the Thomas case stands out for me as a cautionary tale.

When I first met Thomas, he was 19 months old, adopted from our local private shelter at about 6 months. All that his owner, Delia, knew about him was that he was a transfer from another shelter.

He was free-fed a "sensitive-stomach" food until I recommended a better quality food that he did well on. He had a good exercise schedule, walking daily and hiking on Sundays. Delia had been taking him to a traditional training school. What she learned there, she said, had made it possible for her to walk him. He wore a choke chain so she could "control him better."

Thomas is a high energy young dog who fits Jean Donaldson's description of the Tarzan type in her book *Fight! A Practical Guide to the Treatment of Dog-Dog Aggression* (see Resources). She writes on page 12: "Dogs that come on too strong [to other dogs]. They appear hypermotivated and have coarse social skills."

When Delia first adopted Thomas, she would take him to the dog park. That soon stopped when she saw him hyper-aroused and tipping over from play to aggression. He now has occasional play dates with a female dog but wears a muzzle so he does not injure her in his over-the-top play style.

Delia's main concern was Thomas' reactivity to people who came to the house. He would bark, growl, pull on the leash (he was always on-leash when visitors arrived), whine, shake, and, if he could, nip the visitor. Delia would "introduce" him to visitors in the front yard, with Thomas leashed, on his choke chain and muzzle. She would "make" him sit and then lie down. Then she would wait until he "calmed down"—at which point she would either put him in the back yard, out of the way, if the visitor was staying, or take him out so that they could take a walk with the visitor. Once on the walk, Thomas was fine and even allowed the visitor to pet him.

First session
I had asked that Thomas be in the back yard when I arrived so as to avoid an over-threshold introduction. Delia and I sat in the kitchen talking for a while, and then she brought him in. At my request, he was on-leash but not muzzled. He reacted in his usual aggressive manner upon seeing me. I wanted to learn more about him, so I did a few simple training exercises. When I tried to reinforce voluntary eye contact, he remained agitated, so I went back to simply clicking and treating him. He was very interested in the food. As long as I kept it flowing, he was relatively calm, but when I paused for a moment, he resumed his barking and lunging. Next, I tried to teach him to target my hand, and he learned that very quickly—but still reverted to aggressive behaviors when I paused.

I showed Delia how to play Look At That. Thomas learned the game quickly. I asked her to practice the game often but only when there were no triggers present. My plan for our next session was to use Look At That as a first step into BAT.

Second session

At my request, Delia had invited a friend, Ruth, to come and help. Ruth was someone Thomas had previously been reactive to in the front yard but not away from home on walks. Because he knew her and she was a frequent visitor, I decided to use her as our first helper.

We started with Bar Open/Bar Closed, with Ruth and me alternately appearing from behind a wall about 15 feet away. This simple counterconditioning technique seemed like a good foundation before starting BAT. Thomas soon began to give the desired response: see person and immediately turn to handler for his treat. He seemed impervious to Delia's very rough handling—jerking his leash and harshly asking him to sit every few seconds.

We gave Thomas another break outdoors while we discussed what had happened. In our next training period and after I had made a few appearances in a row, I decided to move a little closer. I appeared and took a few steps towards him, reducing the distance quickly to within about 5 feet. On my next appearance, I walked right up to him and offered him a handful of treats. He took them calmly. I repeated that on my next appearance, and he took the treats again. And then suddenly, he started barking, lunging, and trying to nip me. I had exceeded his tolerance for my proximity and inadvertently put him over his threshold. That can happen when the dog suddenly realizes how close the person is. He becomes anxious and reverts to his old behavior.

We gave Thomas another rest outdoors while I explained the objectives and method of BAT. The front yard was not very big, but we managed to plot out a path for BAT. Delia would handle Thomas, while Ruth and I, hidden around the corner of the house, would take turns appearing for the Look At That game. Our starting distance was about 35 feet. When that was going well, Delia and Thomas would gradually shorten the distance from us with each repetition.

To my delight, Thomas did very well. He remained calm and relaxed up to a distance of about 10 feet away. I decided to leave well enough alone and not push him beyond his threshold. We stopped, put him in the back yard to rest, and went indoors to discuss what had happened.

I left Delia that day with instructions to practice Bar Open/Bar Closed and Look At That on their walks, but only in the absence of triggers. Our plan for our next session was to invite Paul, a neighbor, and use him as a helper.

Before leaving, I suggested that Delia talk to her veterinarian about possibly doing a complete thyroid panel, on the chance that hypothyroidism might be contributing to the aggression. I also suggested that she give Thomas Suntheanine, a natural calming supplement. I learned later that she had done neither. I also doubt that she practiced any of the techniques I had shown her.

We scheduled another session which Delia had to reschedule because of her work commitments. After that, we were unable to schedule any more sessions, ostensibly because Delia's work was just too demanding.

In spite of the good results we had seen in Thomas using BAT, it seemed to me that Delia had decided this was not going to work. Delia's force-based "training" of Thomas was, in her mind, the only way to modify his aggressive behavior. She had been skeptical about my methods from the start but expressed willingness to try them. I had taken her at her word.

It's also worth noting what her goals were for Thomas, as expressed in the behavior questionnaire she had filled out before our first meeting: "I want Thomas to be able to play and socialize with other animals, fully and joyfully. I want my friends and family to be able to sit with him and see the beautiful, sweet soul that I experience....I am confident that Thomas will grow into being a perfect dog."

The combination of unrealistic goals and force-based training are deadly to BAT work. BAT requires the full participation of the dog as he learns to make better choices. It also requires commitment and compliance from the owner. The saddest part of this story is knowing that Thomas was ready and willing to do this, if only his owner had let him.

Deepened relationship
Leonard "Buzz" Cecil, CTDI, Cert.CBST
Trainer and Owner of Auf den Hund Gekommen Training and Behavior Modification
Ettingen, Switzerland

I have a client with a fearful dog: people, autos, trams, and other dogs. It took 6 sessions, but now the two of us are like long lost buddies. Last week we did a simple walk through the village (8th weekly "session") and there were no problems with cars, trams or people. At first the client herself was apprehensive, but when she saw how relaxed the dog was with her entire environment, she was gushing.

Approaching dogs are still a problem, but today with a new set-up dog it only took us 25 minutes to get from 40 yards to 3 yards. Meets and greets are next on the list, but the client is now confident that SHE will be able to help her dog when I finish helping and that has to be the goal - their deepened relationship. Looking forward to the full weekend seminar, so that I can optimize MY application of BAT for my clients. Great stuff!

Enhances the relationship with my dogs
Debi Carpenter with Emsie and Harry
USA

I just wanted to say how grateful I am for the BAT training you have made available on DVD. I missed the chance to see you here in Boise when you presented this training so its especially nice to have the DVD format for distance learning. My last dog was a 200-pound English Mastiff and therapy dog named Eli, who had no issues or troubles with anything. He was bulletproof. A year ago Eli passed away so I decided to adopt two Border Terrier puppies this past fall—a boy, Harry and a girl that I named Emsie. At 9 weeks of age, Harry was more shy and Emsie was super outgoing, even though I put a lot of emphasis on socializing both pups, i.e. puppy kindergarten and numerous outings and play dates with safe dogs.

Emsie and Harry at the beach

Emsie somehow began to develop fear reactions around a lot of things like other dogs, men, and many other things commonly found on an average walk. I remembered that I had been given your seminar flyer and decided to look up your work and I am so glad I did. I really appreciate your tips, guidance, and help in choosing the BAT Organic Socialization DVD for my little scared dog, Emsie. I have been working with her using the techniques demonstrated in the BAT Organic Socialization DVD and it has made a huge difference. What I notice most is that her trust in my guidance around what we do together has increased significantly. I can tell that Emsie's confidence in what I ask her to do, and what she tells me she can tolerate (her threshold) based on BAT techniques, is key not only to her socialization but also to our bonding. Rather than exposing her to various situations and hoping for the best outcome I now feel like I have a foundation to work with Emsie from and we have fun doing it. I LOVE working with her in this way!

Most of all, I want you to know what a difference this technique makes and how much it enhances my relationship with my dog.

Dog-centric and versatile

Tena Parker, M.Ed.
Pittsburgh, PA
www.successjustclicks.wordpress.com

What I love about BAT is that there is a ridiculous amount of freedom to work within the protocol and because of this, it has a myriad of uses. What I love more about BAT is that it puts the dog in the driver's seat and it keeps his/her stress level and well-being in the forefront of the behavioral work. The goal of BAT is to work the dogs below their threshold level but to do that, the handler and trainer must be continually evaluating the stress and anxiety the dog may be displaying. The training moves forward not at the rate the handler desires but at the rate the dog feels comfortable: because the work is done based on the dog's level of stress the dog is really in control of the process, he/she isn't thrown into the deep-end and expected to swim. If the dog does go off the deep-end (becomes too stressed and reacts) the handler must advocate for that dog and get him/her out of the situation—the dog doesn't have to struggle through a reaction, the handler takes control and gets the heck out of Dodge. Really, the dog-centric nature of BAT and its versatility really sets it apart from other protocols out there.

I've been using BAT towards a slightly less common goal (or so I gather) with one of my personal dogs. Over the years I'd used a variety of exercises and tools to help her feel more comfortable around other dogs and they had been instrumental in our progress but we plateaued and got very stuck about teaching her to greet dogs appropriately. She wants to greet the other dogs but at the same time, she is not comfortable and gets concerned about the interaction. If she were to greet nose-to-nose with another dog, she'd get stiff, the other dog would get stiff and she would react to the stiffness with a reactive display. She really doesn't know how to offer a calming signal in the situation to help keep the other dog relaxed and she doesn't know how to end the greeting without a reaction (since she learned that if she reacted, the social interaction would end). This has been my project.... teaching her to offer a calming signal during a greeting so we can end the interaction without a reaction. It's a work in progress but she will now offer a calming signal right next to a dog to end the interaction and add distance, which is a great improvement. The next step is a calming signal while doing a circular greeting and eventually a nose-to-nose greeting. While we had gotten stuck using different methods, we've made quite a bit of progress through BAT and I cannot wait to see where we end up!

Tremendous improvement in clients' dogs

Lisa Mullinax, CPDT-KA
Trainer and Owner of 4PAWS UNIVERSITY
Sacramento, California, USA
www.4pawsu.com

I integrated Grisha's BAT approach into my behavior program about two years ago. Since that time, I have seen a tremendous improvement in my clients' reactive dogs. My clients start to see progress right away and love the cooperative approach. Because BAT does not require the use of special equipment or food rewards, dog owners of all skill levels can easily implement the exercises in any environment and situation. I have found BAT to be an invaluable addition to my behavior practice.

Gives the dog an element of choice and control

Chirag Patel
Clinical Animal Behaviourist Centre manager, The Company of Animals Training and Behaviour Centre
Surrey, UK
www.companyofanimals.co.uk/dog-training-and-animal-behaviour-centre

BAT was introduced to The Company of Animal's Training and Behaviour Centre earlier this year. Our caseload is primarily dog–dog and dog–human aggression, so Grisha's visit to us was very welcomed. We love to listen and learn from other trainers and really enjoyed what Grisha had to say about BAT and the workshop she gave with real clients and reactive dogs.

What we really liked about BAT is that it gives the dog an element of choice and control. It's also great that by working through BAT the human end of the leash learns to better read and understand their four-legged friend. BAT is user friendly and we have found it easy to integrate into our client's daily routine and existing training programs. We have found that having BAT as an additional tool in our tool box has been wonderful and would strongly suggest taking the time to learn about it and giving it a go!

(He's also given his permission to share this note: "By the way Grisha, the gorgeous wirehaired Dachshund who we worked with during your visit came back for a follow-up visit and his owner could not believe the difference in his behaviour around other dogs. He was better able to cope with the presence of bouncier dogs; he approached to sniff them and chose to move away instead of growling and snapping. His general demeanor was far more relaxed and happier.")

Coco in Shanghai

Beverley Courtney
Trainer and Owner of Good for Dogs!
Worcestershire, UK
www.goodfordogs.co.uk

I had visited Coco three times for some basic manners training to which she responded extremely well. Coco was an eight-month-old chocolate Miniature Poodle bitch, entire, and with no previous training. She lived in deep Herefordshire countryside up a lane, so saw very few visitors and no passers-by. When she did see them, her response was full-alert shrieky barking, backing off, and if free she would run around barking, uncatchable.

Her owners asked me to board her for ten days while they went to find accommodation in Shanghai to which they had been posted, so I got to know her a whole lot better! And the first thing I discovered was that on our suburban estate with constant comings and goings, I couldn't get out of the door with Coco without her scanning for any noise or movement at all, and then erupting into shrieky barking.

So we started BAT. I chose a quiet time of day, walked her outside and waited for her to spot something, I'd wait for a calm response and then we'd both turn and go back a bit. This was repeated till another distraction came along and we'd work that one. The postman was always a good bet, as he would follow a random progress down the road, up and down driveways, so was continually disappearing and reappearing.

Within a few days I was able to walk Coco about the estate, allowing her time to assess the threat and if necessary back off. Sometimes she would just look at me and say "I'm ok with this," so we could keep walking.

When her owners came to collect her I took them outside to teach them how to handle her this new way. While we talked, a car pulled up directly opposite and the driver helped a very infirm old lady from the car, up her drive to her house. He was leaning over her and they shuffled along together. To the astonishment of Coco's owners, once we'd backed off a few yards she was able to study this scene, then turn quietly and give her attention to them.

I was thrilled to receive this letter from them a month or so after they moved: "I want to thank you for all the help you have given with Coco as so much was achieved in a short time, making a huge difference in her behaviour. We would have still been floundering, doing all the wrong things, without your help. I was concerned how her behaviour was going to be after her journey here. We left her with the cargo people in Heathrow before the flight to Hong Kong. Once we arrived we waited to see her before she was taken to a kennel in Hong Kong for a 3-day stay whilst her paperwork was processed. Coco was brought to us in the airport for a brief visit. She certainly seemed to take in all the new surroundings very well. We continued the journey to Shanghai thinking we may not see her again: it was a very anxious time. When Coco was brought to us here in the apartment she was fine and ran around taking it all in.

Since staying with you Coco's behaviour has changed considerably: she is so much calmer with children and much more biddable when on walks. She still has her moments with wanting to chase cars, barking and lunging at people when on or off the lead. I use the BAT technique: it works really well though I had not had much chance to practice before leaving.

Since being here Coco has been really good in the gardens where I take her for a walk. There's a lot of activity - people walking, doing exercises, gardeners, bikes, children going to school. Using BAT has been a godsend with Coco: she doesn't bark at anyone and passes by, walking nicely by my side so much more confident in herself.

This is amazing as she has experienced so many new things here, along with the general noise, traffic and lots of people around. There are quite a few dogs here, mostly on leads, and I have to say this is still a problem. It's difficult to use BAT in these situations as the other owner walks away very quickly, giving no opportunity to move to a distance, also I am mindful of the noise factor so I go far away too. They speak little English, so I can't explain to them. Soon we move to a house on a compound—there should be some westerners there who may be amenable to allowing their dogs to be used in a "set up" situation like you suggested. We have visited the Pet Park and Coco had great fun. She was more intent on just running free than interacting with the other dogs. She does love to run and this was the first opportunity she has had.

I think that the BAT technique has had a very positive effect on Coco and I am interested in using it further, especially concerning other dogs." BAT has travelled from Seattle to Shanghai, via rural Worcestershire!

BAT has been miraculous for Sam

Sally A. Bushwaller, CPDT-KA
Staff Trainer, AnimalSense Canine Training & Behavior, Inc.
Chicago, Illinois, USA
www.animalsense.com

I have had great success using BAT and other functional rewards for helping heal some broken dogs. One dog in particular is a Pit mix or Heinz 57 dog I've been working with. We'll call him Sam.

In February 2011, we began working together. Sam had spent some significant time at a no kill shelter and had bitten (with punctures) a shelter worker. Another shelter volunteer developed a relationship with Sam and adopted him, determined to fix him. In addition to reactivity to people, Sam was also reactive to dogs.

Initially Sam couldn't look at a dog from more than ½ block away without reacting. He also reacted to most people he encountered on walks, especially "odd-looking" people. I began doing BAT sessions with Sam and his owner, using my dog as a decoy. Each session Sam continued to improve greatly. After just 4 sessions our dogs were able to parallel walk, then meet with a fence between them and then without the fence.

Improvement really snowballed after that. In a short period of time, Sam was walking side-by-side on daily walks with one or two other dog "buddies" and his owner was allowing him occasional off-lead play with a neighbor's dog.

We have now done 11 BAT sessions. The last 4 sessions have been at dog parks. We don't go inside, we work outside at the fence. Sam can sniff just about any dog who comes up to him without reacting, even if the dog inside the park is a little barky. We are still working on surprise dog appearances, but even that is improving. The owner says BAT has been miraculous for Sam, he is truly a different dog than he was just a few short months ago. He hardly pulls on walks anymore, because he's so much calmer and relaxed. Everyone is thrilled with his progress.

During this process, Sam's reactivity to people has mostly disappeared because the owner worked the BAT process each time Sam began to focus on anyone while on walks. Sam's owner is the ideal client. He keeps great notes on Sam's interactions with other dogs and has embraced BAT, using it on all his walks for every dog they encounter. Thanks to his owner's loving heart and dedication to BAT training, an impossible-to-place dog has been rehabilitated.

Turning point
Jude Azaren and Dusty
USA

Two years of working various aggression protocols had not put much of a dent in Dusty's human aggression, but in August of 2009, Dusty had his first BAT session shortly after Grisha introduced BAT to an aggression e-list in which I participated. A friend and I drove to the home of an acquaintance (the decoy). When Dusty got out of the car and saw the decoy in the street, he was very fearful. He tucked his tail and tried to jump back in the car. This surprised me because the decoy wasn't even near us and Dusty was usually not fearful at that particular distance. So I walked him around the street a bit until his tail untucked and he seemed interested in his surroundings.

When Dusty seemed better, we started to work. We did several BAT variations and mixed them all up. The decoy walked towards us; we walked towards the decoy; we did parallel walking; we did pass-bys. Sometimes, my friend walked with the decoy. Most of the time, the decoy walked alone. Each trial showed improved demeanor on Dusty's part.

Distance was the main reinforcer: Dusty and I walked away, ran away, or the decoy moved away. Sometimes Dusty got treats, and I often praised him for making good decisions. Behaviors that were rewarded included every visible degree of relaxation: unfurrowing his forehead, relaxing the jaw, soft eyes, relaxed blinking, eye contact with me, watching the decoy move without stiffening, air scenting in the decoy's direction, passing the decoy without any sign of lunging.

What I loved about this entire session was that Dusty was totally engaged in the work and was happy to try to figure out the right responses to get to run away, to get the decoy moving, to get a treat, etc. This whole experience was so obviously a very good one for him. We stopped to walk at a park on the way home. Suddenly two teenagers ran straight for us from only about 30 feet away. I braced myself for Dusty to lunge and bark and was about to do a fast about turn and run away. But Dusty looked at them and calmly looked at me as they were VERY quickly approaching. His look said, "Can we run away now, Mom?" and we did just that. I was shocked that he figured this out and remained calm with just the single BAT session we had done an hour earlier.

We weren't done training after just one session, of course, but it had a powerful impact and led to Dusty generalizing his new confidence to numerous other fears he had. BAT has been the turning point in Dusty's aggression treatment. He is a much more relaxed, happy dog. I can't express my enthusiasm for this protocol and my gratitude to Grisha for sharing it.

Stealth BAT
Deborah Campbell with Flossy
UK

Flossy is a working Collie who joined my home from a foster career and before that, she was in a less-than-suitable family home where she did not receive the socialisation she should have had. It is possible that strong working stock genetics have played a part in her over-reactivity as well. At the time of writing this, Flossy was around 14 months old. I attended Grisha's first UK seminar straight after rescuing Flossy, after hearing about the technique on US forums and on Patricia McConnell's "At the Other End of the Leash" blog, after initially starting out on the road with general desensitisation and counter-conditioning.

Flossy is overwhelmed with strangers close by and reacts aggressively to normal approaches. This is her overriding issue. She is also nervous towards some dogs and sometimes inanimate objects such a monoliths on walks etc.—things that are out of the ordinary.

When I gave a home to Flossy, I wanted to learn as much as possible about how I could help her and so I purchased the BAT *Organic Socialization* DVD and began doing 'stealth' or 'undercover' BAT in the local high street on lead, all the while attempting to remain below threshold. There were marked improvements towards her ability to switch off from people doing their own thing and walking around, within about a month of 2-3 short sessions a week in the high street.

Other improvements have come off lead. Most of Flossy's walks are off lead in the forests/woods and it is here when strangers can be walking down the same path or can be appearing from nowhere, that Flossy can react. Flossy walks ahead most of the time with my other dog, a well socialized male Collie, but has been known to get out of her depth and react if someone is up ahead—and even worse, should they stop to look at her or talk to her.

Slowly, Flossy has learnt, despite the distance between Flossy and I, to disengage from the stranger walking towards her, by sniffing the grass or looking back for example and I have learnt to watch the moment Flossy stops to look and mark this exact moment she disengages with a YES and a walk backwards and reward (double reward of distance and then a treat!). This then allows Flossy and I the chance to divert off the path or to continue BAT 'trials' until past the stranger, with no reaction. There are still some issues with strangers standing and not walking or strangers talking to her which I am close enough to control, however, but I continue to use these chances to set up mini BAT sessions. Even if Flossy reacts, I use the opportunity for a very short BAT attempt with Flossy on lead or off lead, whilst the offending person is walking off!

I have learnt to use BAT by herself out and about and have found it incredibly easy to do and empowering. I thoroughly recommend the BAT DVD. Watching Flossy learn has been a wonderful thing. Of course, there are setbacks and the journey is not over yet, but time spent with Flossy out on walks is enjoyable for all concerned.

So, away from the home and garden, BAT has given Flossy the knowledge that she DOES have a choice to get herself out of a situation calmly and she can ignore people—just like her other dog! This in turn has meant she is more relaxed around people now out on walks and she can walk past them or with them, off lead without reacting.

I do not need nor expect Flossy to love everyone—I just want her to make better choices in normal situations and to (albeit slowly due to my lack of formal set-ups) learn a skill to get herself out of situations if she feels too close, without aggression.

Simple enough for everyday use
Jonas Valancius
Trainer and Owner of Reksas Dog Training School
Kaunas City, Lithuania
www.reksas.lt

I am a dog trainer in Lithuania. Now here's the time when dog training culture is raising quickly in my country and in all the World. More people like to be responsible owners and are searching for positive ways of communication with their dogs even when they have hard behavior problems. I found Grisha's BAT as one of the most innovative ways.

In my practice BAT techniques are useful in several aspects:

- It teaches the owner non aversive ways of behavior modification
- It makes the owner deepen his knowledge into his dog's body language
- It is simple enough for everyday use (like Mac plug and play), easy to learn, dynamic and very practical
- It is healthy: the owners must move.

I am happy that I've found BAT.

A shelter dog in my arms
Ryan Neile
Animal Behaviourist at Blue Cross
Burford, Oxfordshire, UK
www.bluecross.org.uk

We have a very small female Norfolk/Cairn terrier type called Alice (currently kenneled in our Southampton branch). Alice is under-socialized, fearful of dogs, easily aroused and finds it hard to cope with the slightest degree of frustration. As you can imagine, these ingredients make the perfect recipe for an extremely reactive dog! To make matters worse, her previous owner was an 'old school' dog trainer, who despite my best efforts to help her, became very angry and confrontational with Alice whenever she failed to cope with another dog approaching her. Eventually the owner brought her to us for re-homing.

Prior to me seeing her she was barking, lunging, and spinning whenever other dogs where present. After spending some time with her, and after making a general evaluation, I picked her up. As I did this she immediately relaxed...which got me thinking! I set my replica dog up in the distance, and a few colleagues and I began doing BAT with her from this position (responding to her 'cut offs' by turning and walking away). It was very bizarre to feel a dog operating my entire body, like she was driving a giant forklift truck, or that giant robot at the end of the film Aliens with Sigourney Weaver! The other really interesting thing was feeling her heart beat on our skin as we held her. We became so much more in tune with her, and could really appreciate just how scared she was when other dogs where near. We could feel her heart rate slowing when we turned and walked away!!! It got me thinking how cool it would be to use heart rate monitors for all dogs in training (imagine an iPhone app that could do that?!).

Anyway, this was a huge success. She has come on in leaps and bounds, and we've now progressed to working on the ground, too. She's approached several dogs, and after meeting them appropriately, has gone off walking with them!!

So, now we are all going to the gym to build muscle so we can lift all the larger dogs!! Just joking!

A different and much happier dog
Susan Kennedy with JitterBug & puppy Snickers
USA

Our BAT experience was a happy accident oddly enough. I have always had "soft" pliable dogs in the past, always Border Collies or in one case a BC/Lab mix. When I decided on my McNab I knew they were different but I was not prepared for a houseguest who decided while he watched our dog for a few minutes that we needed to show a 7 week old puppy "who's Boss." He turned him upside down, dropped him, kicked him and when I pulled in the driveway I heard the screaming from my dog. Bottom line is after that day I had a reactive dog and it only became worse over the next few months as I had no clue what to do.

That began my quest. I went online, found TV commercials for "The Perfect Dog," studied with trainers, behaviorists. One suggested Agility and that proved to be a great call but not the answer to the problem. Friends loaned me DVD's and tried to help. I spared no expense and bought the BAT DVD set. I was in the middle of one of the other methods and put BAT aside (BAD idea)!! After hearing about BAT, I ordered the set, forgetting I already had it, found a great BAT trainer who got us started down the correct path and we took it and ran with it.

After seeing how realistic it was, I worked it like a full time job, and while we are not there completely, we are so far ahead from where we were it's a miracle and not a small one either. We can go places now without fear of him going ballistic and I have learned so many little things as we progress that I know how to calm him when we get in tough situations as happens in life. We recently got a puppy and for some odd reason, that seemed to improve his demeanor even more. I think he sees how much good attention the puppy gets and has decided he wants the same. Whatever it is, I know the pitfalls and with our puppy, I'm hoping to never need BAT. Although…if we needed it, I would begin it immediately and nip any potential problem in the bud. I can belabor the "if only I had done BAT sooner" point, but the fact is, we did it, we DO it, and it's made him into a different and much happier dog. Even his agility trainer notices it.

God Bless Grisha, you have changed our lives.

Breathe and trust your dog
Shelly Volsche
Trainer and Owner of Good Paws, LLC Dog Behavior and Nutrition Consulting
Las Vegas, Nevada, USA
www.GoodPawsTraining.com

I have been on the FunctionalRewards.com list for over a year, and I have experience with using BAT with my own dogs as well as client dogs. Initially, I thought of BAT as just another tool in the toolbox. It was great for working with frustrated greeters and fear reactive dogs.

My own dog, Calvin, was a demo dog for the Seattle seminar that can be seen on the Full Day Seminar DVD. It was on that day that I started to understand BAT more completely.

BAT is much more than a behavior modification technique. It is a philosophy on how to work with your dog, much in the way that clicker training is about more than how to mark and reward behavior. When Calvin and I were working on stage with Grisha, she said something incredibly important that I have held on to since. She told me to "breathe, and trust your dog." In that moment, I saw how important it is to let the dog learn and make decisions.

It is always scary to teeter on the edge of your dog's threshold. Yes, it is important to have a "plan B." You must have a way to "get out of dodge" if your dog is about to explode. But it is vital to know when your dog is simply observing and to learn to listen to your dog. You must let your dog collect information from his environment in order for him to learn that the world is not so scary. At some point, you must let go of the handlebars and let your dog learn to ride the bike of life.

In addition to doing setups, I now apply the philosophy of BAT in daily life with my dogs. If they stop on a walk and notice something, I don't immediately assume the worst and pull them away. Instead, I wait. I watch them and listen for signs of concern, but I wait. I wait for them to tell me if they are overwhelmed or ready to leave. Even if I am not doing a formal setup, I wait.

Thanks to BAT, I have learned to truly listen to my dog. I have learned to rebuild confidence in his ability to make decisions. Most importantly, I have learned this: "breathe, and trust your dog."

GLOSSARY

Agonistic display: According to Wikipedia, an agonistic display is "The combative or territorial behavior of an animal that feels threatened by or intends to threaten another animal, usually of the same species." In other words, agonistic displays are what most people, including me, call "aggression" although that's not technically correct. Agonistic displays in dogs can include barking, growling, lip curling, snarling, leaning forward, hackles up, lunging, air snapping, biting, and other negative reactions. Those behaviors are not always agonistic displays, but reading the whole picture can help you determine the dog's intentions.

Airlock: A buffer in front of exits so that the dog must go through two or more doors/gates in order to escape.

Behavior Adjustment Training (BAT): A philosophy and method of training that uses real-life rewards to teach dogs to meet their needs in socially acceptable ways.

Behavior Analysis: The scientific study of behavior (any measurable thing that a person or other animal does), which looks for environmental and biological factors that influence behavior. The term was coined by B.F. Skinner. Applied Behavior Analysis uses behavioral theory to change behavior. This often involves a functional assessment to discover the consequences that maintain the current behavior.

Bite Threshold: Level of stress or stimulation at which the dog resorts to biting.

Body Block: Use your body to back a dog away. Be assertive and move in quick, jerky motions, rather than slow fluid motions. You don't actually touch the dog. You're more like a Border Collie working sheep with intense eyes and quick motions, rather than an Australian Cattle Dog biting the ankle of cattle.

Choice Point: A situation in which the animal's environment prompts her to respond with a behavior. Choice points in BAT are skewed so that the dog is likely to choose to do the behavior you prefer.

Classical Conditioning: A process that gives an emotional charge to a neutral stimulus through association. When one stimulus consistently leads to another (click leads to treat), the emotional value of the second stimulus gets attached to the first one. So a dog who doesn't have any initial response to the clicker can develop one through classical conditioning. If she hears a click and then gets a tasty treat many times, she will begin to look happy and drool after hearing a click. Also known as Pavlovian conditioning.

Counter-conditioning (CC): A process that changes the emotional charge of a stimulus. Counter-conditioning can be classical or operant. For example, if a dog is afraid of children, classical CC would be to pair up the appearance of children with food. Every sighting of a child would earn the dog a treat. Done backwards (treat leads to appearance of child), the dog can be accidentally classically counter-conditioned to avoid cheese. BAT is an example of operant counter-conditioning. Operant CC changes the emotional charge of a stimulus by allowing dogs to self-soothe and influence the stimulus through their behavior.

Cut-off Signals: When two dogs meet, cut-off signals are behaviors that are requests for additional space or a reduction in the stress level of the meeting. Used to avoid conflict.

Decoys: Helpers you have arranged—people and dogs whose distance, motion, and other movements can be controlled so that you can expose your dog to these triggers without too much stress.

Default Behaviors: The set of behaviors a specific dog normally performs in response to an environment or stimulus. For example, many dogs have a default behavior of jumping and barking at the door or sitting on a rug in the kitchen to receive their meals. Default behaviors are what the dog does on his own without a human explicitly cueing him to do a particular behavior.

Discrimination: The process by which an animal learns to offer a behavior in response to certain stimuli and not others. For example, a dog may discriminate between children and adults, i.e., learn to not bark at adults, but may still bark at children. The sight of children and adults elicits different behaviors because they are perceived as different stimuli to the dog. Discrimination is the opposite of generalization.

Event Marker: Signal that indicates the dog's behavior is what you want and has earned reinforcement. Examples are clicker, verbal "Yes," visual hand-flash, or vibration collar for deaf dogs. You are "marking" the behavior when you use an event marker. Delay between event marker and treats is usually no more than about two seconds.

Functional behavior assessment: A formal analysis of the relationship between a target behavior and environmental events.

Functional Reward: If a behavior is done to achieve a particular consequence, that consequence is a functional reward for the behavior. Dogs do what works, i.e., dogs do whatever best earns a functional reward. With BAT, we look for the functional reward of the animal's reactivity ("real life" consequence that reinforces the behavior) and use that to reinforce behaviors that are more appealing to people.

Generalization: The process of learning that two events or stimuli should both trigger the same reaction. This is a critical process in any training, but especially when working with reactivity. Generalization is what makes the dog more predictable—situations that we consider similar are not necessarily similar to the dog, without generalization training.

Graduated Prompting: Series of prompts to help the dog make a good choice in the smallest, least intrusive way that works. If a smaller prompt doesn't work, use a more obvious one.

Lazy Bones BAT: Method to passively train the dog using the principles of BAT. Ideal for fence fighting and territoriality.

Management: Changing your dog's environment to make it impossible or unlikely that he'll do behavior you do not want him to do. Also known as "environmental engineering."

Magnet Effect: There is a certain distance from the trigger at which the dog is forced to deal with it. This is analogous to a magnetic field, where a magnet and a piece of metal can remain apart until they are close enough, at which point they are quickly drawn together. Even if they really want to just get away, many dogs are 'magnetically' drawn in and pull or run toward the trigger, barking and growling. We want to avoid the magnet effect.

Operant Conditioning: Type of learning in which a person or non-human animal changes behavior because of the environmental consequences of that behavior.

Premack Principle: Discovered by David Premack, this principle states that activities can be used as reinforcers. In particular, a behavior can be reinforced by the opportunity to do a more likely behavior. That is, if the animal gets to do a certain behavior right after doing a lower probability behavior, the lower probability behavior will be reinforced.

Problem Behavior: Behavior that you want your dog to stop doing—panic, aggressive displays, jumping up, pulling on-leash, and other negative behaviors.

Pro-social Behaviors: Behaviors used as communication to another dog (play bow, approach, etc.) that generally result in the other dog walking closer and engaging in social activity (sniffing, play, etc.). Pro-social behaviors are a type of social courtship.

Quadrant: In the theory of operant conditioning, learning is split into four quadrants: positive and negative reinforcement and positive and negative punishment. Positive and negative are indications of whether the learning took place because a stimulus was added (positive) or removed (negative).

Raise Criteria: Increase expectations on reinforceable behavior. For example, you might reward a dog for looking at you after looking at the trigger, but then you might raise criteria by waiting until your dog offered something more difficult, like sniffing the ground or a full-body turn. The trick with raising criteria is to only make it a little harder, so that your expectations are still easily met.

Reactivity: Fear, aggression, or frustration responses that are over the level that dog-savvy humans consider "normal."

Reinforcement: An event following a behavior that causes that behavior to be more likely in the future. Can be positive (think addition, like getting something the dog wants) or negative (think subtraction, like relief from stress or social pressure).

Replacement Behavior: Dog behavior you like or do not mind, which your dog can do instead of the problem behavior to earn the same functional reward as the problem behavior.

Setting Event: The general environment in which a behavior occurs. It's not the direct trigger of the behavior, but it is the rest of what is going on that makes the behavior more likely. For example, if the dog is uncomfortable with loud noises and there is a party going on, those may be setting events while the child reaching into her food dish is the trigger. Or say you can clip your dog's nails with no problem, but your dog does not like your veterinarian. When the veterinarian tries to clip his nails, the dog bites her. The trigger was the nail clipping, but the relationship with the vet, combined with the stressful environment of the vet's office is the setting event, because the nail clipping did not trigger biting with a different person. Rephrased in terms of trigger stacking, a stack of triggers just below the bite treshold is the setting event. The stack does not cause the bite, but one additional trigger does.

Set-up: Training session in which you can control the dog's exposure to the trigger.

Systematic Desensitization: Gradual exposure to a trigger with relaxation before the intensity of the trigger is increased. Humans doing systematic desensitization for phobias are taught relaxation exercises to self-soothe. In dog training, systematic desensitization usually means the progressive exposure aspect of systematic desensitization, and it is generally combined with classical counter-conditioning in lieu of self-relaxation techniques. Also called "graduated exposure therapy."

Sub-threshold: Dog is able to cope and self-soothe without panic or aggression. If you were to ask the dog about how stressed she was, she'd say, "not at all" or "just a little."

Sudden Environmental Contrast (SEC): An unexpected, startling change in the level of stimulation. Examples include a seated person at a dinner party standing up and encountering a box that was not in the room before. Also known as "Sudden Environmental Change."

Threshold: The line between levels of stimulation, "dividing where the dog is able to cope and self-soothe without panic or aggression from where the dog is not able to cope without panic or aggression." I think of it as a line between a calm, happy dog and a freaked out, stressed dog.

Trial: One round of successful or unsuccessful exposure to the trigger. A successful trial is Dog Sees Trigger → Dog Does Replacement Behavior → Dog Gets Reward and an unsuccessful trial is Dog Sees Trigger → Dog Does Problem Behavior → Escape/Reset.

Trigger: An event, person, animal, noise, or other factor that causes a dog to react, usually only used when the reaction is abnormal or undesired. If your dog barks at black dogs, then black dogs would be considered to be triggers for your dog's reactivity. A trigger is also known as the "triggering stimulus."

Trigger Stacking: Stress piling up because of exposure to multiple triggers, either simultaneously or close enough in time that the dog's reactivity has not returned to normal. For example, if a sound-sensitive dog who is afraid of children hears a loud crash just before he sees a child, he is more likely to bite than if he had met the child under calmer circumstances.

ABOUT THE AUTHOR

Grisha Stewart, MA, CPDT-KA is a dog trainer and seminar presenter who specializes in the prevention and rehabilitation of dog reactivity. She has created several DVDs and owns Ahimsa Dog Training in Seattle (DoggieZen.com). Ahimsa has earned many awards, including Best of Western Washington. "Ahimsa" is a Buddhist doctrine of nonviolence to all living things, which reflects Grisha's focus on force-free training.

Grisha and Peanut.

Grisha has a Master's degree in Mathematics from Bryn Mawr College. She is now pursuing a Master's in Integrative Studies Psychology with an emphasis in animal behavior at Antioch University, while still running her multi-trainer business and online store. Her thesis research will be on the effectiveness of BAT. Her first career as a theoretical mathematician and college instructor serves her well in dog training and behavior consultations, because she relies heavily on the problem solving, critical thinking, and teaching skills she gained in that field.

Canine behavior fascinates Grisha and she is highly motivated to help improve our techniques for rehabilitating and training dogs. Her professional interest in reactivity, along with the need to find an efficient rehabilitation technique that would work with her own fearful dog, led Grisha to develop BAT. To see Grisha's seminar schedule and learn even more about BAT, visit http://FunctionalRewards.com online. Grisha lives in the Seattle area with her wife and their two dogs.

RESOURCES

Books

Nan Arthur, *Stress in Dogs*

Ali Brown, *Focus not Fear: Training Insights from a Reactive Dog Class*

Jean Donaldson, *Fight! A Practical Guide to the Treatment of Dog-Dog Aggression*

John Fisher, *Diary of a 'Dotty Dog' Doctor*

Barbara Handelman, *Canine Behavior: A Photo Illustrated Handbook.*

Alexandra Horowitz, Ph.D., *Inside of a Dog: What Dogs See, Smell, and Know*

Alexandra Kurland, *The Click that Teaches: A Step-By-Step Guide in Pictures*

Patricia McConnell, Ph.D., *Feisty Fido*

Leslie McDevitt, *Control Unleashed: Creating a Focused and Confident Dog*

Pat Miller, *Do Over Dogs: Give Your Dog a Second Chance at a First Class Life*

Karen Pryor, *Don't Shoot the Dog*

Cheryl Smith, *Dog Friendly Gardens; Garden Friendly Dogs*

Andrew Weil, *Breathing: The Master Key to Self-Healing* (audio book)

DVDs

Trish King, *Abandonment Training*

Patricia McConnell, *Lassie, Come!*

Leslie Nelson, *Really Reliable Recall*

Kathy Sdao, *Improve Your I-Cue*

Pia Silvani, *Chill Out! Dealing with Overly Aroused Dogs*

Kelly Snider and Jesus Rosalez-Ruiz, *Constructional Aggression Treatment: Shaping Away Aggression*

Grisha Stewart, *Behavior Adjustment Training*

Grisha Stewart, *Give Your Dog a Behavior Adjustment: BAT for Aggression, Reactivity, and Fear*

Grisha Stewart, *Organic Socialization: BAT for Aggression and Fear in Dogs*

Sources

Ogata, N., Kikusui T., Takeuchi, Y., Mori, Y. (2006). Objective measurement of fear-associated learning in dogs. *Journal of Veterinary Behavior,* 1, 55-61.

Lohr, J. M., Olatunji, B. O., Sawchuk, C. N. (2007). A functional analysis of danger and safety signals in anxiety disorders." *Clinical Psychology Review,* 27, 114–126.

Murrey, N. (2007). "The effects of combining positive and negative reinforcement during training." (Master's thesis). Retrieved from http://digital.library.unt.edu/ark:/67531/metadc3636/m1/1/high_res_d/thesis.pdf

Snider, K.S. (2007). "A constructional canine aggression treatment: Using a negative reinforcement shaping procedure with dogs in home and community settings." Retrieved from ProQuest Digital Dissertations. (AAT 1452030)

Websites

Ahimsa Dog Training Blog (my blog, in Seattle). http://doggiezen.com/blog

BAT site with my seminar schedule http://doggiezen.com/bat

Functional rewards Yahoo! group http://functionalrewards.com

Ian Dunbar on "Reatreat & Treat." http://www.dogstardaily.com/training/retreat-amp-treat

Premack Principle. http://en.wikipedia.org/wiki/Premack%27s_principle

Shirley Chong on "Loose Lead Walking." http://www.shirleychong.com/keepers/LLW

Washington State Animal Codes. http://www.animal-lawyer.com/html/animal_law_-_washington.html

Virginia Broitman on "Two-Reward System." http://www.cappdt.ca/public/jpage/1/p/Article2RewardSystem/content.do

INDEX

Selected Titles From Dogwise Publishing
www.dogwise.com   1-800-776-2665

BEHAVIOR & TRAINING

Barking. The Sound of a Language. Turid Rugaas

Bringing Light to Shadow. A Dog Trainer's Diary. Pam Dennison

Canine Behavior. A Photo Illustrated Handbook. Barbara Handelman

Canine Body Language. A Photographic Guide to the Native Language of Dogs. Brenda Aloff

Chill Out Fido! How to Calm Your Dog. Nan Arthur

Do Over Dogs. Give Your Dog a Second Chance for a First Class Life. Pat Miller

Dogs are from Neptune. Jean Donaldson

Oh Behave! Dogs from Pavlov to Premack to Pinker. Jean Donaldson

On Talking Terms with Dogs. Calming Signals, 2nd edition. Turid Rugaas

Play With Your Dog. Pat Miller

Positive Perspectives. Love Your Dog, Train Your Dog. Pat Miller

Positive Perspectives 2. Know Your Dog, Train Your Dog. Pat Miller

Stress in Dogs. Martina Scholz & Clarissa von Reinhardt

Tales of Two Species. Essays on Loving and Living With Dogs. Patricia McConnell

The Dog Trainer's Resource. The APDT Chronicle of the Dog Collection. Mychelle Blake (*ed*)

The Dog Trainer's Resource 2. The APDT Chronicle of the Dog Collection. Mychelle Blake (*ed*)

When Pigs Fly. Train Your Impossible Dog. Jane Killion

HEALTH & ANATOMY, SHOWING

An Eye for a Dog. Illustrated Guide to Judging Purebred Dogs. Robert Cole

Another Piece of the Puzzle. Pat Hastings

Canine Massage. A Complete Reference Manual. Jean-Pierre Hourdebaigt

The Canine Thyroid Epidemic. W. Jean Dodds, DVM and Diana Laverdure

Dog Show Judging. The Good, the Bad, and the Ugly. Chris Walkowicz

The Healthy Way to Stretch Your Dog. A Physical Therapy Approach. Sasha Foster and Ashley Foster

It's a Dog Not a Toaster. Finding Your Fun in Competitive Obedience. Diana Kerew

Raw Dog Food. Make It Easy for You and Your Dog. Carina MacDonald

Raw Meaty Bones. Tom Lonsdale

Tricks of the Trade. From Best of Intentions to Best in Show, Rev. Ed. Pat Hastings

Work Wonders. Feed Your Dog Raw Meaty Bones. Tom Lonsdale

Phone in your Order! 1.800.776.2665 8am-4pm PST / 11am-7pm EST

Sign in | View Ca

Search Dogwise

Everything ▼

GO

Browse Dogwise

Books & Products
* By Subject
* Dogwise Picks
* Best Sellers
* Best New Titles

Book Reviews
* Find Out How

Resources & Info
* Dogwise Forums
* Dogwise Newsletters
* Dogwise Email List
* Customer Reading Lists
* Dog Show Schedule
* Let Us Know About Your Book or DVD
* Become an Affiliate
* APDT, CPDT
* IAABC
* CAPPDT

Help & Contacts
* About Us
* Contact Us
* Shipping Policy

Employee Picks!
See which books the Dogwise staff members love to read.
* Click Here!

Dog Show Supplies from The 3c's
* Visit the 3c's Website
* View our selection of 3c products.

Save up to 80% on Bargain Books! Click here for Sale, Clearance and hard to find Out of Print titles!
* Click Here!

Prefer to order by phone? Call Us!
1-800-776-2665
8AM - 4PM M-F Pacific Time

Be the First to Hear the News!
Have New Product and Promotion Announcements Emailed to You.
Click Here To Sign Up!

<u>Free Shipping for Orders over $75 - click here for more information!</u>

<u>Win a $25 Dogwise credit - click here to find out how!</u>

Featured New Titles

 STRESS IN DOGS - LEARN HOW DOGS SHOW STRESS AND WHAT YOU CAN DO TO HELP, by Martina Scholz & Clarissa von Reinhardt
Item: DTB909
Is stress causing your dog's behavior problems? Research shows that as with humans, many behavioral problems in dogs are stress-related. Learn how to recognize when your dog is stressed, what factors cause stress in dogs, and strategies you can utilize in training and in your daily life with your dog to reduce stress.
Price: $14.95 more information...
 DIG IN

 SUCCESS IS IN THE PROOFING - A GUIDE FOR CREATIVE AND EFFECTIVE TRAINING, by Debby Quigley & Judy Ramsey
Item: DTO230
The success is indeed in the proofing! Proofing is an essential part of training, but one that is often overlooked or not worked on enough. We all know the story of the dog who can perform a variety of behaviors perfectly in the backyard but falls apart in the obedience ring. This book is full of great ideas and strategies to help your dog do his best no matter what the distractions or conditions may be. Whether competing in Rally or Obedience, trainers everywhere will find this very portable and user friendly book an indispensable addition to their tool box.
Price: $19.95 more information...
DIG IN

REALLY RELIABLE RECALL DVD, by Leslie Nelson
Item: DTB810P
From well-known trainer Leslie Nelson! Easy to follow steps to train your dog to come when it really counts, in an emergency. Extra chapters for difficult to train breeds and training class instructors.
Price: $29.95 more information...
DIG IN

 THE DOG TRAINERS RESOURCE - APDT CHRONICLE OF THE DOG COLLECTION, by Mychelle Blake, Editor
Item: DTB880
The modern professional dog trainer needs to develop expertise in a wide variety of fields: learning theory, training techniques, classroom strategies, marketing, community relations, and business development and management. This collection of articles from APDT's Chronicle of the Dog will prove a valuable resource for trainers and would-be trainers.
Price: $24.95 more information...
DIG IN

 SHAPING SUCCESS - THE EDUCATION OF AN UNLIKELY CHAMPION, by Susan Garrett
Item: DTA260
Written by one of the world's best dog trainers, *Shaping Success* gives an excellent explanation of the theory behind animal learning as Susan Garrett trains a high-energy Border Collie puppy to be an agility champion. Buzzy's story both entertains and demonstrates how to apply some of the most up-to-date dog training methods in the real world. Clicker training!
Price: $24.95 more information...
DIG IN

FOR THE LOVE OF A DOG - UNDERSTANDING EMOTION IN YOU AND YOUR BEST FRIEND, by Patricia McConnell
Item: DTB890
Sure to be another bestseller, Trish McConnell's latest book takes a look at canine emotions and body language. Like all her books, this one is written in a way that the average dog owner can follow but brings the latest scientific information that trainers and dog enthusiasts can use.
Price: $24.95 more information...
DIG IN

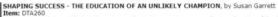

 HELP FOR YOUR FEARFUL DOG: A STEP-BY-STEP GUIDE TO HELPING YOUR DOG CONQUER HIS FEARS, by Nicole Wilde
Item: DTB878
From popular author and trainer Nicole Wilde! A comprehensive guide to the treatment of canine anxiety, fears, and phobias. Chock full of photographs and illustrations and written in a down-to-earth, humorous style.
Price: $24.95 more information...
 DIG IN

FAMILY FRIENDLY DOG TRAINING - A SIX WEEK PROGRAM FOR YOU AND YOUR DOG, by Patricia McConnell & Aimee Moore
Item: DTB917
A six-week program to get people and dogs off on the right paw! Includes trouble-shooting tips for what to do when your dog doesn't respond as expected. This is a book that many trainers will want their students to read.
Price: $11.95 more information...
DIG IN

 THE LANGUAGE OF DOGS - UNDERSTANDING CANINE BODY LANGUAGE AND OTHER COMMUNICATION SIGNALS DVD SET, by Sarah Kalnajs
Item: DTB875P
Features a presentation and extensive footage of a variety of breeds showing hundreds of examples of canine behavior and body language. Perfect for dog owners or anyone who handles dogs or encounters them regularly while on the job.
Price: $39.95 more information...
 DIG IN

THE FAMILY IN DOG BEHAVIOR CONSULTING, by Lynn Hoover
Item: DTB887
Sometimes, no matter how good a trainer or behavior consultant you are, there are issues going on within a human family that you need to be aware of to solve behavior or training problems with dogs. For animal behavior consultants, this text opens up new vistas of challenge and opportunity, dealing with the intense and sometimes complicated nature of relationships between families and dogs.
Price: $24.95 more information...
DIG IN